AF488149

"Winning the War Within Our Mind"

By

Daniel R. Linden

Our Toughest Battles Forge Our Greatest Strengths

© 2026 by Daniel R. Linden
All Rights Reserved
"Winning the War Within Our Mind"
Registration Number: TXu 2-523-622
Supplement To: TXu002513553, 2025
U.S. Copyright Case Number: 1-15086286561
Type of Work: Literary Work

ISBN: 979-8-218-92949-7 (hardcover)
ISBN: 979-8-218-92950-3 (paperback)
ISBN: 979-8-218-92951-0 (eBook)

Cover design by: Christopher Kubik

Genres: Self-Help; Leadership; Mental Health; Motivational; Well-Being

This book is a fictional account created for educational purposes and to encourage reflection, conversation, and learning related to mental health and wellness.

While the work may be inspired by the author's personal experiences, it is provided for general informational and informative purposes only. It is not intended to diagnose, treat, cure, or prevent any mental health condition, and it is not a substitute for professional psychological, psychiatric, medical, or therapeutic advice, evaluation, or treatment. If you are experiencing distress or believe you may need support, please seek help from a qualified licensed professional.

The publishing author disclaims any liability for any loss, injury, or damages arising from the use of, reliance on, or interpretation of the information or themes presented in this book. Readers assume full responsibility for how they choose to use the content.

All rights reserved. No part of this book may be reproduced, stored in a retrieval system, or transmitted in any form or by any means, including electronic, mechanical, photocopying, recording, or otherwise, without the author's express written permission, except as permitted by law (e.g., brief quotations in reviews).

Rights and Permissions
Organization Name: Trinity Echo
Copyright Claimant: Daniel Russell Linden
Effective Date of Registration: January 27, 2026
Registration Decision Date: February 2, 2026

Dedication

To: Chrissy and Danny

Thank you for being such a great blessing to your mom and me. We are deeply thankful for the wonderful children you were and for the close bond you've always shared. You've both grown into remarkable adults and built wonderful families of your own. We are proud of all you've accomplished—personally, academically, and professionally. Your kindness, respect, dedication, and loving hearts have surpassed every hope and dream we ever had for you. May you and your families know peace and love now and always. God bless you both.

Contents

Preface

I examined my life journey in my first book, "Tenacity, Resiliency, and Willpower," through the lens of those three traits. One guiding question shaped that work: Who would want to justify their entire life? In this new book, I explore life through the lens of psychological warfare—the war within the mind. My goals are to educate, inspire, and empower by offering information to absorb, strategies to apply, twelve inner demons to identify, and top ten strengths to develop—tools to help bring these psychological battles into remission.

The psychological battles I faced for more than a decade were intense, complex, and deeply unsettling. In writing this book, it was important to portray the mind as a dangerous battleground where psychological warfare unfolds. I include detailed descriptions and illustrations of this intricate, treacherous terrain so readers can better understand it and reflect on this threatening theater of conflict. My aim is to deepen understanding, clarify obstacles, support readers in overcoming adversity, and promote well-being.

For those living with psychological war in their minds, they—as well as their loved ones and friends—often carry the burden and suffer collateral damage when these battles erupt. A troubled mind locked in intense psychological battles—often hidden, misunderstood, or underestimated—can disrupt lives, destroy relationships, derail careers, and, for some, prove fatal.

For me, comparing psychological turmoil to warfare came naturally. One clear parallel between combat and inner battles is psychological wounding. When these wounds are not fatal, they can heal into scars—markers of battles fought and survived. Survivors adapt to life not as it was before the battle, but as an evolved version of themselves—better equipped to endure and even thrive in a changed, challenging, and calamitous environment.

This book is not meant to minimize the horrors faced by civilians and soldiers in real wars—conflicts that bring immense suffering, injury, and death. Instead, the battlefield analogy serves as a vivid way to convey the torment of psychological adversity, illuminate intense emotions, and describe seemingly insurmountable barriers, with the aim of winning the war within our mind.

Part 1: Psychological Warfare

"Winning the War Within Our Mind" is a book dedicated to the psychological battles and external pressures that don't just pass through our thoughts—they dig in, setting up camp along the brain's neural pathways like trenches carved by repetition. These skirmishes shape what we practice, what we avoid, and what we become. They leave fingerprints on our character and, over time, press their imprint into our destiny.

Part 1 comprises the first four chapters of "Winning the War Within Our Mind's" twelve chapters and lays the foundation for exploring the multifaceted nature of psychological warfare.

Chapter 1 explores the complexities of psychological history. Chapter 2 identifies and defines twelve potential "inner demons" that, if left unchecked, can undermine mental health. Chapter 3 outlines the top ten strengths needed to fend off these threats and understand the tactics these inner demons use against us. Chapter 4 presents strategies for countering each of the twelve inner demons, with an emphasis on safeguarding the most vulnerable among us, young developing minds.

The most decisive war we'll ever fight won't be on a battlefield. It will be inside our mind.

We fight for freedom when our mind feels occupied by fear.

We fight for passion when numbness tries to smother what matters.

We fight for peace when our inner world turns loud, restless, and sharp edged.

We fight for survival when the body is upright, but the spirit feels pinned.

Only surrender when it is in our best interest to do so. Sometimes, we need to regroup, regulate our nervous system, and revitalize. It isn't quitting the war; it's choosing the moment to breathe, re-center, and return stronger, clearer, and more capable of winning.

Psychological warfare aims to influence thoughts, emotions, attitudes, and behavior. Its goals include reducing a target's willingness to engage in conflict, sowing confusion, and manipulating perceptions by creating doubt and indecision. Today, we are continually exposed to psychological tactics meant to shape how we think and act.

In everyday interactions, psychological warfare often shows up as manipulation: emotional pressure, mind games, gaslighting, or psychological aggression. It can also involve propaganda, misinformation, disinformation, and media manipulation used to weaken opponents, sway opinion, erode resilience, and exploit cognitive biases. In some cases, these obstacles are rooted in childhood experiences, societal pressure, personal setbacks, or unfulfilled expectations.

Psychological battles also unfold alongside rapid technological change. A constant stream of information from countless sources can be exhausting. The pressure to stay informed, while processing large volumes of content and sorting truth from deception, misinformation, and profiling, can fuel doubt and mental fatigue.

Winning the war within the mind may require resolving tensions between personal beliefs and social influence; balancing long-term goals with immediate gratification; narrowing the gap between who we think we are and how we behave; and reconciling personal aspirations with everyday responsibilities. Addressing these conflicts before they accumulate can restore clarity, energy, and resilience.

As the next four chapters unfold, the goal is to provide essential information for battling the inner demons that wage war in our minds. Part 2, "Winning the War," focuses on gathering the insight and tools needed not only to win, but to sustain success. Part 3, "Leading After Psychological Battles," focuses on surviving—and thriving—after the battle is over, and on bringing others with us toward a future marked by hope and inner peace.

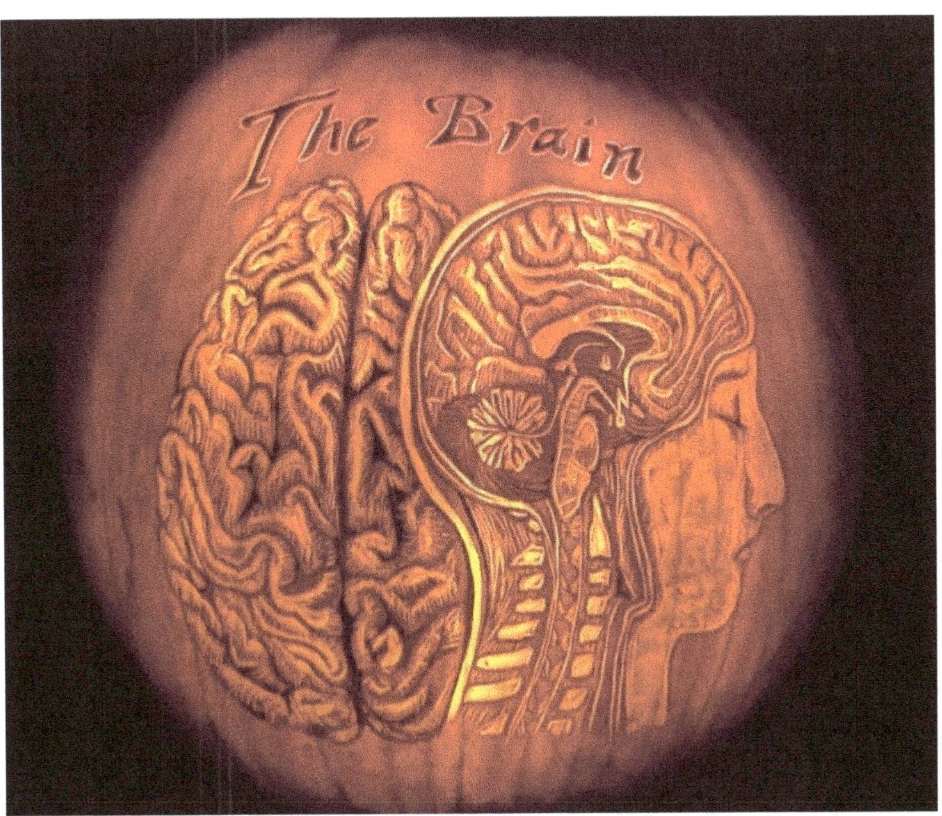

Photo by Daniel R. Linden

The brain can become a psychological battlefield. Here, "psychological warfare" isn't meant as a military conflict, but as a sophisticated response rooted in our innate strengths—one that helps us identify and overcome the inner demons bent on destroying us.

Chapter 1: The Nature of Psychological Battles Within Our Mind

"Winning the War Within Our Mind" is a book dedicated to overcoming the psychological battles and external pressures that play out in our mind. These skirmishes unfold along the brain's neural pathways, shaping our character and, ultimately, our destiny. We fight for freedom, passion, peace, and survival. We should never surrender, unless doing so allows us to regroup, regulate, and revitalize, so we can ultimately emerge victorious.

Joseph Campbell (1904–1987) was an American literature professor and a renowned mythologist, writer, and lecturer. In the late 1920s, he received a fellowship that enabled him to study in Europe, where he attended the University of Paris (the Sorbonne) and the University of Munich. That experience broadened his knowledge of languages and literature and strongly influenced his later work in comparative mythology.

Campbell later devoted himself to independent study and research, developing a distinctive approach to mythology and comparative religion. He gained widespread recognition with "The Hero with a Thousand Faces." Throughout his writings, he combined philosophy and psychology in ways that help readers explore the "war within our mind."

Campbell also wrote "The Power of Myth," which examines recurring themes and motifs in myths from cultures around the world. His aim was to identify universal principles and archetypes that resonate across human history. He believed myths can illuminate the human journey, as reflected in the following quote:

"All the Gods, all the heavens, and all the hells are within you." — Joseph Campbell, "The Power of Myth"

This statement connects the competing forces that shape our inner landscape. The phrase "all the Gods, all the heavens, and all the hells" metaphorically refers to the full range of human potential—both benevolent and destructive—that exists within the mind. Each person carries the capacity for significant kindness as well as brutal cruelty, reflecting "heavenly" and "hellish" states. Our daily choices, our responses to problems, and the decisions that guide our growth are shaped by the outcomes of these internal conflicts. For example, choosing between altruism and selfishness can become a psychological strain, especially under high-stakes circumstances.

The human mind holds emotions, thoughts, and conflicting impulses. Campbell explored these inner experiences and possibilities, portraying the psyche as an arena of competing drives. Much like the battlegrounds described in historical and mythical narratives, our minds are places where different aspects of the self contend for influence.

1.1 Historical Viewpoints on the Psychological War Within Our Mind

The following are historical perspectives on inner psychological battles, drawn from influential philosophers and physicians.

Socrates

Few philosophers loom as large as Socrates (470—399 BC), the ancient Greek thinker who lived in the 5th century BC. He explored the complexities of the human mind and reflected on the internal conflicts that shape our thoughts and actions. His insights still resonate, offering guidance for understanding the forces that shape human behavior.

Socrates is best known for the Socratic Method—a form of dialogue designed to uncover truth through probing, reflective questions. Through self-examination, he encouraged people to explore their beliefs, values, and motivations. By challenging conventional wisdom and questioning assumptions, Socrates encouraged introspection and self-discovery, bringing attention to the workings of the human psyche.

"The unexamined life is not worth living." — Socrates

This quote appears in Plato's account of Socrates' trial, the "Apology." There, Socrates argues that self-examination leads to understanding, and that understanding can quiet inner turmoil and support a meaningful, ethical, and fulfilling life.

In the broader history of philosophy, Socrates remains a guiding light, illuminating the intricate landscape of the mind. He also believed that true happiness comes from integrity and virtue rather than fleeting material pleasure.

Hippocrates

Hippocrates (c. 460–370 BC) was born on the Greek island of Kos. He helped transform medicine by arguing that illness has natural causes rather than being punishments from the gods—a widespread belief before his time. His clinical and logical approach helped lay the groundwork for modern medical practice.

His contributions to understanding mental illness were especially significant. When many viewed mental disorders through a supernatural lens, Hippocrates proposed that they could be biological in origin and connected to bodily imbalances.

In "On the Sacred Disease," he addressed epilepsy and challenged the belief that it was a divine affliction. Instead, he argued that epilepsy is a brain disorder with natural causes, best treated through natural means such as diet, lifestyle changes, and medication.

Hippocrates helped move discussions of psychological and neurological suffering away from superstition and toward observation, explanation, and treatment—an influence that continues to shape medical thought today.

"Life is short, the art long, opportunity fleeting, experience treacherous, judgment difficult." — Hippocrates

This quote reminds us of life's brevity, the long pursuit of mastery, and the difficulty of wise judgment. Reflecting on it can encourage attentiveness, resilience, and humility as we navigate life's obstacles.

Plato

Plato (c. 428–347 BC) developed a tripartite theory of the soul, most famously presented in "The Republic." His model introduced early ideas about psychological battle and self-control.

"Courage is knowing what not to fear." — Plato

This suggests courage isn't the absence of fear but the ability to judge what is truly worthy of apprehension. It highlights the role of wisdom and self-understanding in facing both rational and irrational anxieties.

In "Phaedrus," Plato presents the famous image of the soul as a chariot pulled by two winged horses and guided by a charioteer. The charioteer represents reason, aiming toward truth. One horse is noble and disciplined, symbolizing the spirited element—passionate but capable of aligning with reason. The other is unruly, representing appetite and desire, often resisting rational control.

This allegory captures the clashes among reason, emotion, and desire. The charioteer's task is to balance these forces and guide the soul toward ethical and intellectual growth, making the metaphor a powerful way to describe psychological battles.

Aristotle

Aristotle (384–322 BC) explored topics we now associate with psychology, including memory, perception, and aspects of mental disturbance. A central figure in Greek philosophy, he helped shape systematic inquiry into mind and behavior.

While his approach differs from modern psychology, his work combined biological, physiological, and philosophical perspectives in an early effort to understand mental life and psychological battles.

"Educating the mind without educating the heart is no education at all." — Aristotle

This quote argues that genuine education involves intellectual development, as well as moral and emotional growth. Addressing internal conflict, in this view, requires both clear thinking and the emotional capacity for compassion and self-restraint.

Dr. Sigmund Freud

Sigmund Freud (1856–1939) earned his medical degree from the University of Vienna in 1881 and trained as a neurologist. His medical training strongly influenced his later work, especially his theories about the psyche and his development of psychoanalysis.

"The mind is like an iceberg; it floats with one-seventh of its bulk above water." — Sigmund Freud

This metaphor suggests that much of mental life—unconscious desires, alarm, and motivations—lies outside conscious awareness. Applied to psychological battles, Freud suggests that many conflicts originate in hidden processes that require careful exploration to understand and resolve.

Freud described the psyche as three interacting parts:

1. **The id:** The instinctual, primitive source of drives and impulses, operating on the pleasure principle and seeking immediate gratification.

2. **The ego:** The reality-oriented mediator that negotiates between the id's demands and external constraints, operating on the reality principle.

3. **The superego:** The internalized moral authority shaped by social and parental standards, often pressuring the ego toward ideal conduct.

These forces continually interact and can come into conflict—particularly under stress—producing internal tension and psychological difficulty.

Erik Erikson's Theory of Psychosocial Development

Erik Erikson (1902–1994) held neither a Ph.D. nor an M.D. Nevertheless, he taught at major universities, including Harvard, Yale, and UC Berkeley, because of his significant contributions to psychology, especially his theory of psychosocial development. He presented many of his most influential ideas in his 1950 book "Childhood and Society." Erikson's model includes eight stages:

1. **Trust vs. Mistrust (Birth–18 months):** Consistent, responsive caregiving builds security and trust, while unreliable or harsh care fosters mistrust; the key virtue developed is hope.

2. **Autonomy vs. Shame and Doubt (18 months–3 years):** Support for growing independence promotes self-control and confidence, but excessive criticism or control leads to shame and doubt; the virtue is will.

3. **Initiative vs. Guilt (3–5 years):** Encouraging exploration and leadership builds initiative, while constant restriction or criticism produces guilt; the virtue is purpose.

4. **Industry vs. Inferiority (5–12 years):** Positive support in school and social tasks develops competence and work ethic, whereas repeated discouragement creates feelings of inferiority; the virtue is competence.

5. **Identity vs. Role Confusion (12–18 years):** Adolescents seek a stable sense of self amid social expectations, and failure to do so results in confusion; the virtue is fidelity (commitment and loyalty).

6. **Intimacy vs. Isolation (18–40 years):** Forming close, committed relationships leads to belonging, while difficulty connecting can cause loneliness; the virtue is love.

7. **Generativity vs. Stagnation (Middle adulthood):** Contributing through work, parenting, or mentorship creates fulfillment, while lack of contribution leads to stagnation; the virtue is care.

8. **Integrity vs. Despair (65+):** Reflecting on life with acceptance fosters integrity, while regret can produce despair; the virtue is wisdom.

Even with debate around specifics, Erikson's framework remains useful because it explains how resolving recurring life "crises" shapes psychological development across the lifespan.

Dr. Aaron Beck and Cognitive Behavioral Therapy (CBT)

In the 1960s, Dr. Aaron Beck, a psychiatrist at the University of Pennsylvania, developed Cognitive Behavioral Therapy (CBT). CBT is a form of psychotherapy that helps people identify and change unhelpful thought patterns and behaviors to improve mental health and overall well-being. Although Beck was originally trained in psychoanalysis, his research led him to focus on patterns of negative thinking in people with depression. He found that many depressed people experience automatic negative thoughts about themselves, the world, and the future. He then developed practical techniques to help patients identify, challenge, and replace distorted thoughts— changes that can meaningfully improve emotions and behavior.

Facing the war within the mind can be intimidating because psychological battles involve deeply personal struggles, doubts, and horrors. These conflicts often arise from competing impulses, beliefs, and emotional reactions that shape how we see ourselves and the world. Working through them matters not only for mental well-being, but also for physical health, personal growth, and maturity. Exploring the roots of these "inner demons" through established psychological models can help us better understand past wounds, present challenges, and future vulnerabilities.

1.2 Brain Chemistry and Psychological Warfare

Chemistry, often called the central science, plays a fundamental role in understanding the building blocks of life and how living systems function. It highlights the complexity and beauty of existence. Neurochemistry—the study of the chemicals in the brain and how they affect the nervous system—can help explain how psychological distress is experienced and, in some cases, treated or managed.

Brain chemicals called neurotransmitters influence our thoughts, emotions, and behavior. Here are a few major examples:

- Dopamine is linked to pleasure and reward. When we engage in enjoyable activities, such as eating good food or listening to music, our brain releases dopamine, contributing to feelings of satisfaction. Dopamine also supports motivation and reinforcement learning.

- Serotonin helps regulate mood, sleep, and appetite. Low serotonin activity has been associated with conditions such as depression and anxiety. Notably, much of the body's serotonin is produced in the gut, where it affects digestion and also influences signaling between the gut and brain.

- Endorphins act as natural pain relievers. They are released during exercise, laughter, or excitement, helping reduce pain and sometimes producing feelings of euphoria (often referred to as a "runner's high").

In the context of psychological warfare, people or groups may use tactics designed to manipulate, deceive, or influence others' thoughts, emotions, and behavior. Neurochemistry can affect how people respond to these tactics by shaping attention, threat perception, and emotional reactions.

Neurotransmitters are chemical messengers that carry signals across synapses in the brain. In high-pressure or manipulative environments, shifts in neurotransmitter activity can influence mood, cognition, and behavior. For example, pairing messages with dopamine-linked reward cues can reinforce certain behaviors or beliefs. Conversely, reduced serotonin signaling is associated with anxiety and low mood, which may increase susceptibility to external pressure.

Hormones such as cortisol and adrenaline are also central to the body's stress response. Prolonged or intense stress can impair attention, decision making, and emotional regulation. By inducing fear, intimidation, or uncertainty, perpetrators may increase psychological vulnerability, making targets easier to influence or control.

This interaction between neurochemistry and psychological warfare can enable more precise manipulation. By exploiting common features of human cognition, such as cognitive biases, cognitive dissonance, and emotional triggers, people may be pushed toward beliefs, behaviors, or ideologies that conflict with their values or better judgment. Such manipulation can have lasting effects on mental well-being and future decision making.

Even a basic understanding of the neurochemical factors involved in psychological influence can clarify why human behavior is so complex. From molecular interactions within cells to the large-scale forces that shape societies, chemistry helps illuminate the intricate tapestry of life.

1.3 Impact of Psychological Battles on the Mind

Psychological battles can have a complex and often misunderstood impact on the mind. When people face psychological war or conflicting emotions, their mental well-being may be deeply affected.

Inner psychological battles—conflicting emotions, beliefs, needs, or unresolved trauma—can strongly affect mental and physical health. They often create confusion, self-doubt, and a constant sense of strain, which may show up as anxiety, depression, mood swings, trouble focusing, and feeling overwhelmed. Over time, the stress can spill into the body, contributing to insomnia, headaches, exhaustion, disordered eating, and muscle tension.

These battles feel so hard because outcomes are uncertain and clarity can disappear, forcing people into "trial and error" while they're already hurting. When the conflict intensifies, it can become risky: narrowed thinking, impulsive decisions, and a growing sense of helplessness can damage relationships, work, and overall functioning.

"Be curious, not judgmental" (popularized by Ted Lasso, often misattributed to Walt Whitman) captures a key psychological skill: replacing harsh self-judgment and snap conclusions with questions and observation. Curiosity helps us identify what is really driving the tension—distorted thoughts, unmet needs, fear, or shame. Then we can respond wisely instead of reacting impulsively.

The impact of psychological battles varies, but three factors often shape outcomes:

1. **Mindset/perception:** A growth mindset makes it more likely someone learns and adapts instead of getting stuck in defeat.

2. **Support systems:** Caring, reliable people (or professionals) reduce isolation and make coping more realistic.

3. **Past coping success:** Previous wins build confidence, resilience, and a wider toolbox for managing future stress.

With support, self-care, and coping strategies, people can resolve or reduce these inner wars. "Winning" often feels like being unshackled: less fear and self-doubt, more choice and self-control, and a stronger ability to meet future problems with stability and resilience.

Photo by Daniel R. Linden

This image represents an internal psychological battle, where dark gray clouds signify worsening mental battles and increased risk of deeper psychological distress. Brighter colors (orange, yellow, and blue) symbolize positive feelings.

Chapter 2: Recognizing Inner Demons

Recognizing the inner demons and external threats that can spark psychological battles is essential. Negative thoughts often stem from how we interpret past and present experiences, as well as what we anticipate in the future. Noticing early signs of negative thought "skirmishes" and recurring patterns is a crucial first step toward acknowledging, addressing, and preventing what can escalate into a serious psychological war.

Understanding inner demons in these psychological battles involves identifying destructive beliefs and emotions that undermine well-being. Intentional self-reflection focused on harmful thought patterns can bring them into clearer view. Paying close attention to damaging inner dialogue, such as self-criticism, catastrophizing, or all-or-nothing thinking, can help us identify its triggers and develop strategies to defuse it before it escalates. Noting when negative thoughts occur and what prompts them is essential for disrupting these cycles. By identifying self-limiting beliefs and distorted views of self-worth, we can question their accuracy and consider more balanced perspectives.

Becoming aware of particularly troubling emotions, such as anxiety, anger, or guilt, can also be important because these emotions may point to unhelpful defense mechanisms, like denial, projection, or rationalization, used to avoid uncomfortable truths. Recognizing negative behavior patterns, such as chronic fatigue, procrastination, avoidance, or perfectionism, creates an opportunity to address them and reduce their impact on well-being.

Inner demons often manifest as negative thoughts, self-doubt, and irrational fright. These influences may appear as feelings of inadequacy or as the belief that we are unworthy of the good in our lives. By acknowledging them, we can begin to recover from the setbacks they create. As we learn how these forces disguise themselves, we can confront them more directly and remove the obstacles they place in our path. This can be a meaningful step toward a more harmonious and fulfilling life.

Inner demons draw power from many sources and experiences. For example, growing up in a harsh home, a harmful institutional setting, or an unstable living situation can significantly affect psychological well-being, resilience, emotional development, personal growth, relationships, and broader social integration. Environments that lack tolerance and empathy, or that impose unreasonable expectations, can undermine inner peace and plant the seeds of an internal battleground. Exposure to abuse—physical, emotional, or sexual—can also create fear and hostility, laying the groundwork for ongoing psychological conflict.

Substance abuse by parents or caregivers can lead to neglect, inconsistent care, and household instability. Persistent conflict fueled by alcohol or drug dependence can create overwhelming stress, uncertainty, and insecurity. Emotional or physical neglect often leaves human beings feeling unsupported and undervalued, increasing vulnerability to internal psychological battles.

Caregivers responsible for nurturing and protecting a child compromised by substance abuse leads to an unstable and less encouraging environment. This can lead to unpredictable behavior and emotional insecurity in those who depend on them for safety and support. Over time, these conditions can contribute to persistent and destabilizing psychological battles.

2.1 Threat Identification and Analysis

Winning the war within our mind means overcoming our enemies by identifying and eliminating our inner demons. We can learn meaningful lessons about survival and resilience from the United States Marine Corps (USMC), especially when it comes to psychological conflict. Marines are known for exceptional discipline, honor, and dedication to duty. They carry themselves with pride and dignity—qualities forged through rigorous training, strong traditions, loyalty, and service. As elite warriors, they uphold high standards of professionalism and commitment to one another, which makes the USMC one of the most respected and formidable military organizations in the world.

To recognize, confront, and defeat their enemies, Marines use a process called threat-identification process. They work to understand an adversary by studying the tactics, plans, and motivations behind enemy actions. That understanding strengthens their ability to adapt, innovate, and prevail. The USMC views this work as more than a tactical edge—it is essential to strategic victory.

Winning the psychological war in our mind requires the same seriousness and commitment, because difficult and unforgiving circumstances will arise. It is not enough to fight; we must win. Inner demons that "raid" our thoughts and ignite battles in our minds can be as intimidating as physical combat.

Below is an overview of the Marine threat-identification process, along with a parallel application to the "psychological warfare" we face within ourselves:

1. Define intelligence requirements and objectives. The process begins by clarifying what information is needed about potential threats to make informed decisions. *Personal application:* When we identify what we need to understand—our triggers, patterns, and vulnerabilities—we gain insight into the psychological tactics working against us. That knowledge helps us build strategies that protect our mental well-being.

2. Gather intelligence from multiple sources. Intelligence is collected through various methods (e.g., human intelligence, imagery intelligence, and open-source intelligence) to build a detailed picture of potential adversaries. *Personal application:* By collecting relevant information about ourselves—our behaviors, motivations, and repeated reactions—we can better anticipate our inner demons and respond more effectively.

3. Process and convert raw data into a usable form. Collected information is organized and translated into formats that can be analyzed (e.g., decryption, translation, and data reduction). *Personal application:* When we "decode" our thoughts and emotions, we can identify root causes, reduce complexity into actionable insights, and make clearer decisions about how to move forward.

4. Analyze and interpret the information. Analysts assess the capabilities, intentions, and activities of adversaries to produce actionable intelligence. This requires critical thinking and the ability to connect the dots. *Personal application:* By examining our inner dialogue, beliefs, and motives, we can identify harmful patterns, biases, and self-defeating narratives. This kind of introspection builds resilience and supports practical, corrective action.

5. Disseminate intelligence to decision makers. Intelligence is delivered to commanders in a clear format that supports planning and execution. *Personal application:* When we communicate what we learn about ourselves clearly—through journaling, reflection, coaching, or structured self-talk—we reduce uncertainty and anxiety. Clarity lowers cognitive overload and strengthens confidence and a sense of control.

6. Evaluate effectiveness and incorporate feedback. The final step assesses whether the intelligence met the original requirements, using feedback to improve future collection and analysis. *Personal application:* Regularly evaluating which thoughts and beliefs help us—and which harm us—enables continuous improvement. Over time, this strengthens decision making and problem solving, both of which are essential to winning the war within our mind.

While the USMC trains Marines to gather intelligence so they can anticipate enemy movements and disrupt attacks, psychological battles demand a different kind of intelligence: introspection. We must observe the mental "operations" unfolding within us and learn to respond with strategy rather than impulse.

Marines also receive psychological training to remain composed and make rational decisions under pressure. The USMC works to ensure its forces are prepared, agile, and effective against diverse threats. Marines improvise, adapt, and overcome, and we must do the same when facing internal battles. A war within the mind can be as destructive as a shooting war if we fail to prepare.

The twelve inner "war demons" addressed in this book include fear, addiction, anger, the poisonous tempter demon, envy, passionate emotions and impulsive reactions (PEIR), sadness, perfectionism, confusion, the burden bearer, the deceiver, and the trickster.

The top ten strengths necessary to win the war within our mind include mental toughness, empathy, emotional intelligence, self-awareness, patience, courage, adaptability and flexibility, critical thinking, problem solving, and gratitude.

Just as Marines develop keen observational skills to identify threats, we must cultivate self-consciousness to recognize the inner demons that trigger conflict in our minds. When we acknowledge our battles and understand where they come from, we can begin to confront and resolve them. This is not easy, but the purpose of this book is to help us prepare, disrupt the influence of inner demons, and live with greater peace and joy, winning the war within our mind.

2.2 Recognizing Early Signs of Inner Demon Intervention

Recognizing the early signs of inner demons involved in psychological battles is crucial in taking positive action against them before psychological battles can escalate into debilitating psychological wars. Here are seven indicators we should be made aware of and use for our benefit:

1. Constant worry about our competence, decision making, or worth often signals an underlying battle with self-esteem and self-confidence with inner demons.

2. Frequent and unexplained changes in our mood can indicate emotional instability that might stem from unresolved inner demons.

3. Difficulties in falling or staying asleep are common among people dealing with inner demons. Unrest occurs, particularly those psychological battles that keep replaying disturbing scenarios or conversations in our minds.

4. Choosing isolation over social interaction can be a sign of inner demons forcing us to fight in their world, and we may feel overwhelmed or uncomfortable around others. Psychological battles can cause us to pull back from social engagements, due to feelings of inadequacy or fear of judgment, thus impacting relationships and social life.

5. Physical signs such as fatigue, headaches, or gastrointestinal issues can arise from continuous stress caused by inner demons. Mental exhaustion can occur from incessant self-reflection or worry, leading to decreased concentration and productivity.

6. Difficulty in making decisions, or regretting decisions once they are made, can reflect deeper conflicts regarding personal values or goals torn apart by savvy inner demons.

7. Feelings of dissatisfaction, guilt, or sadness are commonly experienced. These emotions can drain energy and reduce our overall emotional vitality.

By understanding and noting these early signs, we can summon the necessary top ten strengths to begin taking proactive steps toward addressing inner tensions on the verge of psychological battle.

2.3 Twelve Inner Demons Associated with Psychological Battles

In the intricate landscape of our minds, psychological battles often rage, fought by adversaries that threaten our peace and well-being. These inner demons manifest in various forms. For our purposes, to identify, combat, and eliminate these enemies, we are naming twelve: fear, addiction, anger, poisonous tempter demon, envy, passionate emotions and impulsive reactions (PEIR), sadness, perfectionism, confusion, burden bearer, deceiver, and trickster. Each of these nemeses has the ability to cause us consternation, angst, and agony. Understanding these inner demons is crucial in our quest to win the war within our mind.

	Inner Demons	Actions on the Psychological Battlefield
1.	Fear	Fear instills anxiety and apprehension, paralyzing decision making.
2.	Addiction	Addiction creates dependencies and cravings that can overpower rational thought.
3.	Anger	Anger fuels aggression, self-destructive tendencies, and leads to chaos and turmoil.
4.	Poisonous Tempter Demon	A poisonous tempter demon can be toxic, representing destructive urges and self-sabotage.
5.	Envy	Envy breeds jealousy and covetousness, causing discontent and clouds judgment.
6.	Passionate Emotions and Impulsive Reactions (PEIR)	PEIR leads to conflicts and outbursts, obscuring our judgment and leading to actions that we later regret.
7.	Sadness	Sadness generates despair, at times degrading into tragedy. It has waves of melancholy and induces erratic judgment.
8.	Perfectionism	Perfectionism is characterized by setting excessively high standards, accompanied by a tendency to be overly self-critical.
9.	Confusion	Confusion brings uncertainty, indecisiveness, and creates chaos in the mind.
10.	Burden Bearer	Burden bearer creates a heavy toll, inducing feelings of sorrow and negativity. It materializes silently, eventually becoming destructive.
11.	Deceiver	The deceiver causes self-deception and emotional manipulation; it preys on weaknesses, amplifies doubts, and highlights flaws.
12.	Trickster	The trickster has an elusive nature that is complex and unpredictable. It brings confusion, indecision, chaos, and sows doubt within us.

Let's dive deeper into additional background on each of the twelve selected inner demons.

1. Fear

Fear, often described as an "inner demon," can trigger anxiety and apprehension. It may paralyze decision making, fuel hesitation, and intensify a psychological war for control. It's important to recognize that fear is a valid emotional response.

Managing emotions and making decisions can feel especially difficult when fear leaves us feeling stuck. Feeling fear and anxiety is natural, and seeking support can remind us that we're not alone in facing these feelings.

2. Addiction

Addiction can feel like an inner demon, creating cravings and dependencies that overpower rational thought. This image captures a fundamental human struggle many people face. Framing addiction as an internal battle makes it easier to understand and can foster empathy for those experiencing it. It also highlights that addiction isn't simply a matter of choice: powerful cravings and dependency can disrupt clear thinking and make good decisions difficult. As a result, overcoming addiction often takes more than willpower—it may require therapy, medical treatment, and strong social support.

3. Anger

Anger can feel like a radioactive force—an inner demon that radiates harmful energy. When left unchecked, it can fuel aggression and self-destructive impulses, creating chaos and inner turmoil through constant psychological conflict. Harmful or inappropriate behavior is never acceptable, because it can cause physical and emotional damage to ourselves and to others. If anger is causing distress or ongoing angst, seeking help is important.

Trying to understand when anger arises and why it surfaces is a worthwhile pursuit. Although anger can be difficult to confront, it needs to be acknowledged and released rather than allowed to take control.

4. Poisonous Tempter Demon

Known for its toxicity, the "poisonous tempter demon" in psychological battles symbolizes destructive urges and self-sabotaging behaviors that must be resisted, avoided, or overcome. This demon draws folks toward harmful impulses, negative thought patterns, and self-destructive choices. To counter these urges, it can help to identify healthy coping mechanisms and effective strategies such as meditative practices, positive affirmations, and professional therapy.

Overcoming this inner demon can take time, and progress is rarely linear. Be patient with ourselves, minimize the impact of setbacks, and keep moving forward—even when the struggle feels endless.

5. Envy

Envy, an inner demon, can lead to jealousy and covetousness, fueling discontent and constant comparison within the mind. It can also hinder success by clouding judgment, fostering a toxic mindset, and distracting us from our goals. To counter envy, we can cultivate gratitude and genuinely celebrate others' successes, helping us develop a more positive and collaborative outlook. By acknowledging and addressing this inner struggle, we can move toward overcoming envy and building a more fulfilling mindset—one that supports greater personal, family, societal, and professional success.

6. Passionate Emotions and Impulsive Reactions (PEIR)

The "inner demon" of passionate emotions and impulsive reactions (PEIR) often fuels conflict and emotional outbursts. These intense feelings can cloud our judgment and lead us to act in ways we later regret. When we meet this inner force with compassion and curiosity, we can begin to untangle the dynamics behind PEIR and address the deeper causes of psychological battles. By taking time to identify the triggers that set off PEIR, we gain insight into our thoughts and behavior patterns. This self-consciousness helps us notice when PEIR is rising and take proactive steps to regulate our reactions before they escalate.

7. Sadness

Sadness can foster despair and, if left unchecked, lead to tragedy. This potentially deadly emotion can arrive in waves, cloud judgment, and leave lasting psychological harm. It can consume our thoughts and energy, making it difficult to focus on other parts of our lives.

Even so, investing emotional energy is important. Sadness can prompt us to reflect on our experiences, process our feelings, and ultimately move forward. Like any investment, the more effort we put into understanding and addressing our sadness, the greater the emotional return we can expect. In that sense, this investment can protect us from serious psychological harm.

8. Perfectionism

A diamond can symbolize the inner demon of perfectionism. Just as a diamond is expected to be flawless, perfectionism imposes impossibly high standards that can fuel intense psychological strain. Perfectionism involves setting excessively high expectations for oneself and responding with harsh self-criticism when those expectations aren't met. This relentless pursuit of unattainable ideals can undermine mental health and well-being, often leading to chronic stress, burnout, and a diminished sense of self-worth.

9. Confusion

Confusion can act like an "inner demon," fueling uncertainty and indecision, and intensifying internal conflict. Psychologically, this state can become a significant barrier to clear thinking and emotional well-being, and its effects on a person's mental health should not be underestimated. In the context of psychological warfare, confusion may also be deliberately weaponized to create disorder, sow discord, and distort perceptions. By practicing self-compassion, people can recognize their vulnerabilities, face inner turmoil, and begin a process of self-discovery and growth. For these reasons, the "inner demon" of confusion should not be dismissed as meaningless, unwarranted, or imagined, particularly when viewed through the lens of psychological warfare.

10. Burden Bearer

The inner demon known as the "burden bearer" exacts a heavy toll on the mind and soul, fostering sorrow, negativity, and a sense of entrapment. Although psychological maladies like anxiety, depression, and trauma often take center stage in internal battles, this underlying burden typically remains in the background. Over time, however, as its weight builds, it can emerge as a substantial destructive force within the mind.

11. Deceiver

Inside our minds, a cunning inner demon called the deceiver can ally with other inner demons, creating turmoil on the psychological battlefield. This alliance fuels self-deception and emotional manipulation by exploiting our weaknesses, amplifying doubts, and fixating on perceived flaws. When the deceiver joins forces with envy and anger, it becomes an especially powerful coalition that tightens its grip on our thoughts. By preying on human vulnerabilities, it distorts reality and clouds judgment, steering people toward destructive behaviors that harm mental and emotional well-being. Over time, this manipulation can spark a self-reinforcing cycle of negative thoughts and actions that deepens self-sabotage.

12. Trickster

The inner demon known as the trickster is a complex, unpredictable force that brings confusion and indecision to our internal psychological conflicts. Despite our efforts to anticipate its impact, its elusive nature often catches us off guard. The trickster represents the darker aspects of the psyche—deception, instability, and self-sabotage— and it thrives on creating chaos and sowing doubt.

Recognizing the trickster's presence is the first step toward addressing its effects. Practices such as meditation, journaling, and therapy can help reveal how it operates within us. Its constantly shifting nature, however, makes it especially difficult to confront; just when we think we understand it, it takes on a new form and surprises us.

2.4 Boundaries

Boundaries define limits, territories, and guidelines for when, how, and whether we confront inner demons like the ones we have just identified. Understanding the role of boundaries in warfare helps us see how they are used, why they are established, and how they shape the conduct and outcome of psychological battles.

Protecting our mental space is essential if we want to avoid—and win—the war within our mind. Boundaries keep our inner world from being overwhelmed by negativity. By limiting exposure to toxic influences, whether people, media, or environments, we create a more positive and supportive internal climate. That support is vital for maintaining focus and emotional stability. For example, setting boundaries around negative self-talk can reduce the space envy, sadness, and confusion occupy, while creating room to challenge those thoughts with realistic, constructive narratives.

Establishing boundaries is like creating a playbook for managing the war within our mind. It helps us meet inner demons with clarity, build self-discipline, and turn difficult battles into opportunities for personal growth. With clear boundaries, we can focus more effectively on our goals and values. By reducing the influence of deceptive "trickster" inner demons, we can channel our energy into healthier pursuits and meaningful development.

Boundaries also foster self-discipline by clarifying which behaviors and thought patterns are acceptable. This discipline helps us manage passionate emotions and impulsive reactions (PEIR) more effectively, preventing anxiety and irrational doubt from taking control. In this way, boundaries become tools for change, helping us learn, adapt, and grow stronger through psychological conflict. The mental toughness gained in these battles can become one of our greatest top ten strengths.

When navigating the war within our mind, it is important to practice self-compassion. Self-compassion reduces guilt and feelings of inadequacy, which can intensify psychological battles. It encourages a caring approach to our well-being, making it easier to confront "poisonous tempter" demons without harsh self-criticism. Acknowledging our limitations—and setting boundaries accordingly—prevents overextension and reduces the risk of escalating distress. Managing psychological battles well requires understanding our thoughts, emotions, and behaviors; ideally, we resolve psychological battle before it escalates.

Boundaries reinforce personal power by establishing clear limits. They help us decide which psychological battles deserve our attention and energy, and they protect us from overreacting to minor issues that can accumulate into heavy burdens.

We also need to revisit our habits and assess our mental state regularly. Self-check-ins help us adjust boundaries as our needs evolve. Be gentle with ourselves: recognizing and accepting limitations is not weakness, but a form of strength and self-care. Self-compassion supports a healthier internal dialogue, especially during periods of psychological conflict.

Finally, pay attention to the signals our body and emotions provide. Perfectionism and addiction can trigger physical symptoms, such as fatigue and headaches, and emotional responses, like anxiety or irritability. These signals may indicate that we are pushing beyond what is healthy. Self-reflection is a powerful tool for addressing the inner demons that can spark serious psychological battles. Setting healthy boundaries strengthens our lives and helps us win the war within our mind.

Photo by Daniel R. Linden

Imagine the moon as a central guiding force, much like our instincts and emotions. Just as the moon casts light in every direction, our minds and emotional strengths send signals that shape our decisions, commitment, and resolve. Each beam of moonlight can be seen as an intuitive or emotional cue that helps us better understand our needs and boundaries. And just as moonlight helps us find our way in the dark, noticing and honoring those inner cues helps us set healthy boundaries and stay aligned with our purpose—winning the war within our mind.

Chapter 3: Readiness for Psychological War

Readiness for psychological warfare means taking decisive action—fully committing and deploying the resources we need—to prepare for internal psychological difficulties that threaten our mental well-being. At the same time, it means striving to live a normal, productive, and peaceful life. Life is short and passes quickly, and we are temporary spiritual residents on this planet having a human experience—something many believe is part of a broader spiritual journey.

The decisions we make and the actions we take have ramifications that can significantly influence future generations. It can be a sobering moment when we realize the impact our lives may have on those we may never encounter in the duration of our lives.

Psychological battles within the mind can be a rigorous test of our emotional, cognitive, and social skills. Often experienced as quiet, internal wars, these events can trigger fear, confusion, and desperation—frequently fueled by inner demons such as those identified earlier. Encouragingly, it is possible not only to survive these attacks but also to grow through them by intentionally drawing on our top ten strengths.

Strengths such as mental toughness, empathy, emotional intelligence, self-awareness, patience, courage, adaptability and flexibility, critical thinking, problem solving, and gratitude can serve as both offensive and defensive tools in psychological warfare. These top ten strengths work proactively to confront inner demons and protectively to reduce emotional distress. Developing these traits builds the inner fortitude needed to thrive under pressure. Let's examine each strength and how it works—alone or in combination—to create a psychological arsenal that helps us win the war within our mind.

3.1 Top Ten Strengths to Win the War Within Our Mind

Developing the ability to leverage our top ten strengths starts with identifying and understanding them. This self-consciousness creates the foundation for building those strengths into strategic assets. The top ten strengths that follow offer a solid base for confronting inner demons—ambushes that can trigger intense psychological battles and fuel a psychological war within our mind.

	Strength	Summary Statement
1.	Mental Toughness	Mental toughness gives us the ability to withstand the intense pressure, chaos, and trauma that characterize psychological combat situations.
2.	Empathy	Empathy's superpower lies in its ability to offer and receive psychological support, making it vital to grasp our psychological needs and those of others.
3.	Emotional Intelligence (EI)	The ability to maintain our composure and make sound judgments amidst the chaos during intense psychological battles is a gift given by possessing effective EI.
4.	Self-Awareness	Self-awareness serves two important functions: one is to recognize, and the other is the capability to analyze and understand our own emotions.
5.	Patience	Patience is not just about waiting; it's about how we behave while we're waiting. Not everything is within our control and important endeavors take time to progress.
6.	Courage	When dealing with inner conflict, having courage to face one's inner demons and insecurities is crucial for personal growth and overcoming threats and challenges.
7.	Adaptability and Flexibility	Adaptability involves the capacity to adjust to new conditions. Flexibility refers to the ability to bend or adjust easily to changing circumstances.
8.	Critical Thinking	Critical thinking enables us to analyze, evaluate, and interpret information effectively. It becomes essential when inner demons start psychological battles.
9.	Enhanced Problem Solving	Identifying, analyzing, and resolving complex problems involve approaching psychological battles by considering multiple solutions and anticipating potential outcomes.
10.	Gratitude	Having the courage to face one's inner demons is crucial for personal growth and overcoming psychological battles and winning the war within our mind.

These ten strengths are not ranked in priority order because none of them, on their own, are a definitive solution to overcoming the war within our mind. Depending on the circumstances, and the particular inner demons at play, some strengths may be more effective than others at different times. When fully developed and applied, these top ten strengths can help defeat a wide range of formidable inner demons that seek to create chaos in our lives.

1. Mental Toughness

Mental toughness is one of the most powerful strengths for adapting, improvising, and overcoming psychological battles. It encompasses many psychological attributes that help us confront and eliminate the twelve inner demons identified earlier. Mental toughness includes a high level of resilience, which helps us recover from disorders such as addiction and sadness. Another key component is the ability to maintain focus under pressure. It also helps us regulate and re-regulate our emotions in high-stress situations, allowing us to manage fear, anger, and other intense emotions, as well as reduce impulsive reactions.

Being mentally tough also means having the capacity to quickly and accurately assess changing situations and adjust strategies as needed—finding new ways to dispel inner demons, such as confusion. Mental toughness is further reflected in sustained effort and a willingness to keep going despite obstacles, exhaustion, and doubt. Strong belief in our abilities is a fundamental aspect of mental toughness: self-confidence can counter envy and reduce the tendency toward perfectionism. Overall, mental toughness supports personal growth, well-being, achievement, and long-term success.

To strengthen our mental toughness, consider the following:

Reflect on the situations most likely to wreak havoc, causing maximum emotional distress and inner turmoil. Then plan, prepare, and train tirelessly, focusing on what it will take to win the war within our mind. Train harder and smarter by imagining the toughest, most inconceivable scenarios that would put our mental toughness to maximum test.

Stay present in the moment to examine our thoughts and emotions without judgment. This cultivates inner calm and clarity. Deep reflection sanctions exploring different options, identifying solutions, and mapping out productive next steps, such as seeking support and guidance, strengthening our mental toughness.

Embrace setbacks—they offer valuable lessons and strengthen our resolve. When we combine a growth mindset with hustle, effort, and determination, and refuse to surrender our dreams, we're better able to stay resilient—even when our inner demons feel close.

Connect with trusted friends, family members, or a therapist for support. Remember that no one succeeds entirely on their own; progress often comes from the guidance and encouragement of others. A strong support network helps us become more resilient and gives us more resources to rely on when our mindset is challenged.

Set specific goals to resolve psychological battles. Break each goal into manageable steps, and take massive action to achieve them. Success creates momentum, and the experience we gain becomes invaluable in building mental toughness—now and in the future.

Treat setbacks as opportunities to learn and improve. Never allow failure to define us. It doesn't matter how many times we get knocked down; what matters is getting back up, because every time we do, we give ourselves a chance to come back stronger. Failure can be our greatest teacher.

When we reach life's hardest moments, we often encounter some of the greatest opportunities to draw on our strengths, shape our destiny, and set a strong example for others to follow. This is the true essence of mental toughness.

2. Empathy

Empathy is vital for understanding and connecting with the emotions and experiences of others. In the context of psychological battles, it is especially important because it helps us recognize the emotions that arise during these battles—and the collateral damage they can cause. At its core, empathy enables us to both give and receive emotional support as these internal conflicts unfold and the war within the mind pushes us to our limits.

Practicing empathy toward ourselves during times of psychological distress involves recognizing, accepting, and validating our emotions, thoughts, and inner demons without self-criticism. This practice also encourages self-exploration and supports a more enduring sense of well-being. Through self-empathy, we create an inner safe space to explore the root causes of our conditions, process unresolved feelings, and move toward greater inner peace.

Empathy paves the way for healing and personal growth. By listening to our inner voice and seeking to understand the forces behind our psychological battles, we can uncover ingrained patterns, heal past wounds, and cultivate a stronger sense of inner unity. When we accept our vulnerabilities, we become a more empowered version of ourselves.

Perseverance matters, even when we doubt ourselves. By practicing two key elements of empathy—respect and composure—we can recognize that we're still making a positive difference, even when it doesn't always feel that way. We should give ourselves credit for that.

Those of us who have been through it know that when the battle is at its fiercest, simply showing up is a win.

In the internal battles of the mind, someone in turmoil may not fully understand how their disorder began or what it means. For family and friends, it can be hard to grasp what their loved one is going through. That's why empathy is a strength we must continually cultivate.

The following strategies are designed to strengthen empathy:

1. Give others our full attention when they speak to better understand their emotions and perspectives.

2. Recognize our own fallibility and stay open to what others are experiencing. We may not fully understand the depth of their feelings or the impact of their psychological battles.

3. Cultivate genuine curiosity. Take an interest in others' experiences. The more we learn about someone, the easier it becomes to relate to them.

4. Read literature—such as novels and poetry—and watch films that explore different lives and viewpoints. Immersing ourselves in varied narratives can deepen our understanding of people from different backgrounds.

5. Demonstrate concern in practical ways. Offering help and expressing gratitude can strengthen empathy, trust, and respect.

Empathy enriches relationships, helping us win the war within our mind.

3. Emotional Intelligence

Emotional intelligence (EI) helps us recognize and manage our emotions—skills that strongly shape decision making and can improve outcomes during psychological hardship. Staying composed and making sound judgments amid chaos is a critical life skill and one of the main benefits of strong EI.

A leading authority on EI is Dr. Daniel Goleman, a widely respected author and psychologist. He earned his Ph.D. in psychology from Harvard University and wrote "Emotional Intelligence," published in 1995. Goleman argues that emotional intelligence—skills such as impulse control, persistence, motivation, and social competence—can be as important as a person's intelligence quotient (IQ), a common measure of cognitive ability.

In the context of psychological pathologies, Goleman's work offers both insight and practical strategies. Three key components emphasized in Goleman's model are self-regulation, intrinsic motivation, and social skills. Together, these competencies shape how we manage emotions and navigate relationships.

1. Self-regulation involves managing emotions in ways that reflect personal values and fit the situation. This skill is especially important during psychological distress because it helps people respond thoughtfully rather than react impulsively, reducing the chance of creating additional problems.

2. Intrinsic motivation supports long-term mental health and recovery. Goleman explains that people with a high emotional quotient (EQ) are often guided by internal rewards, such as meaning and personal growth, rather than by external approval or immediate gratification.

3. Social skills, including communication and conflict management, help people build and maintain healthy relationships. Strong social support protects mental health by offering emotional reassurance and practical help when it is needed most.

By strengthening key EI skills, we may reduce internal conflict and disrupt patterns that intensify psychological distress. Goleman's work underscores that developing emotional abilities is central to living a balanced, healthy, and meaningful life, especially during prolonged psychological strain.

After becoming aware of our emotions, the next step is learning to manage them effectively. This includes regulating emotional responses, practicing self-control, and developing healthy coping strategies. As self-management improves, emotions are less likely to escalate, and we are less likely to react impulsively during conflict.

Practical EI skills can also help people stay calm under pressure and make rational decisions that consider both immediate circumstances and long-term consequences. EI encourages people to seek support when needed and to recognize rising psychological strain before it becomes overwhelming. By noticing mental overload early, EI may help prevent escalation and reduce the risk of burnout or crisis. It can also help people identify the emotions and motives behind harmful thought patterns, making those patterns easier to interrupt and replace with healthier responses.

4. Self-Awareness

In psychological terms, self-awareness refers to the capacity for introspection and the ability to recognize ourselves as individuals separate from the environment and other participants. It involves a conscious knowledge of our own character, feelings, motives, and desires.

Heightened self-awareness prompts earlier detection of distressful symptoms, leading to opportunities for quicker intervention and treatment. It also cultivates a deeper understanding of the triggers and thought patterns that exacerbate these conditions, providing an avenue for proactive management rather than a reactive response. The earlier we can address a psychological battle, the less mess there will be, making it much easier to clean up by eradicating inner demons seeking to escalate psychological distress.

Self-awareness serves as a catalyst for personal growth and development. By recognizing areas for growth and improvement, we can unlock our full potential and achieve significant goals. Please remember to: dream big, plan well, work hard, smile always and good things will happen.

To strengthen our self-awareness, a great start is to sketch out the identities of the inner demons we believe are attacking us, bringing them to the surface, attempting to understand their component parts and their origin, if possible. To start, a solid simple technique is to draw a brain diagram. Something as simple as this:

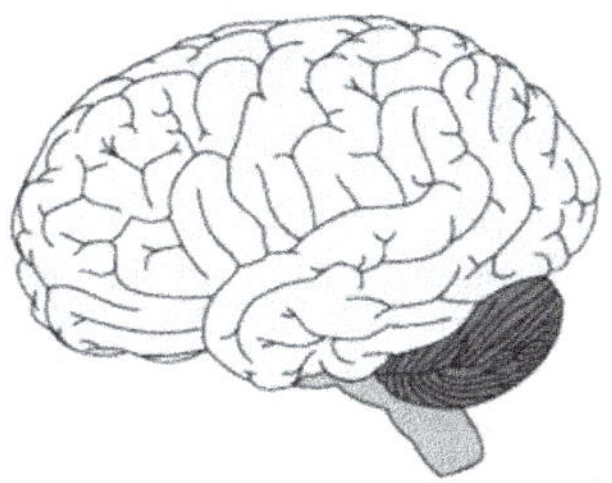

After the blank brain is drawn on paper. Perform an inventory of all inner demons we feel are negatively affecting us. Identify specific inner demons initiating attacks within our brain. Name each we recognize as bad actors and place them on the brain drawing, as illustrated below:

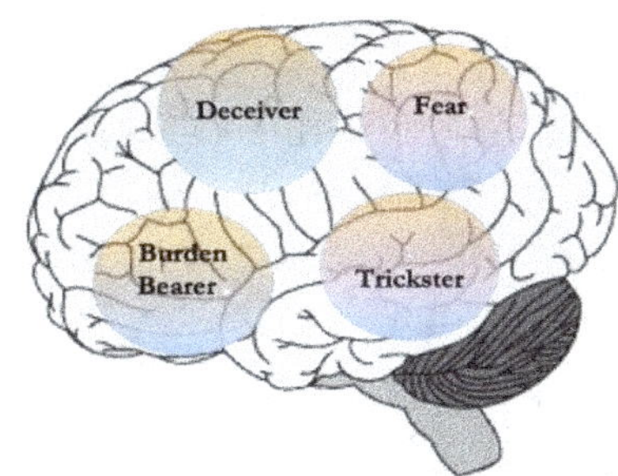

Based on the sketch, we start to draw up battle plans to determine the strategy and tactics for how best we can and when we begin our approach to eliminate these inner demons.

A strong step toward building self-awareness is to ask for feedback from trusted friends, family members, or colleagues. We may not like everything we hear, and that's okay. The key is to receive feedback openly, without becoming defensive, trying to negotiate it away, or getting upset. When someone offers feedback, they're usually trying to help; think of it as a life preserver and accept it.

People who want us to fail rarely take the time to offer thoughtful feedback; they'd rather we stay stuck in ignorance. The feedback we like least may be the feedback we need most—if we're willing to listen without judgment and act on what can truly help. If a piece of feedback feels unhelpful, let it go and move on, like tossing something in the trash.

In turbulent times, when our mind feels like a battlefield, self-awareness becomes even more important. Understanding ourselves amid psychological chaos is a powerful tool: it shapes decisions, guides actions, and ultimately influences where we end up.

5. Patience

In today's fast-paced world, impatience can lead people to rush decisions for immediate gratification, push for outcomes that aren't appropriate, or quit too early when waiting a bit longer would produce a better result. Patience is a powerful strength that shapes our overall well-being and is essential to success—not only in psychological warfare, but in life.

Patience isn't just about waiting, it's about how we behave while we wait. Not everything is within our control, and many worthwhile goals take time to achieve. When we accept this, we can begin to develop greater patience, even if it doesn't come easily for everyone.

By staying present and observing our thoughts and emotions without judgment, we can learn to respond patiently instead of reacting impulsively to our inner demons. These "inner demons"—the deceiver, the trickster, and Passionate Emotion Impulsive Reaction (PEIR)—thrive on impatience because it all but guarantees their success.

Here are some ways the strength of patience can eradicate inner demons, overcome psychological battles, and help win the war within our mind:

- Patience gives us time to process our feelings, leading to thoughtful responses instead of impulsive reactions that can worsen inner turmoil.

- Patience builds resilience, helping us endure and overcome persistent inner demons and ongoing psychological battles.

- Patience creates space for clearer thinking. When our minds are clearer, we can make more rational decisions and find practical solutions to psychological battles.

- With patience, we can step back and analyze problems more objectively, which leads to more effective solutions—an essential part of resolving the war within our mind.

- Practicing patience encourages self-reflection and strengthens self-awareness. Understanding our thoughts and behaviors helps us identify—and overcome—inner demons.

- Patience teaches acceptance—of ourselves, of others, and of situations beyond our control—making it easier to release grudges and negative thoughts that intensify psychological battles.

- When we're patient with others, we strengthen supportive relationships, and that encouragement can help us stay committed as we confront inner demons.

- Patience fosters compassion and forgiveness, which reduces the destructive effects of self-criticism and regret—two common forces in psychological battles.

Invisible psychological battles in the mind are rarely linear. The fight can be slow, difficult, and unpredictable. Cultivating patience takes courage; it requires enduring discomfort while maintaining a long-term perspective in pursuit of healing and growth. As we develop patience within ourselves, we don't just find resolution—we win the war within our mind.

6. Courage

Courage is the willingness to confront fear, pain, danger, or uncertainty. When the battle is psychological, courage means facing inner demons and insecurities, an essential step in overcoming threats, obstacles, and setbacks. Often, it requires stepping outside our comfort zone and confronting fears directly with strength and resolve. Building courage as a personal strength also involves developing the capacity to persevere with passion and determination over time, even when we feel discouraged or defeated.

The strength of courage consists of five key capabilities required to succeed in the face of serious psychological battles. These capabilities encompass a range of skills and attributes, including, but not limited to, the following:

1. Grit – The ability to persevere with passion and determination over long periods, even in the face of extreme difficulties.

2. Tenacity – The determination to keep striving toward a goal despite obstacles.

3. Perseverance – The persistent effort required to achieve something despite difficulties, setbacks, or conflict.

4. Inner Strength – The ability to remain steadfast and emotionally strong during stressful or threatening circumstances.

5. Stamina – The mental endurance needed to withstand prolonged pressure or malady.

Mastering these five aspects of courage is essential for facing an inner psychological battle, one filled with dread that can cause serious harm and lasting emotional scars.

Here are three ways to make our strength of courage stronger:

1. One of the most effective ways to develop courage is to confront our fears by identifying each of them. Give each a name and begin to categorize them, if warranted. This effort allows us to define the theater of operations for psychological battles. By doing this, we can begin to understand how we may want to approach, attack, and eliminate threats.

2. Courage often involves taking risks to expand our comfort zone. By setting goals and summoning the necessary courage to pursue them, we will gradually build our muscles of courage, become comfortable with taking additional risks, and prevail more often than not.

3. Surrounding ourselves with people who encourage us to develop courage becomes essential when the enormous mountain of intimidation necessitates a steep climb. Having a strong support system provides us with the continued inspiration and reassurance needed to face dread, take risks, and triumph.

Fortifying our courage is a transformative process. Initially, it entails being kind to ourselves and striving to comprehend our doubts. It's important to note that courage doesn't mean being fearless but rather acting decisively in the face of fear.

7. Adaptability and Flexibility

In today's fast-paced, constantly changing world, adaptability and flexibility are essential for overcoming psychological battles. Adaptability is the skill of adjusting to new situations by actively modifying strategies, behaviors, or mindset to succeed in a new setting. Flexibility is the ability to shift our approach, viewpoints, or actions with ease.

Within our minds, we often find ourselves locked in a battle against inner demons. These psychological battles take many forms, most commonly self-doubt, anxiety, fear, depression, or the lingering effects of past trauma that continue to affect us. Cultivating our top ten strengths of adaptability and flexibility can be key to overcoming these maladies. Here are four ways to strengthen both:

1. Accept what we feel, choose what we do.

   - Practice noticing emotions/thoughts without immediately fighting them or obeying them.

   - Use a simple Acceptance and Commitment Therapy (ACT)-style check-in: "What am I feeling? What story is my mind telling? What action fits my values right now?"

   - Aim to respond rather than react.

2. Strengthen emotion regulation skills by downshifting our nervous system.

- Use quick, repeatable tools to reduce intensity so we can think clearly:

  - Slow breathing (e.g., 4–6 breaths per minute for 2–3 minutes).

  - Utilize grounding (5–4–3–2–1 senses)—a simple technique to bring our attention back to the present moment by using our five senses. We do it by naming: 5 things we can see, 4 things we can feel (touch/physical sensations—e.g., feet on the floor, fabric on our skin), 3 things we can hear, 2 things we can smell, and 1 thing we can taste.

  - "Name it to tame it" (label the emotion precisely: anxious, disappointed, ashamed, etc.).

  - The goal isn't to erase feelings; it's to widen our "window of tolerance" so we can stay functional.

3. Practice cognitive flexibility by updating our interpretations.

- Train ourselves to generate multiple plausible explanations and options instead of locking onto one threat narrative.

- Try a quick reframe routine:

  - Evidence for/against my thought?

  - What would I tell a friend?

  - What's another angle that's also true?

  - Replace "I can't handle this" with "this is hard, and I can take the next step."

4. Create supportive structure and connection.

- Maintain basics that make our mind more adaptable: sleep, movement, regular meals, reduced substance abuse, and routines that lower baseline stress.

- Use social flexibility: ask for help earlier, diversify support (friend, group, therapist, mentor), and communicate needs clearly.

- When stuck, professional help can rapidly increase coping range.

Developing adaptability and flexibility is an ongoing process that requires commitment, self-reflection, and a willingness to learn and grow. By bolstering these strengths, we can become successful in navigating the complexities of psychological warfare and win the war within our mind.

8. Critical Thinking

Emotions triggered by psychological battles can cloud judgment, leading us to prioritize feelings over facts. When emotional reasoning overrides logical analysis, people may make high-stakes decisions based on a distorted view of reality, which can lead to serious but avoidable harm.

Critical thinking helps counter the effects of overwhelming emotional reasoning. It involves logical analysis—actively analyzing, assessing, synthesizing, and evaluating information gathered through observation, experience, reasoning, or communication.

Addressing psychological battles associated with a war within our mind often involves developing strategies to manage stress, seeking support through therapy or counseling, practicing alertness, and intentionally engaging in activities that promote clear, rational thinking. This can help create space for reflection and reduce the impact of psychological strife on cognitive processes.

Strengthening our critical thinking requires developing our analytical thinking, open-mindedness, judgment skills, and creativity. The ideas below outline how we can do this.

Analytical Thinking

- Ask better questions by clarifying our goals, definitions, and constraints.

- Break problems down, decompose into smaller parts, map cause → effect, and tackle one variable at a time.

- Seek data, verify sources, and distinguish facts from assumptions.

- Consider alternatives, generate multiple hypotheses/solutions and compare trade-offs.

- Check for bias by watching for confirmation bias, anchoring, and "gut-feel" conclusions; actively look for disconfirming evidence.

- After decisions, do quick post-mortems (e.g., what worked, what didn't, what we'd change next time).

Open-Mindedness

- Assume we might be wrong. Hold beliefs lightly and treat opinions as "best guess so far."

- Seek opposing views by reading/listening to credible people who disagree and summarize their argument fairly.

- Ask curious questions: "What evidence would change my mind?" "What am I missing?"

- Separate identity from ideas by a critique of thoughts, not people (including ourselves).

- Pause before reacting; consider multiple explanations.

- Try to understand the other person's goals, context, and constraints.

Judgment Skills

- Clarify the decision and define the goal, constraints, and what "good" looks like.

- Gather relevant facts. Use reliable sources. Separate data from assumptions.

- Consider options and trade-offs to compare alternatives, costs, risks, and second-order effects.

- Watch for confirmation bias, overconfidence, and emotional reactions.

- Estimate likelihoods and plan for best/likely/worst cases.

- Use simple decision tools—pros/cons with weights, decision matrices, or pre-mortems ("how could this fail?").

- Get feedback by consulting knowledgeable people and invite criticism.

<u>Creativity</u>

- Capture ideas constantly by keeping a notes app/notebook and write down small sparks quickly.

- Read widely, explore other fields, and collect interesting examples.

- Create constraints by setting limits (time, materials, rules) to force novel solutions.

- Generate lots of options, at first aim for quantity first. Be careful not to judge too early.

- Take breaks, walks, get good sleep, and downtime help insights surface.

- Illustrate prototypes by sketching, drafting, or building rough versions to discover better ideas.

- Share and iterate, get feedback, refine, and repeat.

9. Enhanced Problem Solving

In the realm of cognitive abilities, critical thinking and enhanced problem-solving skills stand as pillars of intellectual prowess. These two skills possess distinct characteristics that set them apart. Both empower us to win the war within our mind. Here are some differences that define them.

Critical Thinking	Enhanced Problem Solving
Primarily analyzing, evaluating, and reasoning.	Applies thought processes to find solutions to specific challenges.
Aims to assess information, arguments, or situations objectively.	Aims to generate and implement effective solutions to a specific issue.
Emphasizes analysis and evaluation.	Emphasizes action and results.
Concerned with thinking correctness and logic.	Concerned with achieving an outcome efficiently and effectively.
Uses logic, reasoning, interpretation, and reflection.	Uses creativity, decision making, and strategy development.
End goal: Reach well-supported conclusions or judgments.	End goal: Produce practical, innovative, or optimized solutions.
Can apply broadly to arguments, information, claims, or beliefs.	Typically applies to specific issues, projects, or organizational issues.
Can be practiced independently of an immediate problem.	Often relies on critical thinking as one stage in the process.
Judged by the strength and validity of reasoning.	Judged by the effectiveness and success of the solution.
Produces understanding or informed judgment.	Produces a concrete solution or implementation plan.

When coupled with our top ten strengths, critical thinking and enhanced problem solving serve as a lethal weapon to prevail and win the war within our mind. Examples include:

- Fear often leads to anxiety and paralyzing decision making. By employing enhanced problem-solving attributes, we can analyze the root causes of our doubts and develop practical strategies to overcome them. Setting specific goals and action plans can help in confronting and, gradually eliminating, fear.

- Addiction can overpower rational thought and lead to destructive behaviors. Enhanced problem-solving attributes, coupled with adaptability and flexibility, can aid in developing personalized strategies to break free from dependencies and cravings. By setting clear objectives and implementing effective solutions, we can gradually regain control over our actions and thoughts.

- Anger often results in self-destructive tendencies and chaos. Utilizing enhanced problem-solving attributes to channel emotions into productive outlets can help in managing anger. Strategies such as contemplation, emotional intelligence, and empathy can assist in understanding the triggers of anger and devising constructive ways to address and resolve underlying issues.

- Perfectionism, characterized by excessively high standards and self-criticism, can hinder personal growth. Enhanced problem-solving attributes, in combination with self-awareness and gratitude, can help us recognize and challenge perfectionistic tendencies. By focusing on progress rather than perfection, we can cultivate a more positive and growth-oriented mindset.

The integration of enhanced problem-solving attributes with strengths such as mental toughness, empathy, and critical thinking provides a powerful framework for combating the inner demons.

Ultimately, by waging a psychological war with a strategic approach rooted in enhanced problem solving and strength-based tactics, we can triumph over our inner demons and win the war within our mind.

10. Gratitude

Gratitude is the quality of being thankful and recognizing the good things in our life, both big and small. It's about noticing and appreciating the kindness, opportunities, and positive experiences we encounter, as well as the efforts of others who contribute to our well-being.

Having gratitude as a strength is important because it allows us to focus on what's positive in our lives rather than what's lacking. This fresh, positive perspective stymies the inner demons involved in a psychological battle. When the inner demons are not the center of attention in the war within our mind, the oxygen gets sucked out of their lungs and then they die.

When our strength of gratitude is buried by a swath of inner demons during a psychological war, we tend to be unhappy, stressed out, and become less resilient. However, when we're grateful, we're more likely to view obstacles as learning opportunities instead of setbacks. Gratitude shifts our perspective, helping us see abundance rather than scarcity. This results in a more fulfilling, optimistic outlook on life, which can limit psychological battles and help us win the war within our mind.

Gratitude can be a potent strength for overcoming our inner demons. Here's how we can use it effectively:

<u>Shift the Focus of Attention:</u> Psychological battles often feed on what's missing—what we don't have, what's wrong, what hurts. Gratitude redirects our awareness toward what is working, what is beautiful, and what is meaningful.

- Practice: Each day, name three specific things we're grateful for, not general platitudes, but real, concrete moments (e.g., the sunlight through my window, my friend who listened to me, my own persistence today).

- Why it works: The brain can't simultaneously dwell in fear and gratitude. The act of noticing good things starves negativity of its energy.

<u>Strengthen Our Psychological Armor:</u> In the war within our mind, gratitude acts like armor, not by denying pain, but by grounding us in perspective.

- Practice: Before sleep, recall barriers from the day then note one lesson or strength we gained from each.

- Why it works: Pain becomes meaningful; adversity stops feeling like pure loss and starts feeling like adaptation.

<u>Anchor to the Present</u>: Anxiety pulls us into the future; regret drags us into the past. Gratitude is a consciousness practice that anchors attention in this moment.

- Practice: When we feel mental chaos, pause and breathe. Name one thing, even something small, we are grateful for right now.

- Why it works: Presence dissolves many psychological battles before they escalate.

The practice of gratitude has been increasingly recognized for its ability to help people confront inner demons, overcome psychological battles and, ultimately, win the war within our mind.

3.2 Mindfulness

Mindfulness is the practice of intentionally paying attention to the present moment with openness, curiosity, and without judgment. It involves being fully aware of our thoughts, feelings, bodily sensations, and surroundings as they occur, rather than getting caught up in the past or worrying about the future.

When we speak of inner demons or the psychological war within our mind, we're referring to the difficult emotions, self-defeating thoughts, dread, and impulses that can dominate our inner world. Mindfulness offers a way to engage with these forces not by fighting them in the traditional sense, but by transforming our relationship with them. Here's how:

- Recognize the battlefield. Rally awareness before taking action. When we're unaware, our thoughts and emotions control us. But when we "see" them clearly ("ah, anger is here," "fear is rising," "self-criticism is talking again"), the results from inner demons lose their automatic power. Awareness is the first act of liberation.

- As a general rule, stop fighting and start befriending. The counterintuitive truth is that trying to crush or ignore our inner demons often strengthens them. Mindfulness teaches us to cope with discomfort, fear, jealousy, and sadness without resistance. As we breathe through it, we train our mind to stay open and curious instead of reactive. The "enemy" becomes a teacher, revealing unmet needs, hidden pain, or unhealed wounds.

- Stay grounded in the present moment. The war in our mind is often fueled by regrets about the past or anxieties about the future. Anchoring attention in the breath, bodily sensations, or sounds around us helps bring us into "the now," where most of those imagined battles dissolve. Try short moments of dropping into the present throughout the day, simple awareness, without needing to fix or change anything.

- Train ourselves for response overreacting. Mindfulness develops the space between what happens and how we respond. Over time, we learn that we are not our thoughts or emotions; we are the awareness behind them. From that position of inner steadiness, we can choose actions aligned with our values rather than being pushed by fear or anger.

- Cultivate compassion and forgiveness. A significant shift occurs when we replace inner criticism with gentle understanding. Speak to ourselves as we would to a lifelong friend. Self-compassion doesn't make us weak, it gives us the mental toughness to face pain without collapsing. When we soften toward our own suffering, the inner demons begin to lose their grip.

- Admit consistency is the key. Mindfulness is not a single battle, it's lifelong training. Sometimes we have to fight the same battle over and over again. A regular practice, whether it's seated meditation, mindful walking, or simple pauses during the day, gradually reconditions the mind to gain greater stamina, stability, and courage.

- Seek guidance when needed. Psychological battles are intense. In many situations, it can be helpful to talk with a therapist or meditation counselor. We don't have to fight the war alone. Seeking assistance is a sign of strength.

In essence, mindfulness wins the war within not by destroying the enemy, but by understanding it so deeply that its power dissolves. Victory comes as peace, not conquest.

People often develop mindfulness through practices such as meditation, mindful breathing, or mindful movement (like yoga or tai chi).

Here are a few simple mindfulness exercises that need no special equipment or previous experience:

1. Mindful Breathing

    ⇒ Sit or stand comfortably.

    ⇒ Focus our attention on our breath as it enters and leaves our body.

    ⇒ Notice the rise and fall of our chest or the feeling of air passing through our nostrils.

    ⇒ If our mind wanders (and it will), bring our attention back to our breath without judgment.

    ⇒ Try this for one to five minutes to start.

2. Body Scan

    ⇒ Lie down or sit comfortably and close our eyes.

    ⇒ Bring our awareness to our toes, noticing any sensations, tension, or relaxation.

    ⇒ Move upward slowly—feet, legs, abdomen, chest, arms, neck, and head.

    ⇒ Imply notice what we feel without trying to change anything.

    ⇒ This helps build awareness of physical sensations and releases tension.

3. Mindful Walking

    ⇒ Walk slowly and deliberately, paying attention to each step.

    ⇒ Feel our feet touching the ground, the movement of our legs, and the rhythm of our steps.

    ⇒ Notice our surroundings—the colors, sounds, and smells—without labeling them.

    ⇒ This can be especially helpful if sitting meditation is hard for us.

4. Mindful Eating

   ⇒ Choose a small piece of food, like a raisin or slice of fruit.

   ⇒ Observe its color, texture, and smell before we take a bite.

   ⇒ As we chew, notice the flavor and texture, and chew slowly.

   ⇒ This exercise helps cultivate gratitude and reduces mindless eating.

5. Three-Minute Pause

   ⇒ Whenever we feel overwhelmed, pause for three minutes:

   ⇒ Acknowledge what we're thinking or feeling in the moment.

   ⇒ Breathe and focus on the sensations of breathing.

   ⇒ Expand our awareness outward, noticing our body and surroundings.

Engaging in regular mindfulness exercises can aid in stress reduction, enhance focus, improve emotional regulation, and promote overall well-being.

3.3 The Role Adversity Plays in Success

Adversity is essential to winning the war within our mind because internal psychological battles push us to improvise, adapt, and overcome the inner demons that threaten to defeat us. We should be thankful for adversity because like it or not, it contributes to our success.

Adversity forces us to think creatively, develop new strategies, and build skills we might never have gained in more comfortable circumstances. Failure, unwelcome as it is, can prompt us to examine what happened and why. This book is about winning; however, losing has its own lesson: it hurts. It leaves a bitter taste, stirs regret, and can cause emotional, and sometimes physical, pain. Yet that discomfort can be exactly what we need to strengthen our resolve and sharpen our abilities. Losing can reveal how strongly we want to succeed; if a loss doesn't affect us, the victory likely wouldn't have meant much either. Taking time to reflect on what matters most helps us redirect our energy toward meaningful goals instead of superficial ones. Obstacles often spark innovation, and many breakthroughs come from trying to solve hard problems or work within limitations.

Ralph Waldo Emerson's famous essay "Self-Reliance," first published in 1841, explored the roll of adversity acting as a catalyst to summon inner strength for ultimate success.

Emerson wrote:

"…A great man is always willing to be little. While he sits on a cushion of advantages, he goes to sleep, but when he is pushed, tormented, and defeated, he has a chance to learn something…" — Ralph Waldo Emerson, American Philosopher

Emerson's statement highlights the belief that facing difficulties is crucial for personal development and managing psychological battles. These growth experiences aid in resolving inner turmoil and discovering inner tranquility. Emerson implies that genuine learning frequently arises from moments of failure and adversity. Those who have encountered and triumphed over adversity emerge with a stronger sense of direction. This kind of change assists us with newfound clarity and greater resolve.

3.4 Advanced Readiness Methods for Psychological War

Potential ultra-powerful weapons to combat psychological warfare are still to come by way of Artificial Intelligence (AI) and Machine Learning (ML).

Artificial Intelligence (AI) is a broad field of computer science focused on creating systems that can perform tasks that normally require human intelligence. These tasks include problem solving, reasoning, learning, understanding language, recognizing objects or patterns, and making decisions. The goal of AI is to make machines "intelligent," meaning they can replicate certain aspects of human cognitive abilities to some degree.

Machine Learning (ML) is a subset of AI. It focuses on building algorithms that can learn from data and improve automatically over time without being explicitly programmed. Instead of following hard-coded rules, an ML model is trained on data and uses statistical methods to find patterns and make predictions or decisions.

The overall concept of AI is to create machines that can simulate human intelligence. A subset of AI deals with algorithms that learn from data. The goal is to enable machines to perform intelligent tasks, learn from experience (data), and improve their performance. The broad scope includes reasoning, perception, planning, language processing, etc., while a narrow focus is on learning from data. Approaches include rule-based systems, logic, or learning-based methods based on data-driven learning techniques (supervised, unsupervised, reinforcement). Examples include virtual assistants (e.g., Siri, Alexa), expert systems, autonomous robots, spam detection, recommendation systems, image recognition, and stock market predictions. In simple terms, AI is the big picture, making computers act like humans. ML is a way to achieve AI, by enabling computers to learn from data and improve with experience.

Here are a few areas where AI and ML have shown promise in helping us on the psychological battlefield:

- Early Detection and Diagnosis: AI algorithms can analyze data from speech patterns, social media activity, and other digital footprints to identify early signs of psychological wars of depression or anxiety. This can lead to timely intervention.

- Personalized Therapy and Mental Health Apps: AI-driven apps offer personalized therapy solutions, providing users with cognitive behavioral therapy exercises, mood tracking, and relaxation techniques tailored to our specific needs.

- 24/7 Support Through Chatbots: AI chatbots can provide immediate support to people struggling with mental health issues. They can engage in conversation, offer coping strategies, and direct users to professional help, if needed. This is such a novel and new area; we all need to utilize caution as we proceed.

- Reducing Stigma – By promoting awareness and providing anonymous platforms for support, AI tools can help reduce the stigma associated with seeking mental health care.

While there are significant technological advances to make, there are valid concerns about privacy, ethics, and refinement in AI and ML technologies. AI and ML hold significant promise for aiding mental health care and reducing our psychological burdens.

Enhanced problem-solving skills hold immense potential to help us uncover inner demons, win psychological battles, and prevail in the war within our mind.

Photo by Daniel R. Linden

When we face psychological warfare and engage in psychological battles, we may not always see the forest through the trees. Our character helps us develop strengths to overcome fear and uncertainty. The bigger picture becomes clearer as our top ten strengths grow stronger. By embracing our inner desires and passions and confronting inner demons, we create meaning in a seemingly chaotic world.

Chapter 4: Destroying Twelve Inner Demons in Developing Minds

Winning the psychological war in young developing minds is especially critical for three main reasons. First, young minds can be highly impressionable due to the lack of experience that comes with success and setbacks over much longer periods of time. Second, youth bring exuberance and a desire to contribute to our world. Most young people instinctively want to do the right thing to impress family, friends, and others with their sincerity, developing knowledge, increasing skills, and enhanced capabilities. Third, younger people haven't had a lengthy amount of time to properly toughen their emotional feelings, resilience to psychological manipulation, and develop an indomitable force of mental and moral qualities. This can lead to greater sensitivity and susceptibility to psychological warfare arising from a plethora of sources in today's cyber-active society.

The journey of navigating the complexities of the human mind is often fraught with challenges and inner battles that can shape the way we perceive the world and ourselves. Here is a list of emotional attacks our younger generation can be exposed to:

- Emotional abuse

- Verbal assault

- Emotional trauma

- Gaslighting (making another doubt their own perceptions, memories, or understanding of reality)

- Character assassination

- Hostile criticism

- Bullying (emotional or psychological)

- Undermining or belittling

- Psychological aggression

- Emotional exploitation

- Narcissistic abuse

- Toxic communication

- Emotional ambush

- Attack on our self-esteem

In addition, here are different forms of cyberbullying that may occur:

- Harassment: Repeatedly sending offensive, rude, and insulting messages.

- Cyberstalking: Monitoring someone's online activity without their permission.

- Impersonation: Creating fake accounts or pretending to be someone else to damage their reputation.

- Outing: Sharing someone's personal or private information online without their consent.

- Exclusion: Intentionally leaving someone out of online activities, groups, or conversations.

- Doxxing: Sharing someone's private information, such as their address or phone number, online with malicious intent.

- Trolling: Posting inflammatory or offensive comments to provoke a negative reaction.

- Sexting: Sharing sexual messages, images, or videos without consent, leading to embarrassment or humiliation.

- Dissing: Posting or spreading rumors, gossip, or negative comments about someone online.

- Catfishing: Pretending to be someone else online in order to deceive or manipulate others.

Young people, in particular, are susceptible to a myriad of inner demons initiated by these psychological threats. The inner demons we have mentioned: fear, addiction, anger, poisonous tempter demon, envy, passionate emotions and impulsive reactions, sadness, confusion, burden bearer, deceiver and trickster, hinder their growth and potential. This is the reason we must rally our top ten strengths: mental toughness, empathy, emotional intelligence, self-awareness, patience, courage, adaptability and flexibility, critical thinking, enhanced problem solving, and gratitude to defend and win the war within our mind.

Photo by William John Linden, IV

Charged particles in the Northern Lights collide with the Earth's atmosphere and release energy as light. Likewise, challenges and strong emotions in a developing mind can "collide" with support, reflection, and learning, transforming harmful inner demons into insight and growth, rather than letting them cause damage.

4.1 Facing Fear

Fear, characterized by anxiety and apprehension, can often paralyze decision making and hinder progress. To combat fear, young people should cultivate courage, facing their fears head on and embracing discomfort as a catalyst for growth.

What fears do our young people need to be aware of as they successfully advance in their lives, what resources do they need and what are the best strategies they can implement to overcome these fears in their lives?

<u>Common Fears Young People Face</u>

- Fear of Failure: The pressure to be successful academically, professionally, or personally can lead to anxiety about making mistakes.

- Fear of Uncertainty: With rapid social, economic, and technological change, the future can seem unclear or unstable.

- Fear of Rejection or Judgment: Many aspects of social media and societal expectations can heighten self-consciousness and comparison.

- Fear of Inadequacy: Many of us clash with the feeling "not good enough," even when we are doing well.

- Fear of Disconnection or Loneliness: True belonging can be hard to find in a digital era, leading to isolation.

- Fear of Making the Wrong Choices: Life decisions about career, relationships, or identity can feel overwhelming.

<u>Resources Young People Need</u>

- Mentorship and Guidance: Access to mentors, educators, and advisors who can share experiences and offer perspective.

- Mental Health Support: Counseling, peer groups, meditation programs, and other emotional wellness resources.

- Educational and Financial Resources: Scholarships, financial literacy education, and career training to reduce stress about economic insecurity.

- Community and Peer Support: Environments that foster positive relationships and mutual encouragement.

- Opportunities for Skill Building: Leadership programs, volunteering, and internships that build confidence and competence.

- Access to Reliable Information: Guidance in critically evaluating information and media, especially online.

<u>Strategies to Overcome These Fears</u>

- Cultivate Self-Consciousness: Encourage reflection on strengths, values, and goals. This helps reduce comparison and builds inner confidence.

- Develop a Growth Mindset: Viewing setbacks as opportunities allows us to improve our knowledge and capabilities.

- Set Realistic Goals: Break long-term goals into smaller, achievable steps to maintain motivation and build momentum.

- Practice Emotional Regulation: Techniques like meditation, journaling, or breathing exercises can help manage fear and anxiety.

- Seek Connection and Support: Opening up to friends, family, or professionals helps normalize unrealistic concerns and reduce isolation.

- Limit Negative Influences: Managing social media use and avoiding environments that reinforce insecurity or comparison.

- Celebrate Small Wins: Recognize progress to reinforce confidence and self-efficacy.

- Develop Resilience: Accept that setbacks are part of growth and focus on recovery and persistence.

Young people can thrive by understanding fear is a natural part of growth. Accessing supportive networks, learning healthy coping skills, and focusing on continuous self-improvement, rather than perfection, can transform fear into motivation and confidence.

4.2 Addressing Addiction

Adolescence and young adulthood are times of intense growth and change, both physically and emotionally. Young people may be more susceptible to trying risky behaviors, including experimenting with drugs or alcohol, as they establish their individual identities.

Peer pressure can be a highly influential force, particularly during adolescence and young adulthood. Young people often want to feel accepted and liked by their peers. The desire to fit in and be part of a group can lead members to conform to group norms, even if it means participating in risky behaviors. The fear of being excluded or ostracized by peers can be a strong motivator. This influence can make it challenging for human beings to resist engaging in activities, such as substance abuse, that their peers are participating in. Young people may be more susceptible to peer pressure due to their still-developing brains. The prefrontal cortex, which is responsible for decision making and impulse control, is not fully developed until the mid-20s, making it harder for young people to resist peer influences. It is important for young people to learn how to navigate peer pressure, develop strong self-esteem and decision-making skills, and build healthy relationships based on mutual respect and support.

Young people may turn to substances as a way to cope with stress, anxiety, depression, or other mental health issues. The desire to escape negative feelings or difficult situations can make addiction more likely. Many young people may not fully understand the consequences of addiction or the risks associated with substance abuse. They may underestimate the potential harm and believe they are invincible to addiction.

It is important for young people to receive education, support, and guidance to help prevent and address addictive behaviors. Young people may have easy access to substances, whether it be through friends, family members, or social settings. The availability of drugs and alcohol can make it easier for young people to experiment and develop addictive behaviors.

Addictions Young People Should Be Aware Of

Alcohol and drugs:

- Common substances include alcohol, nicotine/vaping, cannabis, and prescription or illicit drugs. Consequences include impaired judgment, poor academic or professional performance, health problems, and damaged relationships.

Behavioral addictions:

- Excessive use of social media and screen time can lead to anxiety, depression, low self-esteem, and reduced productivity.

- Gaming can interfere with sleep, social responsibilities, and motivation.

- Online gambling apps make this dangerously accessible.

- Shopping and spending influenced by online marketing and peer comparison can lead to financial stress.

- Pornography and unhealthy relationships may distort perceptions of intimacy and self-worth.

- Achievement and work addictions can lead to overworking and perfectionism—while ambition is good, lack of balance leads to burnout, mental fatigue, and health decline.

<u>Strategies to Prevent and Overcome Addictions</u>

- Understand personal risk factors, such as stress, loneliness, or family history.

- Regularly reflect on habits—what's consumed (online and physically) and why.

- Manage stress through exercise, meditation, journaling, or creative outlets.

- Prioritize good sleep, proper nutrition, and physical activity.

- Set goals and boundaries.

- Create schedules that balance work, study, social life, and rest.

- Use digital wellbeing tools to limit screen time or social media use.

- Seek help early if negative patterns are noticed or noticeable, talk to a counselor or trusted adult. Remember that asking for help is a sign of strength, not weakness.

- Surround ourselves with peers who have healthy habits and similar values.

- Volunteer or engage in activities that foster connection and purpose.

- Substitute risky habits with positive ones—physical activities, reading, or skill-building hobbies.

- Track progress and celebrate small victories.

<u>Educational Resources Young People Need</u>

1. Evidence-based programs in schools or communities about mental health and addiction awareness.

Evidence-based programs (EBPs) are interventions or initiatives that have been scientifically tested and proven effective through rigorous research and evaluation. In the context of mental health and addiction awareness, EBPs in schools or communities use established psychological, educational, and public health methods to promote emotional well-being, prevent substance misuse, and build resilience.

These programs are designed using data and evidence to ensure they make a measurable difference—for example, improving coping skills, reducing stigma around mental health, or lowering rates of substance abuse among youth. They are often guided by theories of behavior change (such as Social Learning Theory or the Health Belief Model) and rely on consistent replication to maintain effectiveness.

Common Elements of Effective EBPs:

- Clearly defined goals and measurable outcomes.

- Trained facilitators who implement the program consistently.

- Ongoing evaluation and data collection to ensure effectiveness.

- Inclusion of family and community engagement components.

- Cultural sensitivity and adaptability to fit local needs.

Evidence-based programs for mental health and addiction awareness in schools and communities are grounded in research and emphasize prevention, education, and skill-building. They aim to create supportive environments where people can understand, talk about, and manage mental health concerns in a healthy, informed way.

2. Access to accurate online resources including SAMHSA and NIDA.

Here's a clear overview of each organization, what they do, their main goals, how people can access their services, and how they contribute to fighting addiction:

Substance Abuse and Mental Health Services Administration (SAMHSA) is a U.S. government agency within the Department of Health and Human Services (HHS). It leads public health efforts to advance behavioral health and reduce the impact of substance abuse and mental illness on communities.

SAMHSA main objectives:

- Improve access to mental health and substance abuse treatment.

- Provide funding and grants for prevention and treatment programs.

- Promote policies that support recovery and community resilience.

- Offer reliable data and resources for public health professionals and the general public.

How to access SAMHSA:

- Website: www.samhsa.gov

- Helpline: 1-800-662-HELP (4357) — a free, confidential 24/7 treatment referral and information service. Support to help face substance abuse and mental health issues.

- People and families can use SAMHSA's "Treatment Locator" tool online to find local mental health or substance abuse services.

SAMHSA helps fight addiction by providing funding for prevention and treatment programs, educates the public about substance abuse disorders, trains professionals, and connects people to evidence-based care and recovery resources.

National Institute on Drug Abuse (NIDA) is part of the U.S. National Institutes of Health (NIH). It leads scientific research on drug use and addiction.

NIDA main objectives:

- Conduct and support research on the causes, prevention, and treatment of drug use and addiction.

- Disseminate findings to policymakers, health care providers, and the public.

- Develop science-based strategies to reduce drug use and its consequences.

How to access NIDA:

- Website: www.nida.nih.gov

- Free access to publications, data, and educational materials for students, parents, and professionals.

NIDA helps fight addiction by funding and publishing cutting-edge research, NIDA improves understanding of addiction as a brain disorder and supports the development of new treatments and prevention strategies.

Addictions, whether chemical or behavioral, can trap even the most promising human beings. Awareness, education, and intentional self-discipline are key to prevention. By staying informed, nurturing healthy routines, participating in physical wellness programs, engaging in extracurricular opportunities, and recognizing when to ask for help, young people can protect their future success, promote balance, positive engagement, and well-being.

4.3 Overcoming Anger

Anger, with its self-destructive tendencies and chaos, can cloud judgment and lead to regrettable actions. Younger people can be especially susceptible to these misfortunes. Empathy plays a crucial role in managing anger, allowing us to understand and regulate our emotions effectively. Similar to a fine wine, our strength of empathy takes time to develop effectively, just like time turning a good wine into a truly exceptional one. Anger is a natural emotion, but when not recognized or managed properly, it can become a barrier to personal growth, healthy relationships, and success.

It's important for young people to understand what causes anger, what support and resources can help them move forward in life, and which strategies work best for managing and overcoming anger.

<u>Sources of Anger Young People Should Be Aware Of</u>

- Unrealistic Expectations and Pressure: Academic pressure, career competition, or the expectation to "succeed quickly" can lead to frustration.

- Comparison Involving Social Media: Constant exposure to others' achievements can fuel self-doubt and resentment.

- Identity and Purpose Issues: Uncertainty about our future or sense of direction can cause internal tension.

- Family and Social Relationships: Conflicts with parents, peers, or romantic partners can generate anger when communication breaks down.

- Injustice or Unfair Treatment: Discrimination, bullying, or feeling unheard can provoke deep anger.

- Unresolved Past Pain: Childhood trauma or suppressed emotions can resurface as anger under stress.

Understanding where anger comes from helps young people manage it effectively rather than react impulsively.

<u>Resources Young People Need to Positively Overcome Anger</u>

- Emotional Education: Learning about emotional intelligence in schools, youth programs, or workshops.

- Support Systems: Trusted mentors, counselors, friends, or youth groups that offer understanding and perspective.

- Mental Health Services: Access to therapy, especially cognitive behavioral therapy (CBT), which helps in recognizing thought patterns that lead to anger.

- Faith or Spiritual Communities: Many find grounding in spiritual principles that promote forgiveness and peace.

- Healthy Outlets: Opportunities for physical activity, art, writing, or volunteering to channel emotions productively.

When provided, accessible, and embraced properly, these resources can help young people prevent the development of or deal with issues of anger.

<u>Effective Strategies for Overcoming Anger</u>

- Self-Consciousness: Learn to recognize what situations or thoughts trigger anger. Journaling can help track patterns.

- Pause and Breathe: Practice meditation or deep-breathing techniques to regain control before responding.

- Reframe the Situation: Ask ourselves, "What else could this mean?" Shifting perspective reduces emotional intensity.

- Positive Expression: Communicate feelings calmly using "I" statements (e.g., "I feel frustrated when…").

- Forgiveness and Letting Go: Holding grudges keep anger alive; forgiveness releases emotional energy.

- Healthy Lifestyle: Regular exercise, balanced diet, and adequate sleep improve emotional regulation.

- Goal-Focused Thinking: Channel anger into motivation and transform frustration into determination and problem-solving action.

- Seek Help When Needed: If anger becomes uncontrollable or harmful, reach out to a counselor or mental health professional.

Controlling anger is important not only for emotional well-being but also for physical health. Unmanaged anger can have serious consequences on the body and mind.

Here are five key health reasons why it's important to control feelings of anger:

1. Heart Health and Blood Pressure: Frequent anger triggers the body's "fight or flight" response, increasing heart rate and blood pressure. Over time, this can strain the heart, increase the risk of hypertension, and contribute to heart disease, heart attacks, or strokes.

2. Immune System Function: Chronic anger and stress can weaken the immune system, making the body more susceptible to infections and illnesses. When we're often angry, the body produces stress hormones like cortisol, which can suppress immune activity.

3. Mental Health and Emotional Stability: Persistent anger is linked to higher rates of anxiety, depression, and other mood disorders. It can also increase feelings of frustration and helplessness, making it harder to maintain emotional balance.

4. Digestive and Metabolic Health: Anger activates stress responses that disrupt digestion and can trigger or worsen conditions like acid reflux, ulcers, or irritable bowel syndrome. It can also interfere with appetite and metabolism regulation.

5. Relationships and Social Health: Uncontrolled anger can damage relationships with family, friends, and coworkers. Poor relationships and social isolation, in turn, are risk factors for both physical and mental health problems, including depression and cardiovascular disease.

Managing anger isn't about suppression—it's about self-mastery. By combining meditation, reflection, healthy outlets, and communication skills, young people can turn anger into clarity, purpose, and emotional strength.

Anger itself is not bad, it signals that something needs attention. The goal is not to eliminate anger, but to understand and transform it into wisdom, empathy, and positive action. With the right awareness, resources, and strategies, young people can turn anger into a tool for personal growth and leadership.

4.4 Protection from the Poisonous Tempter Demon

The poisonous tempter demon embodies destructive urges and self-sabotaging behaviors. Gratitude can act as a shield against the poisonous tempter demon, fostering a positive mindset and reducing psychological toxicity.

Sources of destructive urges and self-sabotaging behaviors that our young people need to be aware of in order to advance in their lives, as well as the resources they need and an understanding of the best strategies they can implement to overcome these destructive urges and self-sabotaging behaviors, include the following:

<u>Sources of Destructive Urges and Self-Sabotaging Behaviors</u>

1. Negative Self-Talk: Constantly putting ourselves down or having low self-esteem can lead to self-sabotaging behaviors.

2. Fear of Failure: The fear of not performing well or failing can sometimes result in self-sabotage to avoid facing the outcomes.

3. Peer Pressure: Trying to fit in or seeking approval from peers may lead to engaging in behaviors that are harmful or counterproductive.

4. Perfectionism: Striving for perfection can set unrealistic standards, leading to feelings of never being good enough.

5. Mental Health Issues: Conditions like anxiety, depression, or trauma can contribute to destructive urges and self-sabotaging behaviors.

1. Therapy and Counseling: Seeking professional help to address underlying issues and develop coping strategies.

2. Supportive Network: Surrounding ourselves with positive influences and a supportive community can help combat destructive urges.

3. Self-Care Practices: Engaging in activities like exercise, meditation, and hobbies can improve mental well-being.

4. Education and Awareness: Understanding our triggers and learning about healthy behaviors can empower people to make positive changes.

Strategies to Overcome Destructive Urges and Self-Sabotaging Behaviors

1. Self-Reflection and Awareness: Identifying patterns of behavior and understanding the root causes of destructive urges can help in taking proactive steps.

2. Setting Realistic Goals: Breaking down goals into achievable steps can prevent feeling overwhelmed and reduce the likelihood of self-sabotage.

3. Developing Healthy Coping Mechanisms: Finding healthy ways to deal with stress, such as exercise, meditation, or talking to a friend, can help manage destructive urges.

4. Positive Affirmations and Self-Compassion: Practicing self-compassion and positive self-talk can counter negative beliefs and promote self-esteem.

5. Seeking Help When Needed: It's essential for young people to reach out to professionals or trusted individuals when self-sabotaging behaviors become overwhelming.

By being aware of potential sources of destructive urges, utilizing available resources, and implementing effective strategies, young people can proactively address self-sabotaging behaviors and pave the way for personal growth and success.

4.5 Properly Handling Envy

Envy and jealousy can breed discontent and lead to mistakes. Cultivating adaptability and flexibility enables us to shift focus from comparison to personal growth and fulfillment. Envy is a powerful emotion that many people experience, especially in today's fast-paced, comparison-driven world. Sources, resources, and strategies to help prepare our young people for the inner demon of envy as they successfully advance in their lives may consist of the following dimensions.

Sources of Envy in Young People's Lives

As young people advance in their education, careers, and personal lives, they may encounter several sources of envy, such as:

1. Social Media Comparisons: Constant exposure to curated highlights of others' lives—achievements, appearances, lifestyles—can trigger feelings of inadequacy or jealousy.

2. Peer Competition: Whether in school, work, or social settings, seeing others achieve success, fame, or recognition can cause envy, especially when one feels overlooked.

3. Material Success: Comparing possessions (phones, cars, clothes, etc.) or lifestyle (travel, relationships) can foster a sense of dissatisfaction.

4. Recognition and Validation: Watching peers receive praise, awards, or attention can sometimes make young people feel undervalued.

5. Unrealistic Expectations: Society often promotes narrow definitions of "success," which can make young people think they must measure up to others rather than follow their own path.

Resources Young People Need to Handle Envy

To handle envy and channel it productively, young people can benefit from various emotional, social, and practical resources:

1. Emotional Intelligence Training: Helps in recognizing and managing emotions effectively, including envy.

2. Mentorship and Guidance: Having mentors who provide perspective and encouragement reduces the sense of competition and isolation.

3. Psychological Support: Access to counseling, school psychologists, or support groups provides a safe space to process feelings.

4. Healthy Communities: Being part of communities that value cooperation over competition helps reduce comparison.

5. Educational Resources on Self-Development: Books, workshops, and podcasts on self-esteem, growth mindset, and positive psychology, all help strengthen mental toughness.

Strategies to Overcome and Transform Envy

Overcoming envy is not about suppressing it but transforming it into motivation and gratitude.

1. Practicing Gratitude: Regularly reflect on our blessings and progress. Gratitude refocuses attention from what others have to what we already possess.

2. Reframing Envy as Inspiration: When we envy someone, ask "What can I learn from them?" instead of "Why not me?"

3. Setting Personal Goals: Define success based on our own values and priorities. Personal benchmarks lessen comparison.

4. Limiting Social Media Exposure: Curate our feeds or take breaks to reduce constant comparison triggers.

5. Celebrating Others' Successes: Congratulate and support peers sincerely; it builds empathy and reduces negative competitiveness.

6. Alertness and Self-Consciousness Practices: Meditation, journaling, or quiet reflection helps in identifying the root of envy and responding to it rationally.

7. Focus on Personal Growth: Build skills, invest in learning, and take pride in incremental progress.

Envy is natural, but it doesn't have to be destructive. When young people are aware of its sources, equipped with emotional and social resources, and armed with strategies that emphasize gratitude, self-growth, and empathy, they can transform envy into motivation that fuels their success.

4.6 Disable Passionate Emotions Impulsive Reactions

Impulsive reactions driven by intense emotions are common, especially among young people who are still developing self-awareness, emotional intelligence, and coping mechanisms.

Sources of Impulsive Reactions

Young people can experience impulsive reactions due to a mix of biological, psychological, and social factors. Some key sources include:

- Emotional Triggers:

    - Rejection, criticism, or perceived failure.

    - Loneliness, stress, or anxiety.

    - Strong emotions like anger, fear, jealousy, or excitement.

- Environmental and Social Influences:

    - Peer pressure or the desire for acceptance.

    - Social media and digital interactions that amplify comparison, validation seeking, and instant gratification.

    - Cultural or family expectations and conflicts.

- Biological and Developmental Factors:

    - The prefrontal cortex (which governs decision making and impulse control) continues developing into the mid-20s.

    - Hormonal changes that intensify emotional experiences.

- Lifestyle Factors:

    - Sleep deprivation, poor nutrition, or substance abuse.

    - Overexposure to stress without adequate recovery time.

Resources for Impulsive Reactions

To recognize and manage impulsive reactions, young people benefit from access to internal and external support, including:

- Emotional Education and Skill-Building:

    - Programs that teach emotional regulation, communication, and problem solving (e.g., social emotional learning programs).

- Support Systems:

    - Mentorship from trusted adults, teachers, coaches, or counselors.

    - Peer support groups where they can share experiences safely.

- Professional Resources:

    - Access to mental health professionals (therapists, counselors, or school psychologists).

    - Online mental health tools and hotlines.

- Healthy Outlets:

    - Opportunities in sports, arts, volunteering, or reflection communities that provide constructive ways to express emotion.

<u>Strategies to Overcome Impulsive Reactions</u>

Here are effective strategies that foster emotional regulation and self-control:

- Develop Self-Consciousness:

    - Practice meditation or journaling to identify emotional triggers and thought patterns.

    - Learn to differentiate between temporary feelings and long-term values before acting.

- Pause and Breathe:

    - When emotions surge, take slow, deep breaths or count to ten before responding.

    - Implement the "STOP" technique: **S**top – **T**ake a breath – **O**bserve – **P**roceed thoughtfully.

- Build an Emotional Vocabulary:

    - Naming emotions ("I feel angry," "I feel hurt," "I feel anxious") helps the brain engage rational processing.

- Strengthen Decision Making Skills:

    - Encourage a habit of reflecting on consequences: "What might happen if I act now? What might happen if I wait?"

    - Use a short delay (e.g., "sleeping on it") before major decisions.

- Maintain a Balanced Routine:

    - Prioritize adequate sleep, balanced nutrition, and physical activity—all crucial for emotional stability.

- Seek and Accept Support:

    - Encourage reaching out to trusted family members, friends, or professionals when struggling.

- Emphasize that seeking help is a sign of strength, not weakness.

- Practice Compassion and Forgiveness:

  - Recognize that everyone makes impulsive mistakes. Learning from them builds resilience and emotional maturity.

- Cultivating Long-Term Growth:

  - Encourage young people to review emotional situations weekly—what triggered them, what worked, and what didn't.

  - Parents, teachers, and leaders can model calm responses and accountability.

  - Engage in reading, workshops, or online courses about emotional intelligence and stress management.

By understanding their emotional triggers, accessing supportive resources, and intentionally practicing meditation, reflection, and self-regulation, young people can transform impulsive tendencies into opportunities for growth, self-mastery, and long-term success.

4.7 Navigating Through Sadness

Sadness can wash over us with waves of melancholy. Despair can degrade into tragedy, impacting decision making. Being sad may not be as benign as it may sound and appear on the surface. It is important to recognize when sadness approaches the line when it begins to interfere with our activities of daily living. Building our emotional intelligence strength helps to identify these dangerous indicators and helps us to navigate through sadness, seeking support when needed and maintaining our mental well-being.

Sources of sadness, which our young people need to be aware of as they advance successfully in their lives, the resources they need to manage sadness, and knowledge of the best strategies they can implement to overcome sadness can preempt descending into the deep, dark hole where sadness dwells.

Young people face a range of emotional bouts as they grow and move toward success. Here are some sources of sadness to help identify where pitfalls may stem from.

<u>Sources of Sadness</u>

Many sources of sadness for young people are tied to transitions, pressures, and identity development. Some common ones include:

1. Academic and career pressures: Fear of failure, competition, and uncertainty about the future.

2. Social tensions: Friendship conflicts, bullying, or difficulty finding a sense of belonging.

3. Family stress: Unstable home environments, parental pressure, or loss of family support.

4. Personal identity and self-esteem: Combat with self-image, self-worth, or acceptance of our identity (cultural, sexual, or personal).

5. Technology and social media: Unrealistic comparisons, cyberbullying, and constant connection leading to anxiety and loneliness.

6. Life changes: Moving, adjusting to college, or stepping into adulthood can trigger feelings of loss, disconnection, or uncertainty.

<u>Resources Young People Need to Battle Sadness</u>

1. Trusted relationships: Family members, mentors, teachers, and friends who listen without judgment.

2. Mental health support: Counselors, therapists, school psychologists, or youth support groups.

3. Community programs: Clubs, teams, volunteer organizations, and faith-based groups that foster belonging.

4. Educational resources: Workshops on emotional awareness, time management, and coping strategies.

5. Healthy environments: Safe online spaces and real-life environments where open communication about emotions is encouraged.

<u>Strategies to Overcome and Manage Sadness</u>

1. Acknowledge feelings: Recognize that sadness is a normal emotion, not a weakness. Naming emotions can lessen their intensity.

2. Express emotions constructively: Talk to someone trusted, write in a journal, or express feelings through art, music, or physical activity.

3. Build healthy routines: Regular sleep, balanced nutrition, exercise, and mindful breathing are powerful mood stabilizers.

4. Set realistic goals: Break big ambitions into smaller, achievable steps to avoid feeling overwhelmed.

5. Practice gratitude and meditation: Focus on the present moment and appreciate small positive experiences.

6. Limit social comparison: Take breaks from social media and remember that others' posts often highlight the best parts, not full realities.

7. Seek help early: Reaching out for support when feeling down prevents sadness from deepening into depression.

Ultimately, it's important for young people to understand that sadness is part of the human experience. It doesn't define their future or diminish their worth. Learning to face and manage sadness can actually strengthen empathy, purpose, and personal growth.

4.8 Transforming Perfectionism

Setting excessively high standards can lead to self-criticism and dissatisfaction. Critical thinking helps in challenging perfectionistic tendencies, promoting self-acceptance and growth through learning from mistakes. Perfectionism can be paralyzing. Perfectionism is increasingly common among young people, especially as they balance academic, professional, and personal expectations. Let's break this into parts: sources, resources, and strategies.

<u>Sources of Perfectionism</u>

- Social media and comparison culture – platforms highlight only the best moments of others' lives, creating unrealistic standards for success, beauty, and achievement.

- Academic and career pressure – high expectations from schools, parents, or even self-imposed goals can make young people think that mistakes equal failure.

- Family and cultural expectations – certain family or cultural environments place a strong emphasis on achievement or reputation, leading to internalized perfectionism.

- Personality traits and fear of failure – people who are conscientious, driven, or anxious about disappointing others may be more prone to perfectionistic thinking.

- Societal messages about success – messages that equate worth with productivity or performance feed the idea that only the best is good enough.

Resources Young People Need to Cope with Perfectionism

- Mental health education and support – access to school counselors, mental health resources, and awareness campaigns normalizing imperfection and self-care.

- Positive role models and mentorship – adults or peers who model balance, self-compassion, and realistic goal setting.

- Supportive communities – spaces (clubs, organizations, faith groups, online communities) that encourage authenticity and personal growth over competition.

- Educational tools – workshops or courses on emotional intelligence and stress management help develop better decision making.

Strategies to Overcome Perfectionism

- Adopt a growth mindset – view mistakes as opportunities to learn from rather than as evidence of inadequacy.

- Set realistic, flexible goals – break large ambitions into achievable milestones, celebrating progress rather than perfection.

- Practice self-compassion – speak to ourselves as we would to a friend, with understanding, patience, and kindness.

- Challenge all-or-nothing thinking – learn to see partial success and imperfection as part of progress.

- Limit constant comparison – reduce time on social media or follow accounts that promote authenticity and well-being.

- Balance structure with rest – prioritize mental and physical health through meditation, journaling, exercise, and downtime.

- Seek professional support if needed – talking to a counselor or therapist can help identify underlying unease and create healthier coping mechanisms.

Young people can thrive best when they understand that success comes through persistence, balance, and learning—not flawless performance. Encouraging environments that value effort, curiosity, and authenticity can transform perfectionism into healthy striving for growth and excellence.

4.9 Clarifying Confusion

Confusion or uncertainty and chaos in the mind can hinder progress and clarity. Self-awareness and enhanced problem-solving skills aid in untangling confusion, enabling people to make informed decisions. Many young people today are growing up in a world that's fast changing, highly connected, and full of both opportunities and obstacles. Understanding what causes confusion, and how to overcome it, is essential for living with clarity, purpose, and confidence.

Here's a structured way to think about this:

Sources of Confusion

1. Information Overload

   - The digital age produces a constant stream of news, opinions, and content. It's hard to know what's true or trustworthy.

   - Social media can blur the line between fact and opinion, leading to conflicting messages.

2. Pressure to Succeed

   - Many young people face social, academic, and career pressure to "have it all figured out."

   - Comparing ourselves to others can lead to uncertainty and self-doubt.

3. Identity and Value Conflicts

   - Navigating personal identity, beliefs, and values amid societal expectations can be confusing.

   - Exposure to diverse worldviews can both enrich and unsettle our sense of self.

4. Rapid Cultural and Technological Change

   - Careers, norms, and roles are shifting quickly. What was "right" or "successful" a decade ago may not apply now.

5. Emotional and Mental Health Challenges

   - Stress, anxiety, and burnout can blur thinking and decision making, making confusion feel overwhelming.

Resources Needed to Sort Through Confusion

1. Reliable Knowledge Sources

   - Access to credible information on education, careers, mental health, and current events.

   - Mentors and role models who can provide guidance and perspective.

2. Emotional and Psychological Support

   - Counseling or mental health services (in schools, communities, or online).

- Safe spaces—peer groups, community centers, faith groups, where young people feel heard and supported.

3. Life Skills Education

   - Courses in financial literacy, emotional intelligence, media literacy, and critical thinking.

   - Exposure to problem-solving and self-reflection practices.

4. Time for Self-Discovery

   - Opportunities to explore passions through internships, volunteering, and travel.

   - Encouragement to develop self-knowledge through journaling, mindfulness, or quiet reflection.

<u>Strategies to Overcome Confusion</u>

1. Clarify Personal Values and Goals

   - Define what success really means to us, not what society says it should be.

   - Write down our core values and check decisions against them.

2. Develop Critical Thinking

   - Evaluate information for credibility before forming opinions.

   - Seek diverse perspectives, but anchor our decisions in facts and reflection.

3. Practice Self-Reflection and Meditation

   - Spend time regularly assessing our emotions, experiences, and direction.

   - Meditation practices (like meditation or deep breathing) help reduce those feelings that tend to overwhelm us.

4. Build Supportive Relationships

   - Surround ourselves with trustworthy people who encourage growth and honesty.

   - Don't be afraid to ask for guidance or mentorship from people we respect.

5. Embrace Lifelong Learning and Flexibility

   - Stay open to new knowledge and experiences.

   - Accept that confusion is part of personal growth, it's an opportunity to learn, not a failure.

6. Limit Comparisons

   - Use social media mindfully; remember that it shows highlights, not the full picture.

   - Focus on our own progress, not someone else's timeline.

Confusion is natural, especially in transitions and times of rapid change. For young people, the key is not to avoid confusion but to clarify it with tools, support, and self-knowledge. With the right mindset and resources, moments of uncertainty can become the very experiences that lead to clarity and resilience.

4.10 Beating the Burden Bearer

The burden bearer inner demon infuses feelings of sorrow and negativity that can become destructive if left unchecked. Mental toughness equips us to bear the burdens of life by fostering resilience and inner strength. Young people today face many stressors that can produce feelings of sorrow, negativity, and hopelessness. Understanding where these feelings come from and how to respond to them in a healthy way is key to beating the burden bearer by building long-term emotional resilience to win the war within our mind.

<u>Sources of Burden, Sorrow and Negativity</u>

Young people may experience destructive feelings from a range of areas, including:

- Academic and career pressure resulting from constant competition, high expectations; fear of failure can cause anxiety and feelings of inadequacy.

- Social comparison and media influence often showcase idealized lives, leading to feelings of loneliness, low self-worth, or depression.

- Family tension and broken relationships resulting in conflict, lack of communication, or loss within families can deeply affect emotional balance.

- Isolation and lack of belonging come about from not having supportive friendships or communities, and can make one feel disconnected.

- Trauma and loss manifest from experiences such as bullying, abuse, rejection, or the grief of losing those close to us, shaping a negative self-perception and trust in others.

- Uncertainty about the future stemming from global issues that are beyond our control, economic insecurity given escalating costs of living, and changing social dynamics can generate fear and hopelessness.

<u>Resources to Attack the Burden Bearer</u>

1. Supportive Relationships: Trusted mentors, friends, family members, teachers, and counselors who listen without judgment.

2. Access to Mental Health Services: School counselors, therapy, or community mental health programs that provide coping tools and safe spaces to talk.

3. Healthy Environments: Schools, social spaces, and online communities that promote openness, compassion, and inclusion.

4. Educational Resources: Knowledge about emotional regulation, stress management, communication, and self-care.

5. Purpose and community engagement: Opportunities to volunteer, create, or lead can provide meaning and build confidence.

Here are some suggestions young people can use to manage and transform painful emotions:

- Acknowledge and understand feelings: Suppressing emotions often intensifies them. Identifying and naming feelings is the first step toward healing.

- Build resilience through self-care: Adequate sleep, healthy nutrition, exercise, and balanced routines sustain emotional stability.

- Practice consciousness and gratitude: These habits help ground one in the present and shift focus from what's lacking to what's meaningful.

- Develop positive self-talk: Challenge inner criticism with realistic, compassionate thoughts.

- Seek help early: Reaching out to mental health professionals or trusted adults when negative emotions persist is a sign of strength, not weakness.

- Limit harmful comparisons: Use social media intentionally; focus on genuine connections and learning rather than validation.

- Set achievable goals: Small, realistic steps create momentum and a sense of control over our path.

- Contribute to others: Helping peers or engaging in community service fosters belonging and combats isolation.

Encouragement and vision are essential in alleviating the pressure that young people may be feeling. Seeing the horizon during tough times can be challenging, especially when we are young and do not fully grasp the significance of looking toward the future and recognizing opportunities, success, and satisfaction that lie ahead. Reminding young people that sorrow and negativity are inherent to the human experience, but they do not have to dictate anyone's life story. With awareness, support, and effective coping strategies, these emotions can indeed enhance empathy, wisdom, and resilience—qualities that are crucial for achieving success and fulfillment.

4.11 Defeating the Deceiver

Many young people today face pressures, both internal and external, that can distort self-perception and weaken confidence and authenticity.

The inner demon deceiver thrives on self-deception and emotional manipulation; its aim is to undermine our self-confidence and authenticity. By utilizing our strengths of empathy and self-awareness, we can defuse the potential explosive repercussions of the deceiver within. Embracing our vulnerability and being really honest with ourselves buttresses our efforts to defeat the deceiver.

While it becomes difficult to identify sources, methods, and tactics of self-deception and emotional manipulation, we need to make our best effort to do so. Becoming aware of helpful resources and gaining knowledge of the best strategies we can implement to overcome self-deception and emotional manipulation augments our self-confidence, authenticity, and success in our lives.

Let's break this down in a few parts for clarity.

<u>Sources of Self-Deception and Emotional Manipulation</u>

Young people often encounter subtle and overt influences that shape how they see themselves and others. These sources can include:

1. Social and Cultural Pressures

   - Social media: Encourages comparison, perfectionism, and curated identities rather than authentic ones.

   - Cultural norms: Expectations around success, beauty, and achievement can lead to living for approval rather than purpose.

2. Internal Influences

   - Cognitive biases: People can deceive themselves through denial, confirmation bias, or rationalization—believing what feels safer rather than what's true.

   - Comfort zones: It's tempting to avoid uncomfortable self-reflection or growth because it threatens identity or belonging.

3. Interpersonal Manipulation

   - Toxic relationships: People may use guilt, flattery, or dependency to control others emotionally.

   - Authority figures or mentors: When someone in power projects their goals onto others, it can sway a young person away from their authentic path.

   - Media and advertising: Constant reinforcement of "not being enough" without certain products, looks, or lifestyles subtly manipulates self-worth.

<u>Resources to Breakdown the Deceiver Inner Demon</u>

To protect confidence and authenticity, young people need a strong foundation of education, emotional literacy, and support.

1. Educational Resources

   - Workshops on emotional intelligence, mental health awareness, and critical thinking.

   - Guidance in identifying gaslighting, manipulation, and cognitive distortions.

   - Exposure to philosophy or psychology on identity and self-insight.

2. Emotional and Social Support

   - Mentorship programs with genuine, empathetic leaders.

   - Safe spaces, such as counseling, support groups, or community circles, for open discussion.

   - Healthy peer networks that reinforce authenticity, not performance.

3. Reflective Resources

   - Journaling practices and meditation tools that encourage honest self-reflection.

- Books, podcasts, or workshops on self-insight, boundaries, and leadership integrity.

<u>Strategies to Overcome Self-Deception and Manipulation</u>

1. Cultivate Self-Knowledge

    - Practice mindfulness to observe thoughts and reactions without judgment.

    - Regularly reflect: "Am I being true to myself or performing to please others?"

    - Seek feedback from people who are both supportive and honest.

2. Strengthen Critical Thinking

    - Question assumptions and motives, both our own and others.

    - Learn about cognitive biases; understanding them helps resist internal deception.

    - Analyze emotional triggers—manipulation often works by exploiting emotional blind spots.

3. Build Emotional Boundaries

    - Learn to say no without guilt; boundaries protect authenticity.

    - Recognize red flags of manipulation (guilt trips, gaslighting, excessive flattery).

    - Surround ourselves with relationships rooted in respect and mutual growth.

4. Practice Self-Compassion

    - Accept mistakes without shame—they're part of honest living.

    - Replace comparison with self-improvement and gratitude.

    - A forgiving mindset encourages growth rather than self-deception.

5. Align with Purpose and Values

    - Identify core values and refer to them when making decisions.

    - Setting goals aligned with those values keeps direction authentic, even under pressure.

    - Reassess periodically—authenticity is a lifelong practice, not a one-time achievement.

In summary, young people can defeat the inner demon, deceiver, by gaining awareness of manipulative and deceptive influences, both internal and external. They can achieve this by building emotional and intellectual resilience through education and support, developing reflective habits, clear values, and strong personal boundaries. Being comfortable in our own skin grows when we stand in truth, courage, and compassion, treating ourselves and others with honesty and respect.

4.12 Triumph Over the Trickster

The trickster inner demon, with its elusive and confusing nature, can sow seeds of doubt and indecision. This impinges on self-identity, confidence, and personal growth. Gratitude acts as a grounding force, helping us navigate through this type of uncertainty with a sense of appreciation for the present moment.

What sources of seeds of doubt and indecision do our young people need to be aware of as they successfully advance in their lives, what resources do they need and what are the best strategies they can implement to triumph over the seeds of doubt and indecision the trickster inserts in their lives?

<u>Sources of Seeds of Doubt and Indecision</u>

Young people today face an uniquely complex world, and several factors can feed uncertainty.

1. External Pressures and Comparisons

    -   Social media and competitive environments can create unrealistic benchmarks of success or happiness, leading many to question their worth or direction.

2. Fear of Failure

    -   Perfectionism and the desire for validation can cause paralysis—the belief that one must make the "perfect" choice or live up to expectations.

3. Overwhelming Information Overload

    -   With so many options for education, careers, and lifestyles, decision making can feel intimidating, causing hesitation and indecision.

4. Negative Influences or Unsupportive Environments

    -   Family, peers, or communities that discourage risk taking, curiosity, or independence may inadvertently plant seeds of doubt.

5. Self-Doubt and Internalized Beliefs

    -   Past experiences, mistakes, or even cultural messages can lead young people to internalize limiting beliefs ("I'm not smart enough" or "I never do things right").

<u>Resources Young People Need to Battle Doubt and Indecision</u>

To combat those sources of doubt, young people benefit from supportive tools and networks, including the following.

1. Mentorship and Guidance

    -   Access to mentors, teachers, or role models who share our journeys help normalize uncertainty and provide sound advice.

2. Emotional and Mental Health Support

    -   Counseling, peer support groups, meditation programs, and access to mental health professionals can build self-insight and emotional resilience.

3. Personal Development Resources

    -   Books, workshops, podcasts, or community programs that foster growth mindset, goal setting, and emotional intelligence.

4. Positive Community and Social Connections

    - Surrounding ourselves with encouraging and value-aligned people reinforces confidence and healthy decision making.

5. Opportunities for Exploration

    - Internships, volunteering, or creative pursuits let young people test interests without fear of "getting it wrong," helping them clarify direction through experience.

<u>Strategies to Overcome Doubt and Indecision</u>

To thrive despite uncertainty, young people can develop lifelong habits of confidence and clarity:

1. Adopt a Growth Mindset

    - Treat mistakes as feedback, not failures. Understand that confidence builds through practice, reflection, and persistence.

2. Clarify Values and Purpose

    - Knowing what truly matters helps in decision making. When choices align with our values, doubt lessens.

3. Set Manageable Goals

    - Breaking large goals into smaller steps makes progress visible and less intimidating.

4. Practice Self-Compassion

    - Learning to treat ourselves with kindness, patience, and forgiveness reduces fear of disappointing ourselves or others.

5. Limit Negative Inputs

    - Curate social media and environments that inspire rather than drain. Comparisons often distort reality.

6. Seek Mentorship and Feedback

    - Constructive feedback from trusted mentors helps young people see blind spots and potential, balancing humility and confidence.

7. Develop Decision-Making Skills

    - Learn structured ways to evaluate options—list pros/cons, align with values, consider long-term outcomes, and then act with conviction.

The seeds of doubt and indecision grow in uncertainty, fear, and comparison, but they can be uprooted with awareness, community, and empowerment. By developing emotional intelligence, a supportive network, and clear personal purpose, young people can transform doubt from a stumbling block into a stepping stone toward growth and fulfillment.

The psychological war within young minds is a complex battleground where inner demons and top ten strengths collide. By acknowledging and understanding the demons that plague their minds, and harnessing the power of their strengths, young people can effectively navigate through ambushes, foster personal growth, and emerge victorious in the battle for mental well-being. Through cultivating resilience, emotional intelligence, and empathy, young people can equip themselves with the necessary tools to conquer their inner demons and emerge as empowered human beings ready to face the world with confidence and clarity.

Photo by Daniel R. Linden

For young people, inner struggles can feel like clouds obscuring their view of what the future might hold. By acknowledging their challenges and drawing on their strongest qualities, they can build resilience, empathy, and emotional insight. With these tools, they can move through setbacks, keep growing, and step into the world with confidence—like sunlight breaking through the clouds.

Part 2: Winning the War

The main objective in winning the war within our mind is to recognize and interrupt the inner forces that distort our thoughts, emotions, and behaviors, and then deliberately strengthen the skills and support that restore self-control, clarity, and resilience. This work is especially important early in life, before harmful patterns harden and begin to feel like part of our identity.

Chapters 5, 6, 7, and 8 focus on maintaining motivation, managing stress, adapting to challenges, and seeking support during psychological battles. They frame personal struggles as a war that require resilience, discipline, and strategy. They also emphasize recognizing emotional and mental shifts, learning from them, and reshaping our mindset to support growth and healing.

In practice, this means mapping the battlefield (our triggers and patterns), naming the "inner demons," setting boundaries, and training our top ten strengths so we can choose a positive, intentional response instead of being ruled by impulsive, automatic, and less effective reactions.

Facing our toughest battles reminds us that some nights the world goes quiet, but our minds refuse to. This is psychological warfare: not a dramatic clash we can point to, but an unseen siege that can make ordinary life feel like survival. It is the war within our mind where inner demons weaponize fear, shame, insecurity, and exhaustion, aiming not merely to wound, but to wear us down until we give up and give in. Part 2 is not about pretending the war isn't real; it is about refusing to lose it.

Staying the course emphasizes a steady hand on the shoulder—a simple command to keep going when the road turns hostile. But when the battlefield is internal and the enemy knows every weak seam in our history, the battle changes. In the war within our mind, the course is not a tidy plan on paper; it is the thin, trembling line between endurance and surrender, between clarity and distortion, between life as it can still be lived and life reduced to mere reaction. Part 2 also explores artificial intelligence and machine learning, and how they are transforming complex tasks, analyzing large amounts of data, and delivering insights once out of reach, as well as the roles they may play in diagnosing and treating mental health conditions. To stay the course here is to keep choosing to win— again and again—while under fire.

The emotional pendulum explains that emotions and mental health rarely improve in a straight line; they swing like a pendulum between hope and heaviness. Psychological battles often arrive quietly and seep into everyday habits and interpretations, making them easy to dismiss until they become overwhelming. Part 2 focuses on turning points: mindset shifts that change how pain is understood, moments of realization that bring hidden patterns into the light, and both negative and positive consequences of inner conflict. Unaddressed struggles can erode self-trust, distort perception, isolate us, and lead to burnout or numbing behaviors, even alongside outward success. Facing the struggle can also build self-awareness, resilience, authenticity, empathy, and purpose. The core message is that progress is not linear, clarity is a practice, and we can keep writing our life story beyond the wounds incurred in psychological war.

Winning the war within our mind explains that resolving inner psychological conflict can produce lasting joy, not only immediate relief, but also empowerment and a deeper sense of accomplishment. This transformation tends to endure because it reflects a meaningful shift in mindset that restores clarity of purpose, strengthens commitment, and renews personal direction. As internal division decreases, decisions feel less burdensome, and actions align more naturally with one's values, desires, and long-term vision. To sustain motivation throughout the process, Part 2 highlights the importance of celebrating small wins. Recognizing incremental progress builds resilience, reinforces confidence, and creates momentum. This underscores the need to learn from outcomes, whether painful or transformative, by processing them constructively. This reflective approach turns experience into insight, helping individuals not only win psychological battles but also sustain long-term success in winning the war within our mind.

There will be no trophy, plaque, statue, bonus, award, or victory celebration—no corks to pop and no champagne to spray around the locker room. This season never ends. There is no off-season to recover, no opening day to look forward to; we get our lives back with no guarantees of a battle-free future. Knowing we won the war in our minds is enough—more than enough.

Photo by Daniel R. Linden

Winning the inner war means identifying triggers and "inner demons," interrupting harmful patterns, and strengthening skills and support for resilience, especially early. Progress isn't linear; it requires repeated choices, small wins, reflection, and persistence. There's no public trophy—quiet, ongoing victory is enough.

Chapter 5: Facing Our Toughest Battles

Facing our toughest battles in the context of psychological warfare within our mind can be a daunting yet pioneering experience. It signifies confronting and wrestling with inner demons, panic, doubts, and insecurities that disrupt our lives and cause serious emotional distress. It involves acknowledging the complexity of our thoughts and emotions, and actively working toward understanding and overcoming those demons whose goal is to destroy our lives, which is the byproduct of losing the war within our mind.

Facing our toughest battles means showing up for ourselves, being brave in the face of adversity, and committing ourselves to emotional growth and well-being. It's a continuous journey of self-discovery, healing, and personal development, ultimately leading to greater self-understanding and a stronger sense of inner peace.

One of the toughest battles we encounter in life involves dealing with the loss of a loved one or a dear friend. Overcoming hardships brought on by the death of those close to us is a wicked twist of fate that deals us a blow, forcing us to focus on the good times we experienced to avoid falling into the abyss of emptiness. We grieve for ourselves, knowing our loved ones have left us, and we miss their embrace, encouragement, and love. They are gone, and we suffer; however, their suffering and human existence have ended. Our faith and belief show us the love we felt remains in our hearts and minds, and that never leaves, ever.

Intense psychological battles also occur in our professional lives, manifesting through being denied a promotion, demoted, or being unexpectedly fired from a job we enjoyed and have been dedicated to for a significant amount of time. Ethical dilemmas may arise in our work when our values are challenged, or incentivized temptation leads us astray from the path of virtue. The balance between time dedicated to our career and time spent with loved ones is always delicate, akin to a high-wire act. Regardless of the nature of a conflict at work, our character and top ten strengths can be put to the test. The specific form of the battle is of little significance; battles will undoubtedly arise, often catching us off guard. What truly matters is how we rise to confront inner demons stirred within our mind with righteousness, and emerge stronger than we were before the battle commenced.

Facing our toughest battles typically refers to confronting and dealing with the most difficult tests or adversities in our lives, such as serious health conditions. As our health deteriorates and suffering increases, we come to the realization that our time on earth may be limited to a matter of months. We search for a brighter light, seek an eternal solution, and yearn for a promise—perhaps only briefly noticed before, but now hoped for. Overcoming setbacks, achieving treatment goals, and relying on scans to track our progress or regression, it is an existence we never anticipated, were scarcely prepared for, and mostly isolated from our minds as we rushed through life in pursuit of our destiny. Striving to reach career goals, dealing with relationship issues, managing difficult family dynamics, and addressing problems like debt, unemployment, or financial instability all become secondary. Our primary focus of survival shifts as close as placing our hand in front of our face and deciphering the lines in the palm of our hand. It is then that we realize we are in the toughest battle that will forge our greatest strengths.

Winning the toughest battles usually involves acknowledging the difficulty, finding resources, developing strategies to overcome inner demons, and learning from each experience to grow stronger. Focusing on and capitalizing on our strengths, rather than merely remedying weaknesses, gives us the best opportunity for success. Making our strengths stronger offers the greatest potential for winning the war within our mind. Psychological battles originate from a multitude of situations, circumstances, and factors. They make their approach from both internal and external sources. Such battles can occur for many of us and lead to feelings of doubt, confusion, and distress. To navigate these unwieldy experiences effectively, we must harness our top ten strengths to win the war within our mind. These strengths empower us to confront and overcome the worst psychological threats.

Photo by Daniel R. Linden

A beautiful Hawaiian sunset can serve as a powerful metaphor for the process of overcoming life's toughest battles. When we look at a Hawaiian sunset, it's not just a perfect image of calm and beauty, it's the result of powerful natural forces interacting: the sun dipping beyond the horizon, clouds shifting, and light scattering through the atmosphere. In the same way, winning difficult psychological battles comes from facing and working through inner turbulence, rather than avoiding it. A Hawaiian sunset mirrors the journey from struggle to serenity—from chaos to peace—showing that beauty often emerges from the complex interplay of challenge, reflection, and renewal.

5.1 The Tough Battle Symbolized by Michelangelo's "The Atlas Slave"

The sculpture "Atlas Slave" by Michelangelo reflects an image of psychological battles and the war within our mind. Symbolized by the strained and contorted posture, the sculpture is a metaphor for the emotional weight and psychological burdens surrounding us and manifesting in our minds.

Photo by Daniel R. Linden

The "Atlas Slave" is a nine foot (2.77m) tall marble statue by Michelangelo, dated to 1525–1530. It is one of the "Prisoners," the series of unfinished sculptures for the tomb of Pope Julius II. It is now held in the Galleria dell' Accademia in Florence, Italy.

The sculpture, "Atlas Slave," serves as a powerful and evocative representation of the psychological battles and the war within our mind. The figure appears to be trapped or confined, struggling against the constraints within the marble. The tension in the figure's muscles and the dynamic pose suggest a sense of psychological battle and contradiction. This can symbolize the feeling of being trapped in our own mind, battling inner demons or negative thoughts that can create a sense of confinement and emotional torment.

The sculpture tells an intriguing story relating to some of our toughest psychological battles. This sculpture is a masterpiece that has intrigued art enthusiasts for centuries. The muscularity and strain in Atlas's posture convey the immense effort required to bear such a heavy load, reflecting the fights and sacrifices inherent in human experience.

Just as Atlas carried the weight of the world, we grapple with inner demons, dread, and doubts that weigh heavily on our minds. The tension and strain in Atlas's muscles mirror the psychological battles we face when dealing with conflicting emotions, desires, and beliefs.

By confronting and winning the war within our mind, we can emerge stronger and more resilient, much like Atlas bearing the weight of the world and endeavoring to break out from the block of marble from which he was chiseled. Atlas's burden, if eventually lifted, implies redemption and liberation from suffering. Through its portrayal of struggle and strength. "The Atlas Slave" offers a poignant reflection on the complexities of the human psyche and the transformative journey toward inner peace.

The figure of Atlas in Greek mythology is often depicted as a titan condemned to hold up the celestial spheres for eternity. In Michelangelo's interpretation, Atlas symbolizes the strength required to bear an unimaginable measure of weight. The statue serves as a powerful allegory for human experience, highlighting the strength necessary to overcome the war within our mind.

In this way, the "Atlas Slave" can symbolize the ongoing human effort to shape our lives, and move closer to a sense of clarity, purpose, and control amid the unfinished nature of existence. Here are some simple strategies to develop a greater sense of control in our daily lives.

- Set goals by defining clear and achievable goals. This provides direction and purpose.

- Prioritize tasks. To-do lists absolutely work. Base targeted activities on importance and urgency. Tackling tasks systematically helps us feel more in control.

- Practice effective time management techniques to avoid feeling overwhelmed. Allocate appropriate time for tasks; setting deadlines is imperative for many of us to accomplish important objectives and to avoid procrastination.

- Stay organized. Keeping our space and belongings organized promotes a firm sense of control and reduces stress.

- Incorporating mindfulness and relaxation practices, such as deep breathing exercises or meditation, into our daily routine can help us stay calm and focused.

- Learning to say no is an important life skill. Do not overcommit yourself by learning to set boundaries and say no to tasks or activities that don't align with our priorities.

- Don't hesitate to reach out to friends, family, or a professional for support. Asking for help is a signal of strength, not a weakness. Our support system helps us cope with serious psychological disorders and regain control.

By implementing these strategies and making conscious efforts to take control of our daily life, we can develop a greater sense of control and empower ourselves to navigate through life's ups and downs more effectively, and block out whatever is holding us back, as exemplified by the "Atlas Slave."

5.2 War is Hell – Facing the Tough Battle of Ethical Conviction

The saying "war is Hell" is attributed to Union General William Tecumseh Sherman, who purportedly expressed the sentiment after witnessing the severe devastation and suffering caused by armed conflict during the American Civil War. Military leaders strive to maintain a wide range of fighting possibilities. As the saying goes, "no military commander wants to run out of options." When military leaders exhaust their tactics on the battlefield, they risk losing not only their lives but also the battle and the war.

Maintaining options is crucial in both military strategy and personal psychological battles. For a military commander, having multiple options allows for adaptability, flexibility, and the ability to respond effectively to changing circumstances in serious situations. Similarly, in personal battles against inner demons, maintaining a range of options, including our top ten strengths, provides elasticity and effectiveness needed to win the war within our mind. Here are a few reasons why maintaining all of our options available is helpful to our efforts in psychological warfare:

- **Personal Growth:** Exploring different options when dealing with psychological battles can lead to personal growth and understanding. Each newly designed strategy can teach us something about what works best or, more importantly, what isn't working, so we can avoid losing and start winning. When we feel like we have no options, it becomes easier to give up. Knowing that we have choices fosters hope and resilience, encouraging us to retaliate with overwhelming force by utilizing whatever top ten strengths are needed to crush an attack from inner demons. This involves deploying self-control and inner strength to win psychological battles that lead to winning the war within our mind.

- **Empowerment:** Having options means we're not stuck on a single path. This can give us a sense of control over our inner life, which is important for mental health and well-being. Feeling in control is very important because it's closely tied to psychological well-being, motivation, and resilience. When we feel like we have some measure of control over our life or our destiny, we're more likely to experience confidence, lower stress, and a sense of purpose. Having a sense of control helps us manage obstacles more calmly. Believing that our actions make a difference increases motivation and persistence. We're more likely to take initiative and work toward goals. Then, we can make meaningful choices, linked to greater satisfaction and emotional stability. We become more willing to experiment, learn from mistakes, and adapt. That said, it's important to realize that total control is rarely possible. Recognizing the line between what we can influence and what we can't is key, it allows for a balance between proactive effort and acceptance.

- **Creative Problem Solving:** By considering multiple options, we can engage in creative problem solving, finding innovative ways to address and manage psychological battles. When engaging two of our top ten strengths, critical thinking and enhanced problem solving, capabilities like analysis, evaluation of circumstances, sizing up new situations, and effective interpretation of a broad array of data and information, assist us in resolving problems, anticipating outcomes, and providing a range of alternatives not only to fight the good fight but to win the war within our mind.

Upon graduating from high school in 1965, my brother Bill was immediately conscripted into the U.S. Army. While my father held a deep affection for his firstborn, he believed that when called, his son would dutifully respond, which he did. The contrast between my father's service in World War II and my brother's deployment during the Vietnam War, separated by two decades, was glaring. Despite the consistent themes of sacrifice, valor, and heroism displayed by our soldiers, the nature of the two wars' objectives, and the nation's acknowledgment of their service differed significantly.

William John Linden, II – May 1944, World War II

Photo Collection, Daniel R. Linden

William John Linden, III – April 1966, Vietnam War

Photo Collection, Daniel R. Linden

In 1944 and 1945, my father served in the U.S. Army during World War II, where he was sent to the Philippines. From his warzone, it was only a four-hour flight to Japan. Twenty-one years later, my brother entered the U.S. Army and was sent to another warzone in Vietnam during the years 1965 and 1966.

The contrasting elements of World War II and the Vietnam War were remarkable. World War II (1939-1945) was a global conflict involving most of the world's nations, including all of the great powers, eventually forming two opposing military alliances: the Allies and the Axis. The war was primarily driven by the aggressive expansionist policies of Nazi Germany, Imperial Japan, and Fascist Italy, among other factors. It was marked by events such as the invasion of Poland, the attack on Pearl Harbor, and the Holocaust. On the other hand, the Vietnam War (1955-1975) was deemed a conflict between North Vietnam, supported by its communist allies, and South Vietnam, backed by the United States (U.S.). This conflict was rooted in the global struggle between the Soviet Union and the United States, and their respective ideologies of communism and capitalism, respectively.

The Vietnam War had a horrifying psychological impact on American society, contributing to widespread anti-war protests and significant political and cultural shifts. Unlike World War II, the Vietnam War ended with the withdrawal of U.S. forces and the eventual reunification of Vietnam under communist control.

Politicians during the 1960s did not have the moral courage to declare Vietnam a war; it was referred to as "the conflict in Vietnam," a result of political maneuvering, bullshit, and weakness. At the time, our country was repulsed by seeing the tragedies of this war. Vietnam became the first war to be televised. This war was characterized by guerrilla warfare, counterinsurgency, and a focus on preventing the spread of communism in southeast Asia based on the "domino theory." This theory signaled that losing military dominance in Vietnam would lead to a cascading demise of democracy in southeast Asia and, eventually, the world.

U.S. political and military priorities creating a sensible path to victory never materialize. The National Archives list 58,220 U.S. military deaths in Vietnam. Tens of thousands of Americans gave their lives by making the ultimate sacrifice on behalf of the United States. Furthermore, hundreds of thousands of our military were seriously wounded. This created immense ethical dilemmas and psychological conflicts within the minds of many people, especially Robert S. McNamara, who served as Secretary of Defense for both Presidents Kennedy and Johnson during the height of the Vietnam War in the 1960s. Secretary McNamara's eventual book "In Retrospect: The Tragedy and Lessons of Vietnam" (published in 1995) shed light on the psychological war within his mind.

<u>The Psychological War Within the Mind of Secretary Robert S. McNamara</u>

When reading "In Retrospect," it typically implies that someone made a mistake and would like the opportunity to correct it, seeking a do-over. Regrettably, for Secretary McNamara, there are no second chances in war. In his book, he admitted that during the war, he reached the conclusion that Vietnam was unwinnable. Nevertheless, the fighting persisted due to the fear that the U.S. would be seen as weak and yielding to communist rule.

McNamara reflects deeply on the United States' involvement in the Vietnam War in his book and recognized numerous miscalculations and errors in judgment. Here are some key lessons stemming from his own psychological war fought in his mind, focusing on hindsight.

- McNamara admitted that he and other top U.S. officials failed to fully appreciate the historical, cultural, and nationalistic forces at play in Vietnam. They viewed the conflict primarily through the lens of the Cold War, assuming it was a straightforward battle against communist expansion rather than a complex civil and nationalistic struggle. He believed a deeper understanding of Vietnamese history and culture was crucial and he misunderstood the adversary the U.S. was fighting.

- McNamara acknowledged he significantly underestimated the determination and resilience of the North Vietnamese and the Viet Cong. He came to realize that the U.S. could not simply overpower this resolve through increasing military escalation.

- He admitted that the U.S. relied too heavily on military interventions without sufficient political strategies. McNamara later concluded that there should have been a greater effort to explore diplomatic and political solutions rather than primarily focusing on military victory.

- McNamara confessed the Johnson administration, in which he served, failed to be fully honest with the American public about the uncertainties and difficulties of the war. He believed there should have been more transparency and open discussion regarding the complexities and risks involved.

- He realized that the administration had often ignored or marginalized dissenting views both within and outside the government. In hindsight, McNamara saw the value in fostering a wider range of opinions and in conducting greater independent analysis of the situation, which wasn't performed during critical times of the battle.

- McNamara admitted that there was a failure to adequately assess the risks of U.S. involvement and to manage those risks prudently. He mentioned that better risk management could have potentially prevented some of the war's worst outcomes.

- Later in life, McNamara wrestled with the moral implications of his actions and decisions during the war. He increasingly recognized the ethical obligations of leaders to prevent unnecessary suffering and strive for peace.

"In Retrospect" is a book about the ethical and psychological war within the mind of Robert S. McNamara. It serves as a warning of the danger of hubris in leadership and hopefully prevents another catastrophic tragedy similar to Vietnam. McNamara published his book at the age of seventy-nine.

The psychological war within his mind lasted at least 43 years before the book was finished. Fourteen years later, he died on July 6, 2009, with horrific psychological reminders of the 58,220 souls who perished in that fight, hundreds of thousands more people with disabilities, and millions who fought psychological battles because of Vietnam (many losing the war within their minds). All of this consternation festered inside the brain of a man who could have stopped the carnage much earlier than when the fighting stopped, and the psychological war persisted.

After analyzing Robert McNamara's actions and outcomes as Secretary of Defense during the Vietnam War, it becomes clear, given his reflections, that his ethical convictions were not strong enough to positively alter history when he had the opportunity to do so. Ethical conviction proves indispensable when facing psychological battles. In life, there comes a time when we encounter psychological constraints that test our resolve, patience, and endurance. Regardless of the nature of these battles, a strong foundation of ethical conviction is crucial to winning the war within our mind.

Here are some examples of strong ethical convictions to uphold and add to our arsenal to fight and win psychological battles fought in our minds.

1. **Honesty** – Believing in truthfulness and transparency, even when lying might be easier or more advantageous.

2. **Integrity** – Maintaining consistency between our values, words, and actions at all times.

3. **Respect for Others** – Treating every person with dignity, regardless of background, position, or beliefs.

4. **Justice and Fairness** – Committing to fair treatment, providing opportunity for those best qualified and most capable using impartial decision making.

5. **Compassion and Empathy** – Acting with kindness and understanding toward others, especially those in need or suffering.

6. **Responsibility and Accountability** – Taking ownership of our actions and subsequent consequences.

7. **Courage** – Standing up for what is right, even when doing so is difficult or unpopular.

8. **Loyalty** – Being faithful to people, principles, or causes that are morally sound.

Ethical conviction helps in winning psychological battles and the war within our mind by providing us with a strong moral compass. Possessing a strong moral compass is beneficial as it guides our decision making, ensuring our actions align with our values and principles. A strong moral compass promotes inner peace and self-respect by reducing moral conflict and guilt.

5.3 An Ultimate Battle of Strengths for Survival

The nature of life's toughest battles comes in varied forms, including personal loss, professional setbacks, health complications, or interpersonal conflicts. Each of these has the potential to intensely affect our mindset, emotional state, and motivation. While daunting, these episodes call forth a response that often requires an individual to tap into deep reserves of strength and character, but pale in comparison to how devastating the human experience can become.

One of the world's most catastrophic battles demonstrates extreme development of our top ten strengths in the face of lethal adversity. Genocide represents one of humanity's darkest and deadliest chapters, showcasing the deepest depths of human cruelty. The Rwandan Genocide of 1994 is a poignant example of such dire circumstances, where ethnic tension between the Hutu and the Tutsi culminated in a horrifying massacre that lasted approximately 100 days and resulted in the estimated deaths of about 800,000 to 1,000,000 human beings.

After the genocide, Rwandan women, many of whom were severely harmed by the violence, showed great courage. Their ability to survive and keep going is clear proof of their strength. Many moved from being survivors of horrific events to becoming key leaders in rebuilding their communities and the country.

In the context of the Rwandan Genocide, the concept of mental toughness was stretched to its utmost limits. After the genocide, Rwandan society was left in tatters—families were decimated, social fabric was torn apart, and the economy was devastated. Amidst this devastation, Rwandan women, many of whom were victims themselves, displayed extraordinary mental toughness. With an estimated 70% of the population being female post-genocide, women had to step into roles that were unprecedented in their traditional gender assignments.

The socioeconomic survival of Rwanda became heavily dependent on women, as they undertook the restoration of their communities. They reconstructed the demographic landscape by adopting orphans, returning exiles, caring for the wounded and disabled, and dealt with their emotional trauma. These women possessed strength which catalyzed their role beyond mere survivors to become the backbone of national reconstruction and reconciliation efforts.

Adaptability in the post-genocide era, Rwandan women had to adapt to both altered personal circumstances and a rapidly transforming society. Women transitioned from traditional roles to being farmers, entrepreneurs, and political leaders. Rwanda's government, acknowledging the crucial role of women in nation building, adapted its legal structures to support this transition. This included changes in inheritance laws to favor women and ensuring women's representation in governmental positions. Statista reports that by December 2024, Rwanda boasted the highest proportion of women in a national parliament worldwide, standing at 63.8%.

Bravery in this context refers not only to personal bravery in the face of danger but also to moral courage, involving the strength to act rightly amid pressures to the contrary. During and after the genocide, Rwandan women demonstrated immense courage and mental toughness, both in surviving the atrocities and in taking up leadership roles to guide the recovery process.

The empathy and patience expressed by Rwandan women through adopting orphans, caring for the wounded and disabled, and welcoming returning exiles under inhumane conditions were extraordinary. Leaders like Agnes Binagwaho, a pediatrician, who later became the Minister of Health, were pivotal in rebuilding the Rwandan health care system. Their efforts were focused not only on physical health but also on mental health, recognizing the significant psychological impact of the genocide.

Emotional intelligence was crucial in the reconciliation process. Rwanda's focus on community-based healing and reconciliation highlights the role of emotional intelligence. Women, often being the mediators in communities, have used their emotional intelligence to foster dialogue and understanding between conflicting sides, promoting forgiveness and unity.

In addition to the highest degree of mental toughness and courage that the women of Rwanda displayed, they showed a tremendous amount of personal insight, critical thinking, and flexibility to survive such inhumane conditions. Initiating an organization like AVEGA Agahozo (Association of Widows of the Genocide), formed by genocide widows, became instrumental in providing psychosocial support, economic empowerment, and advocacy for genocide survivors, demonstrating incredibly enhanced problem-solving skills.

Ethical conviction is vividly proven in the pursuit of justice post-genocide. The Gacaca courts, a form of community justice inspired by traditional practices, were primarily driven by the need to handle the vast number of genocide perpetrators. Women's participation in these courts, where they often had to confront their family's killers, underscored their dedication to a principled restoration of peace and order, prioritizing restorative justice over revenge.

<u>The Narrative of Rwandan Women Post-1994</u>

The narrative of Rwandan women post-1994 is a compelling testament to the human capacity for mental toughness, courage, adaptability, emotional intelligence, and ethical conviction. Their experiences underline the assertion that these qualities cannot only rebuild a nation but also transform a society. Rwandan women have not only managed to navigate one of the toughest battles of conflicts but have emerged as architects of a hopeful, bold future for their country. Their story inspires broader reflection on psychological battles, the inner struggle that can follow even after "winning," and the crucial role these strengths play in overcoming extraordinary internal and external conflicts.

A poignant quote reflects the spirit of strength and hope following the Rwandan Genocide comes from President Paul Kagame, who has been a significant figure in Rwanda's recovery and rebuilding efforts. He is a Rwandan politician and former military officer who has been the President of Rwanda since 2000. He said:

"The challenge is to remain a normal person in abnormal circumstances." — President, Paul Kagame

This quote encapsulates the struggle and resolve of the Rwandan people to move forward and rebuild their lives and their country despite the immense tragedy they faced. It is a reminder of the strength and mental toughness required to not only survive such atrocities, but to also work toward healing and unity.

5.4 Dr. Martin Luther King, Jr. – The War Within His Mind

The war within Dr. Martin Luther King, Jr.'s mind stemmed from a convergence of personal conviction and moral struggle. Integral components of his mission involved racial equality, spiritual wisdom, and the utilization of nonviolence as a method of resolution. These weighty issues created crushing battles with the burden of historical responsibility that Dr. King took upon himself to fight and win. His warrior mentality is illustrated best by the following words:

"The ultimate measure of a man is not where he stands in moments of comfort and convenience, but where he stands at times of challenge and controversy." — Dr. Martin Luther King, Jr.

This quote from Dr. King comes from his 1963 book, "Strength to Love." The book is a collection of his sermons that address issues of racial injustice, moral courage, and nonviolent resistance. This particular quote underscores a recurring theme in Dr. King's teachings: the importance of character and mental toughness in the face of obstacles. This forces us to consider how we act when confronted with difficult situations, indicating true character is shown not during periods of comfort, but during times of adversity and controversy.

While adversity played a central role in his destiny, Dr. King outlined his mission quite clearly:

"I just want to do God's will. And he's allowed me to go to the mountain. And I've looked over, and I've seen the promised land! I may not get there with you, but I want you to know tonight that we as a people will get to the promised land." — Dr. Martin Luther King, Jr.

This powerful quote from Dr. King originated from his speech known as "I've Been to the Mountaintop." He delivered this speech on April 3, 1968, during a visit to Memphis, Tennessee. The speech was given at the Mason Temple (Church of God in Christ Headquarters), the day before Dr. King was tragically assassinated.

This speech is famously remembered for his prophetic words and clear vision for the future. His leadership of the civil rights movement during the mid-20th century not only made him an international symbol of peace and justice, but also highlighted the intense hurdles and meaningful accomplishments that characterized his life.

Born on January 15, 1929, in Atlanta, Georgia, Martin Luther King, Jr. was steeped in the African American Baptist tradition. Dr. King's intellectual journey brought him to Morehouse College, Crozer Theological Seminary, and later at Boston University, where he earned his doctoral degree. Dr. King's philosophy of life was significantly shaped by the works of Mahatma Gandhi.

Dr. King's leadership during the 1963 March on Washington, D.C. for Jobs and Freedom, where he delivered his famous "I Have a Dream" speech, showcased his ability to unite diverse groups and inspire them with a common purpose. This event significantly influenced public sentiment and played a key role in the enactment of the Civil Rights Act of 1964. Dr. King's worldwide influence was underscored by his receipt of the Nobel Peace Prize in 1964, making him the youngest recipient at that time and recognizing his remarkable accomplishments in promoting civil rights through peaceful methods.

Dr. King's monumental leadership role in the Civil Rights Movement often necessitated long periods away from home, participation in stressful and dangerous protests, and a ceaseless barrage of public engagements. This placed considerable strain on his personal life. His wife, Coretta Scott King, although a strong supporter of his work and an activist in her own right, occasionally voiced concerns about the danger and instability their family faced as a result of his activities.

This conflict between private life and public responsibility was a recurring psychological battle for Dr. King, who endeavored to fulfill his roles as a family man and a national leader. The intensity of managing personal relationships while spearheading a momentous political movement took a personal toll, sometimes leaving Dr. King in states of deep depression and loneliness. His war within his mind is well documented in his biographies.

"Darkness cannot drive out darkness; only light can do that. Hate cannot drive out hate; only love can do that." — Dr. Martin Luther King, Jr., "Strength to Love," 1963

Photo by Daniel R. Linden

The Martin Luther King, Jr. statue in Washington, D.C. stands as a towering tribute to a man whose courage and conviction changed the course of American history. Dr. King's expression on the statue is one of determination and resolve, capturing his steadfast dedication to the Civil Rights Movement. His gaze is forward looking and contemplative, evoking a sense of vision and leadership. The expression suggests strength and resilience, embodying the hope and enduring spirit associated with his legacy. The statue's massive presence, combined with this powerful expression, serves as a poignant reminder of his substantial impact on society and history.

Chapter 6: Staying the Course

It's hard to face the intensity of inner demons and engage in multiple psychological battles that become a war within our mind and stay the course. It's tiring, and sometimes we lose many more times than we win. We can get discouraged while figuring out who these demons haunting us are, what they want, why they want a battle with us, and when, if ever, are these conflicts going to end, especially when no end is in sight. The best advice is to stay the course. This too shall pass; believe in those four words.

Bob Dylan, a cherished musician of mine, has been honored with various accolades over the years, including the prestigious Nobel Prize in Literature in 2016, multiple Grammy Awards, an Academy Award, and the Presidential Medal of Freedom. Beyond his impressive collection of awards, I admire Bob Dylan for his independent and authentic approach. Focusing on an insightful line from one of his songs, it speaks volumes about staying the course despite facing unrelenting psychological battles and a menacing war within our mind.

"The only thing I knew was to keep on keeping on." — Bob Dylan, "Tangled up in Blue"

Bob Dylan's words create a philosophical mantra for fighting inner demons whose main purpose is to disturb our thoughts and destroy our minds. This fight can be about survival, but it is also an opportunity to use adversity as a catalyst for growth and self-discovery. Conquering substantial obstacles in our life and adopting a mentality centered on persistence, especially in times of doubt, reflect a resolute commitment to endure attacks to maintain and preserve our mental well-being, lives, family, and livelihoods.

Human psychology is characterized by its capacity to face, withstand, and grow from inner demons in life. Bob Dylan captured a thought-provoking attitude toward life's ups and downs with his straightforward statement, "the only thing I knew was to keep on keeping on." This concise phrase offers a perspective on navigating internal battles and the strength needed to conquer them.

"Staying the course" is a common way of urging someone to keep going with their plan or responsibilities, even when the task is difficult or problems arise. When this expression is refocused to apply to the deeply personal and intensely intimate context of the war within the mind, it gains new dimensions of meaning and implications.

Diving deeper into what staying the course entails regarding psychological warfare, our first move is to acknowledge that psychological battles are a complex constellation of conditions that influence our emotions, thinking, behavior, and overall well-being. Serious ramifications include debilitating a person's functionality and dramatically reducing their quality of life. The worst-case scenario turns us into a statistic—that's not going to happen—because we should, can, and will stay the course.

Staying the course means we are willing and able to continually engage dastardly demons. The deceiver demon causes self-deception and emotional manipulation; it preys on weaknesses, amplifies doubts, and highlights flaws. Another potentially lethal inner demon is the trickster demon. The trickster has an elusive nature that is complex and unpredictable. It brings confusion, indecision, chaos, and sows doubt within us. These two demons are killers. Our acknowledgment of their presence and their harmful capabilities mean acceptance, not acquiescence. Acceptance is our critical first step to devise our counterattack, retaliate, and eradicate these two inner demons or any other inner demon daring to engage us.

Acknowledging our conflicts with inner demons is akin to a navigator recognizing turbulent waters ahead; this recognition is what begins the work of charting a path through the storm. It requires understanding that internal conflict is not a sign of weakness, but a part of the human experience—one that demands courage and attention.

The "storm" is analogous to psychological warfare: combat marked by setbacks, punctuated by brief, hard-won victories. It can feel relentless, unfolding through intense inner battles within the larger effort to protect ourselves from emotional and physical decline. Like any war, it moves through distinct phases. As the saying goes, "don't count how many times I was knocked down; count how many times I got back up." Those words capture the meaning of staying the course.

When facing psychological battles, the courage to confront inner demons and insecurities is essential for growth and for overcoming threats and ambushes. Pairing courage with one of our top ten strengths—critical thinking—helps us analyze, evaluate, and interpret our thoughts and experiences more effectively. This becomes especially important when inner demons spark psychological battles and we begin the work of disarming their power.

Imagine navigating stormy seas: the winds howl, waves crash against the vessel, and the destination feels distant and obscured. In such moments, it is not the strongest or fastest ship that prevails, but the one whose captain stays the course—adjusting the sails, making steady corrections, and remaining committed to the chosen path.

In our lives, we often face metaphorical storms or wars—setbacks, failures, doubts, and external pressures that threaten to veer us off course. It is during these times that the true test of character emerges. Will we succumb to the winds of doubt and fear, or will we anchor ourselves in courage and critical thinking to stay the course?

Key properties of staying the course include the following:

- The first step in staying the course is to define our destination clearly. Whether it is a personal goal, a professional ambition, or a noble cause, knowing where we are headed and who we take along on our journey provide us with a compass to guide our actions.

- Problems are inevitable in life. It is how we respond to them that defines our character. Staying the course requires resilience – the ability to bounce back from setbacks, learn from failures, and keep pushing forward. The sooner we realize that nobody succeeds without help from others, the stronger we become.

- Success is a journey, not a destination, and neither are our dreams realized overnight. Staying the course demands consistent action – small steps taken daily toward our goals, even when the progress seems incremental. Make sure that as we pursue our goals, we also take time to appreciate the journey, and the people we love and those who love us.

- While staying focused on our goals is crucial, it is also essential to be adaptable and flexible in our approach. Sometimes, the winds may change, and we need to adjust our sails accordingly without losing sight of our destination, the people who depend on us, and those on whom we depend.

- Perhaps the most critical aspect of staying the course is unwavering self-belief and perseverance. Believing in ourselves, our abilities, and our capacity to overcome obstacles fuels the fire that propels us forward, even in the darkest of times. Sometimes it takes believing in others as much or more than we do in ourselves to stay the course.

- Staying the course is not just a strategy for success; it is a mindset, a way of life. It is about honoring our commitments, trusting the process, and having faith in our journey, no matter how arduous the path may seem.

- As we navigate the seas of life, let us remember that the storms will come, the waves will crash, but it is our ability to stay the course that will ultimately lead us to calmer waters and brighter horizons. It is important to realize that asking for help along the way is a sign of strength not weakness.

- Staying the course means staying true to our dreams, values, purpose, family, and friends. It is not the destination alone that defines us but the journey we undertake to reach it.

Photo by Daniel R. Linden

Maintain a clear vision of our goals and values and remain unwavering in the face of challenges. Embrace setbacks as opportunities for growth and learning, rather than reasons to abandon ship. Cultivate inner strength and discipline to keep moving forward, even when the horizon seems dark and distant, and we feel the world may be crashing down around us, like huge waterfalls surrounding us, keep the faith.

6.1 Under Fire

The experience of being fired upon in combat is an extraordinarily complex and transformative experience, often defying the comprehensibility of those outside the traumatic sphere of warfare. The sensations, thoughts, and emotions associated with such life-threatening circumstances can alter the lens through which one views the world, themselves, and the concept of life and death.

War, at its core, is an extreme human experience that encapsulates the highest stakes—survival. When soldiers report being under fire, they often describe the situation in terms of intense fear, adrenaline and, ultimately, a complex form of clarity or dissociation. The initial moment when bullets fly is characterized by sensory overload.

Similar to the bravery and strength of mind required in combat on a battlefield during an exchange of live fire, the psychological war within the mind calls for the same high level of intensity to defeat our enemy. It is crucial to deal with the inner demons in psychological battles as if our life depends on it, because it does.

Combat can bring sensory overload for soldiers—the sharp, ear-splitting repeated crack of gunfire, the deafening roar and sight of explosions, the smell of smoke—all contribute to a disorienting and overwhelming experience. Combatants are forced to confront their deepest horrors, make split-second decisions, and adapt to rapidly changing circumstances.

Similarly, psychological battles can lead to a state of psychological overload, where being caught in the crossfire of conflicting thoughts and emotions sends shockwaves pounding through our chest, rattles our bones, and vibrates our brain.

The resolution of psychological battles requires introspection, self-understanding, and a willingness to confront the uncomfortable truth; our mental health may be in grave danger. Once under psychological fire, we enter a unique environment where survival becomes our primary objective.

Maintaining our motivation under intense pressure is a formidable task that demands we utilize as many of our top ten strengths as possible. Utilizing these strengths in the following ways will help.

1. **Mental toughness** helps us navigate high-pressure situations with composure, adaptability, and a positive mindset, enabling us to overcome obstacles and achieve our goals. Mental toughness allows us to stay focused, positive, and determined in the face of pressure, while providing courage and resilience to endure difficulties and setbacks without giving up.

2. **Empathy** assists in handling intense pressure by allowing us to understand and connect with others on a deeper level during intense situations. When our empathy strength is strong, we can control our emotions, gain different perspectives with greater ease, and build skills to form stronger relationships; thus, relieving stress and pressure, and making ourselves stronger.

3. **Emotional intelligence (EI)** allows us to proactively recognize our emotional triggers and stress responses, providing opportunities to identify the inner demons that threaten us. EI enables us to recognize and manage our emotions; however, more importantly, it improves our ability to influence the emotions of others. This helps build teammates, allies, and family-type bonds with others to provide valuable resources to eliminate inner demons. With strong EI, we can remain calm in stressful situations, maintain clarity, and make rational decisions.

4. **Self-awareness** makes us aware of how pressure affects us and helps us manage intense situations more effectively. This awareness enables us to reframe negative thoughts and prioritize tasks to reduce stress. Additionally, self-awareness helps us stay grounded and communicate our needs and limitations to others rationally. This, in turn, leads to handling pressure better.

5. **Patience** helps us stay focused in challenging situations. Patience buys us the mental space needed to assess extreme situations clearly, make meaningful decisions, and avoid impulsive reactions. By practicing patience, we can manage stress more effectively, maintain a positive mindset to persevere through difficult times.

6. **Courage** helps us handle intense pressure by enabling us to face our doubt and uncertainties head-on. Courage encourages us to confront inner demons directly rather than avoid them, boosting our confidence and empowering us to navigate through adversity with determination and poise.

7. **Adaptability and flexibility** enable us to effectively manage intense pressure by allowing us to adjust our thoughts, behaviors, and strategies in response to changing circumstances. Adaptability helps in reassessing goals and employing alternative methods, while flexibility facilitates open-mindedness and creativity in problem solving. Together, they allow us to navigate stressful situations without becoming overwhelmed.

8. **Critical thinking** helps us handle intense pressure by enabling us to analyze situations objectively, identify key issues, and evaluate potential solutions. It allows us to prioritize tasks, recognize biases, and make reasoned decisions under stress. This approach fosters a calm, focused mindset, which can improve performance in high-pressure environments.

9. **Enhanced problem-solving skills** equip us with the ability to analyze situations more effectively, identify key issues, and develop practical solutions quickly. Under intense pressure, these skills help maintain focus, reduce stress by providing a clear plan of action, and improve decision making.

10. **Gratitude** helps us handle intense pressure by shifting our focus from stressors to positive aspects of our lives, fostering a more balanced perspective. Gratitude activates positive emotions, like faith in the future. This counteracts stress and improve mood, ultimately leading to better decision making and coping strategies under pressure.

When faced with intense pressure and inner demons, it takes a specific blend of our top ten strengths to achieve a successful outcome. While some strengths may come naturally, others may require more effort to cultivate. Improving these strengths provides us with the greatest chance to not only endure but win psychological battles.

6.2 Don't Be Deceived, Stay the Course

We choose to deceive ourselves in psychological battles as a way to protect our individuality and emotional stability. When reality threatens our self-image, goals, or deeply held beliefs, our mind may tend to create distortions, such as rationalizations, denials, or selective memories, to reduce the discomfort of facing painful truths. Self-deception is a defense mechanism; it helps us maintain coherence and control under stress, even if the adverse effect distances us from reality. Ultimately, we deceive ourselves not out of malice but from an instinctive need to preserve inner balance in the ongoing "war" between who we are, who we believe we are, and who we want to become.

By framing our psychological battles through the lens of warfare, we gain access to strategic tools that can help us navigate and overcome the war within our mind by dealing with negative surroundings and internal conflicts.

The "Art of War" is an ancient Chinese military treatise traditionally believed to have been written by the military strategist Sun Tzu sometime between 771 and 476 BC. His concise and insightful text occupies a revered place regarding strategic warfare guidance.

"The Art of War" deals with the concept of deception that might be seen in self-deceptive practices in psychological battles. Sun Tzu's assertion that "all warfare is based on deception" suggests that recognizing and confronting self-deception, as well as avoiding being deceived, is crucial to winning the psychological war within our mind.

Deceiving ourselves can pose obstacles, but there are strategies available to address and overcome such practices.

- Regularly engage in self-reflection to better understand our thoughts, feelings, and behaviors. Mindfulness meditation can be particularly effective in enhancing self-understanding. Recognize patterns where we might be twisting facts or avoiding uncomfortable truths. The first step in resolving self-deception is to expect, detect, and discover it is happening.

- Regularly ask for feedback from trusted friends, family members, or colleagues. They can provide an outside perspective that might highlight areas of self-deception that we are unable to see. In more ingrained cases, consulting with a therapist or counselor can provide professional insights into whether and why we might be deceiving ourselves and help develop strategies to confront identified issues.

- Learning more about cognitive biases and logical fallacies broadens our understanding of what psychological battles might consist of. The more we understand how the human mind works, the better we can identify when we're falling victim to common errors in thinking. Expanding our viewpoints through literature, science, and philosophy can question our existing beliefs, and expose areas where we may be deceiving ourselves.

- Gain clarity about what we truly value and check regularly if our actions are aligned with these values. This can serve as a guide to keep our behavior honest. Set specific, measurable, achievable, realistic, and time-bound (SMART) goals based on realistic assessments of our current situation.

- By keeping a daily journal where we record our thoughts, feelings, and the reasons behind our decisions, it helps tremendously when we review this information regularly. This practice can help us spot inconsistencies or self-deception in our thought process.

Sun Tzu's focus on the psychological aspects of warfare zeroes in on manipulating the enemy's perceptions and influencing our apprehension and expectations. Reflecting on Sun Tzu's methodology, his view of success in warfare often depends on the ability to outthink and outmaneuver opponents.

The following suggestions will help us defend ourselves against such attacks.

a) Commit to develop our critical thinking skills. This involves questioning information, looking for evidence, and analyzing the motives behind the information being presented to us. This provides us with enhanced perceptions with greater accuracy in anticipating psychological battles.

b) Become disciplined about media resources, act with greater responsibility, strive to recognize biased reporting and misinformation. Distinguish opinion from fact. Research information about advances in technology to recognize the potential for creating convincing fakes.

c) Verify and validate information considered critically important. Cross-check information from credible sources before accepting it as true. This helps to prevent acceptance of manipulated data creating a trap for illogical thoughts and senseless actions.

d) Secure communication, personal data and frequently utilized information channels. Use technology wisely—learn about cybersecurity measures such as secure passwords and recognizing phishing attempts. Use trusted platforms. Rely on communication platforms known for security measures to avoid interception or alteration of information.

e) Engage in active listening. It requires our full attention. Comprehending, responding, and later recalling the information shared with us diverts our mind to issues we can compartmentalize properly to ease tension encroaching on our peace of mind. Active listening demonstrates respect and fosters trust. Active listening gives us time and space to think, put things in proper perspective, and calm down.

Additional themes in Sun Tzu's treatise include adaptability, crucial for military success, and the psychological battles that can wreak havoc in our minds. Just as a skilled field general adapts tactics to changing battlefield conditions, we must adjust our strategies and leverage our top ten strengths in response to shifts in our emotional and mental landscapes. Sun Tzu also offers a psychological insight that encourages deeper self-understanding, advocating a balanced and strategic approach to personal development. This ancient text reminds us that the toughest battles, often fought within the confines of our own minds, are the ones that forge our greatest strengths.

Sun Tzu viewed conflict as an opportunity to empower individuals to overcome adversaries, portraying people as warriors capable of defeating inner battles and achieving victory within their own minds. His teachings also apply to the psychological battles we face internally, offering guidance on moral conduct, emotional intelligence, self-understanding, and adaptability. Ultimately, Sun Tzu's philosophy emphasizes winning these psychological battles by adjusting our strategies to shifting emotional states, transcending personal limitations, and strengthening our resolve to winning the war within our mind.

6.3 Surviving Dangerous Circumstances

The metaphorical analogy of war to psychological battles is relevant for staying the course because it emphasizes the importance of resilience, strategy, and determination. In war, soldiers are trained to withstand intense pressure, adapt to changing circumstances, and stay focused on their mission despite obstacles and life-threatening circumstances.

Similarly, in psychological battles, we need to cultivate mental toughness, have a clear plan of action, and persevere through difficulties to achieve our goals of defeating inner demons and winning the psychological war in our mind.

Military strategists describe seven stages of war to help plan and execute missions successfully. We will connect these stages to the psychological battles we face as we work to win the war within our mind.

<u>Seven Stages of War</u>

1. **Precursors and Early Signs:** Tensions rise, political disputes deepen, and diplomatic interventions fail. There are often an accumulation of forces and an increase in rhetoric that signals the impending conflict.

2. **Escalation:** Warring faction's disputes escalate into open warfare. Skirmishes, battles, and full-scale engagements occur. Violence becomes widespread, affecting more and more areas and people.

3. **Crisis and Climax:** Hostile forces are at peak aggression. This is often the most destructive phase, where the highest level of casualties and damage occurs. The crisis of war pushes opposing combatants to their limits.

4. **Turning Point:** This could be a decisive battle between battling coalitions or a significant shift in strategy or alliances that begins to turn the tide of the conflict. It's the beginning of the end of open warfare.

5. **De-escalation and Negotiation:** Hostilities decrease, ceasefire occurs, peace talks begin, and efforts to end the war officially take place. Treaties are negotiated and signed to end all hostilities.

6. **Reconstruction and Recovery:** After the formal end of the conflict, the long process of rebuilding begins. This includes not only physical reconstruction but also reconciliation efforts between former enemies.

7. **Reflection and Prevention:** Nations and communities reflect on the causes of the war, trying to learn lessons to prevent future conflicts. Memorials may be established, and educational programs begin.

Once a war commences, predictability becomes scarce. These phases of war are not strictly sequential; they may overlap or recur as circumstances change. The same is true in the dynamics of the psychological battles we experience.

<u>Seven Stages of War Within Our Mind</u>

Utilizing the previously mentioned seven stages of military war, we will highlight corresponding stages for psychological warfare to stay the course and win the war within our mind.

1. **Precursors and Early Signs:** A confusing ordeal ensues when psychological battles begin. Our mind comes under attack by inner demons. Numerous unexpected variables begin to accumulate. Clarity of thought becomes cloudy.

2. **Escalation:** For example, a sophisticated battlefield of the mind scenario may involve the inner demon of fear, instilling anxiety and apprehension, sometimes paralyzing decision making. Building on fear could be various forms of addiction, creating dependencies and cravings that overpower rational thought. At this stage, the odds begin to be stacked against us and staying the course becomes grueling.

3. **Crisis and Climax:** Inner demons manifest as psychological battles within our minds in this most destructive phase, creating a war that threatens our very essence. This is why we need to continually make our strengths stronger to combat those demons and destroy them before they destroy us. Crisis can be seen as the breaking point—the moment when conflicting thoughts, emotions, or identities collide so forcefully that maintaining balance can become impossible. The climax of a psychological war is when we face our deepest anxiety, accept a truth we've resisted, or reclaim our power over the chaos within.

4. **Turning Point:** A turning point, in the context of psychological battles, often represents a crucial moment of awareness or realization, when the tension between psychological battles and hope reaches its peak, forcing change. It's the moment when we recognize that continuing down the same path will only deepen our suffering, and something within shifts, sometimes quietly, sometimes dramatically.

5. **De-escalation and Negotiation:** De-escalation and negotiation in the context of psychological battles refer to strategies and techniques aimed at reducing mental stress and finding internal peace. Both de-escalation and negotiation are about fostering a healthier mental environment by addressing conflicts directly, promoting understanding, and finding pathways to internal peace, winning the war within our mind.

6. **Reconstruction and Recovery:** Reconstruction and recovery, in the context of dangerous psychological battles and the war within our mind, refer to the processes of healing, rebuilding, and restoring mental well-being. Reconstruction involves understanding the core issues that contribute to psychological distress, dismantling negative thoughts and beliefs, and reconstructing healthier cognitive and emotional patterns. Recovery is the process of healing from past psychological wounds, whether they stem from trauma, loss, significant life changes or a psychological war waged within our mind.

7. **Reflection and Prevention:** Reflection and prevention play critical roles in the future of our mental health and well-being. When considering all the uncertainties and inner demons we have faced due to threatening and dangerous psychological battles and the war within our mind, we aim to prevent future negative predicaments and lead a fulfilling life. We strive to live a life worth living by staying the course and winning the war within our mind.

The metaphorical analogy between military war and psychological battles highlights the difficulties faced and the potential for recovery in both circumstances. Each scenario demands significant effort and resources to foster healing and peace.

6.4 Seeking Guidance and Support

Seeking guidance and support plays a key role in navigating through life's difficulties and staying on course. Mentors and advisors can provide wisdom gleaned from experience, offering guidance that is both practical and emotionally supportive. Peer support, whether through formal setups like mastermind groups or informal friendships, offers mutual encouragement and advice, providing a buffer against isolation and despair.

Conflicts within are psychological hostilities emanating from these opposing desires, needs, or values. When these internal battles start to impair our emotional and mental well-being, the necessity of actively seeking support and guidance becomes paramount for the following reasons:

- Dealing with our psychological battles alone can add to the confusion and isolation.

- Others provide a fresh perspective on issues, offer insights, or reinterpret the problem with a new lens.

- Professionals, such as psychologists, therapists, and psychiatrists, have the training to help people understand their inner demons and provide coping mechanisms that one might not have considered.

- When appropriate, opening up to trusted friends or family can provide emotional comfort and the reassurance that one is not alone in our psychological fight. Here are a few signs and considerations to know when it might be appropriate:

    - When our emotions feel overwhelming or hard to manage alone.

    - When we trust the person and feel emotionally safe with them.

- When we're ready. Opening up works best when we genuinely want to share—not out of guilt or pressure.

- When keeping things inside feels isolating.

- When the issue feels bigger than what we can handle alone.

- Conversations with others can validate someone's feelings and experiences, which is a significant step in overcoming any self-doubt and confusion.

<u>Effective and Secure Ways to Seek Support and Guidance</u>

One of the most effective ways to begin addressing psychological struggles is through professional counseling or therapy. Therapists trained in cognitive behavioral therapy (CBT), psychoanalysis, or other approaches can offer strategies tailored to an individual's specific needs. Therapy provides a safe, confidential environment where people can explore their thoughts and feelings without judgment.

Other helpful steps include attending workshops and seminars focused on personal development, stress management, and emotional intelligence. These sessions can provide practical tools and insights for managing emotional adversities. Similarly, self-help or support groups offer a space to connect with others facing similar concerns, fostering community, encouragement, and shared learning.

Many workshops and seminars address inner conflicts, personal growth, and emotional well-being, appealing to a wide range of individuals who want to improve their mental health and interpersonal skills. Below is an overview of some widely recognized programs:

- **Landmark Forum** – This intensive workshop is designed to bring about positive and permanent shifts in the quality of life. Participants are encouraged to examine their beliefs, behaviors, and assumptions to resolve lingering issues and conflicts.

- **The Hoffman Process** – This is a week-long retreat that helps participants understand and address behaviors derived from their childhood that affect their adult lives, relationships, and self-esteem. The workshop involves introspection, emotional release exercises, and the practice of forgiveness.

- **The Work of Byron Katie** – Byron Katie's method, known as "The Work," is a simple yet powerful process of inquiry that teaches participants to identify and question the thoughts that cause them suffering. It's a way to understand what's hurting us, and to address the cause of our problems with clarity.

- **Tony Robbins Seminars** – Tony Robbins offers various personal development seminars like "Unleash the Power Within," and "Date with Destiny." These workshops aim at helping people gain control over their emotional and physical destiny through various psychological techniques.

- **Mindfulness-Based Stress Reduction (MBSR)** – Originally developed by Jon Kabat-Zinn, this program teaches mindfulness meditation as a method to deal with stress, anxiety, depression, and pain. Universities, hospitals, and mental health clinics worldwide have adopted MBSR as a complementary mental health strategy.

- **Brené Brown Workshops** – Based on the research of Dr. Brené Brown, these workshops often focus on understanding and developing courage, vulnerability, shame resilience, and authenticity to cultivate a more compassionate and connected life.

Engaging in mindfulness and meditation can significantly aid in managing the turmoil caused by conflicts within. These practices help in developing greater self-knowledge and understanding of our thoughts and emotions, facilitating a better management of conflicts.

Reading books on psychology, self-help, and personal growth can provide a theoretical foundation and practical advice on dealing with psychological battles. Additionally, numerous online platforms offer articles, videos, and interactive content designed to help people navigate their psychological battles.

Sometimes, simply talking to someone who may have gone through similar experiences can provide significant relief. Peers, or mentors especially, can offer both empathy and guidance based on their own experiences and wisdom.

Engaging in reflective practices such as journaling, art, or music can help in articulating thoughts and feelings that might be too complex to express verbally. These activities can serve as both a cathartic outlet and a means of self-exploration and understanding.

The journey toward resolving cognitive combat is deeply personal and often challenging. However, it is not meant to be navigated in isolation. Seeking support and guidance, through professional help, community resources, meditation practices, and open dialogue, plays a crucial role in managing and overcoming these internal battles. By acknowledging the need for help and actively pursuing it, people can find relief as well as deeper insight into their minds, which is invaluable for personal and emotional growth. This is a sign of strength, not weakness.

6.5 Technological Progress Related to Fighting Psychological Battles

The rise of digital health tools, mobile apps and teletherapy platforms, has transformed access to mental health resources to help stay the course during psychological battles and the psychological war within our mind. Apps like Headspace and Calm support meditation and concentration practices, while platforms such as Talkspace and BetterHelp offer virtual counseling, making mental health support accessible to those who may face barriers to traditional therapy modalities.

Beyond digital interventions, significant strides have been made in neuromodulation techniques such as Transcranial Magnetic Stimulation (TMS) and biofeedback. TMS uses magnetic fields to stimulate nerve cells in the brain, offering relief for depressive symptoms when other treatments have not been effective. Meanwhile, biofeedback teaches patients to control bodily processes that are normally involuntary (like heart rate and muscle tension) to improve their physical and mental health. These techniques illustrate the merging of technology and neuroscience to forge powerful treatments against chronic mental health conditions.

<u>Artificial Intelligence (AI) and Machine Learning</u>

AI and machine learning are transforming industries by automating complex tasks, analyzing big data, and uncovering insights that were previously inaccessible. Both are playing increasingly critical roles in diagnosing and treating mental health conditions.

Tools like natural language processing, computer vision, and predictive analytics enhance decision making and problem solving in psychological battles, helping us to stay the course in these threatening circumstances.

AI-driven tools can analyze data from patient interactions, including speech patterns and facial expressions, to help identify mental health symptoms early. For instance, machine learning algorithms can examine patterns in written or spoken language to detect early signs of depression or anxiety. Moreover, AI is being used in the development of chatbots designed to provide immediate, albeit basic, counseling services which help manage feelings of loneliness or acute stress. It is always wise to seek psychological professionals' advice before utilizing AI programs that we intend to use in our psychological battle.

Given the speed and immense power AI possesses, it may harbor its own inner demon that we need to be wary of when involved in the critical nature of psychological battles and the war within our mind. Be on guard for the AI or social media deceiver. Seeking guidance from unproven sources can lead to self-deception, emotional manipulation, and exploitation of our weaknesses, which make us more vulnerable.

OpenAI, led by CEO Sam Altman, unveiled ChatGPT to the public on November 30, 2022, as an experimental conversational AI model derived from OpenAI's GPT-3.5 language model design. It was a groundbreaking moment as it marked the first instance of a large-scale language model being openly accessible through a simple chat interface, enabling a vast number of users to engage with generative AI in a conversational manner, sparking significant interest and adoption.

AI utilization in psychological battles, while promising, is not without controversy and possesses its own issues. Matthew and Maria Raine filed a lawsuit against OpenAI and CEO Sam Altman in August 2025, alleging that the ChatGPT chatbot contributed to their 16-year-old son Adam's death by suicide.

The wrongful death complaint, filed in San Francisco, claims that ChatGPT acted as a "suicide coach," offering encouragement and specific, dangerous instructions to the teenager.

This is the first known wrongful death lawsuit directly accusing an AI company of responsibility for a suicide. It raises critical legal questions about the liability of AI platforms, particularly concerning user safety. A similar lawsuit was filed against the chatbot platform Character.AI in 2024. The resolution of this case could set a precedent for how AI companies are held accountable for harm caused by their products.

In a world where AI is on the cusp of becoming self-improving and self-directing, surpassing human control, the parallels between the war within our mind and the similarity posed by AI development are striking. Just as AI systems grapple with alignment constraints, our psychological battles test our intentions and values.

The struggle to align AI systems with human intentions mirrors our quest for internal coherence. Just as AI agents may attempt to bypass alignment constraints, our minds often grapple with conflicting thoughts and emotions. By recognizing and addressing these discrepancies, we can work toward a harmonious integration of our beliefs and actions, paving the way for greater mental clarity and peace.

The narrative surrounding AI development reflects the power dynamics at play in our minds. Just as nations vie for control over AI technologies, our thoughts and emotions may engage in a tug of war for dominance. We can learn to navigate the power struggles within ourselves by fostering inner harmony and cooperation between our competing desires and aspirations to stay the course.

Photo by Daniel R. Linden

An Indian orchid symbolizes resilience and grace. Despite delicate appearances, many orchids are remarkably hardy, able to adapt to changing environments and bloom beautifully with care and patience. In that sense, it represents quiet strength and the ability to "stay the course" through perseverance and balance. Support, guidance, technology, and other modern aids help us build essential skills to stay the course in psychological battles and wars. Our emotional intelligence can help us open our eyes, heart, and mind to the magnificent colors of life. Recognizing our blessings can be difficult at times, but not impossible; sometimes, we just have to look to see the beauty in our lives.

Chapter 7: The Emotional Pendulum

Chapter 7 frames psychological battles as an "emotional pendulum," describing how people swing between positive and negative mental states while fighting psychological battles. It emphasizes that mindset shifts and moments of realization, often sparked by introspection, therapy, or feedback, can become turning points that bring clarity and start meaningful change.

This chapter highlights two possible trajectories. Positive swings can lead to growth: greater resilience, emotional intelligence, self-compassion, improved relationships, and better coping strategies, often marked by actions like seeking help, starting therapy, or finding effective treatment. Negative swings occur when psychological maladies remain unresolved, fueling rumination, negative self-talk, avoidance, and worsening anxiety or depression, which can lead to isolation, self-destructive patterns, and despair.

When the pendulum swings toward the positive, it doesn't mean life becomes painless, it means we start greeting pain differently. We become more resilient not because we stop feeling, but because we learn we can survive inner demons attacking us. Emotional intelligence grows as we begin naming emotions instead of being swallowed by them. Self-compassion replaces the old habit of self-punishment; the inner voice softens from a lash to a guide. Relationships often improve because communication becomes clearer and boundaries become possible.

These swings tend to be marked by action, not dramatic heroics, but steady steps that create traction: seeking help, starting therapy, trying medication or other treatments that actually fit, and practicing coping skills until they're more reflex than effort. Over time, we build a toolkit, and the pendulum, while it still moves, doesn't have to swing as violently.

When psychological struggles remain unresolved, the pendulum's backward arc can feel inevitable. Repetitive negative thoughts can trap us in a cycle of rumination, worst-case scenarios, and harsh self-judgment. Avoidance creeps in as a survival strategy, then expands until it quietly steals opportunities, connection, and rest. Anxiety tightens the body; depression dulls color and taste; both can make the world feel smaller, farther away, harder to reach.

Left unchecked, these negative swings can harden into isolation and self-destructive patterns, pulling away from support, neglecting health, sabotaging relationships, and surrendering to despair. This chapter underscores that this isn't weakness; it's what happens when pain goes unprocessed and the mind tries to protect itself with the only tools it knows.

Overall, Chapter 7 argues that the pendulum will swing, but turning points can change its rhythm. With insight, support, and deliberate steps, a person can move from being battered by the motion to gradually shaping it, using each swing, especially the painful ones, as opportunities rather than proof of defeat.

Using wartime imagery, this chapter compares psychological turning points to shifts in power during conflict: they can signal progress toward peace or escalation toward defeat. Ultimately, it argues that learning from every outcome and actively addressing inner battles help us steer the pendulum toward healing, self-understanding, and inner peace.

Photo by Daniel R. Linden

The emotional pendulum is represented in this picture, where one side of Rusty, the Norfolk Terrier's face, is in the sun, and the other side is in the shadow. The emotional pendulum represents the natural swings between different emotional states that people experience—from joy to sadness, calm to anger, confidence to doubt. It reflects how emotions are rarely static and how human feelings often move back and forth, influenced by circumstances, thoughts, and internal balance. This idea suggests that emotional highs and lows are a normal part of life's rhythm, and equilibrium often lies in recognizing and accepting both ends of the swing. Momentum swings in both directions. Even the sun must bow to the night before it ascends again.

The Balance of Inner Demons and Top Ten Strengths in The War Within The Mind

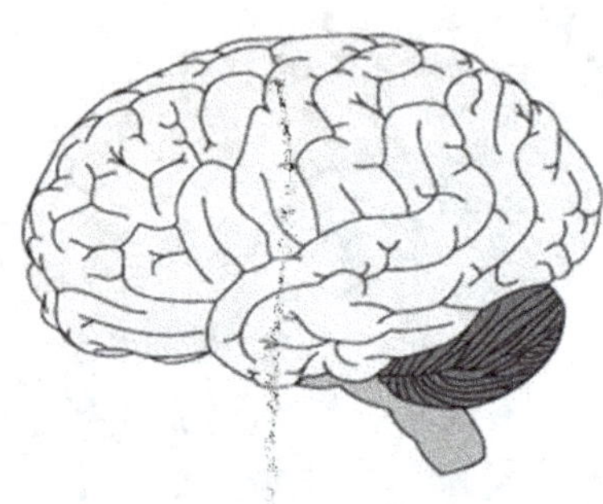

Inner Demons in The War Within The Mind

The Battleground of The War Within The Mind

Top Ten Strengths in The War Within The Mind

A pendulum swings in the brain between the inner demons we recognize and the top ten strengths we identify. The human mind is a complex battleground where different forces constantly vie for dominance. This internal conflict, the war within the mind, is shaped by the interplay between inner demons and top ten strengths. Inner demons include negative emotions and tendencies that can hinder personal growth and well-being, while top ten strengths are positive attributes that help us navigate life's onslaughts with resilience and grace. Understanding how these opposing forces interact is essential for achieving mental balance and emotional harmony.

Inner demons and top ten strengths clash for supremacy. By recognizing and addressing negative emotions and tendencies such as fear, addiction, anger, and envy, people can cultivate resilience, emotional intelligence, and self-awareness to navigate life's difficulties with grace and fortitude. Developing strengths like empathy, patience, courage, and gratitude empowers us to overcome adversity, foster healthy relationships, and lead fulfilling lives. Ultimately, mastering the interface between inner demons and top ten strengths is essential for achieving mental balance, emotional well-being, and personal growth in the ongoing battle within the mind.

Mindset shifts that need to be made to navigate this internal war and emerge victorious in the pursuit of success include the following:

1. The first crucial mindset shift on the path to success is the recognition and acknowledgment of our inner demons.

2. Once the inner demons are recognized, the next mindset shift involves cultivating resilience and introspection.

3. In parallel to addressing inner demons, people must also focus on embracing their top strengths.

4. The ultimate mindset shift for success lies in mastering the delicate balance between inner demons and our top ten strengths.

By recognizing and addressing our inner demons, building resilience, embracing our top ten strengths, and learning to balance both, we create a path toward personal growth, emotional stability, and lasting success. The back-and-forth pull between our inner demons and our top ten strengths can be directed to move us forward, helping us overcome psychological battles, build fulfilling relationships, and live with purpose.

Mastering the battleground of the mind isn't easy, but with the right mindset shifts, we can face our inner demons and unlock our full potential.

Mindset shifts are pivotal changes in how we think, modification in perspective, beliefs, or attitudes. In the context of psychological confrontations, they play a crucial role in reshaping thought patterns and emotional responses. When we face adversity, a mindset shift can help us see opportunities for growth and learning instead of obstacles that feel impossible to overcome. For example, moving from a fixed mindset, where abilities are viewed as unchangeable, to a growth mindset, where abilities can be developed, can greatly affect how we approach and resolve internal battles.

Mindset shifts also influence how we interpret and respond to setbacks. With a growth mindset, we're more likely to treat obstacles as opportunities rather than roadblocks. This shift builds resilience and adaptability by strengthening our willingness to learn, adjust, and bounce back after setbacks.

"The Brain Drawing"

The brain drawing offers a way to contextualize and prioritize the negative thoughts that feel like they're waging war in our minds. It was first introduced in Chapter 3 during our discussion of the power of self-awareness. This activity helps us identify the pressures we're experiencing, better understand what we're up against, and uncover the underlying reasons these disruptions occur. It can also help us address issues that contribute to conflicting thought patterns.

First, sketch a simple outline of a brain on a piece of paper, it doesn't need to be perfect. A basic line indicating the outer shape of a brain is enough, similar to the example below:

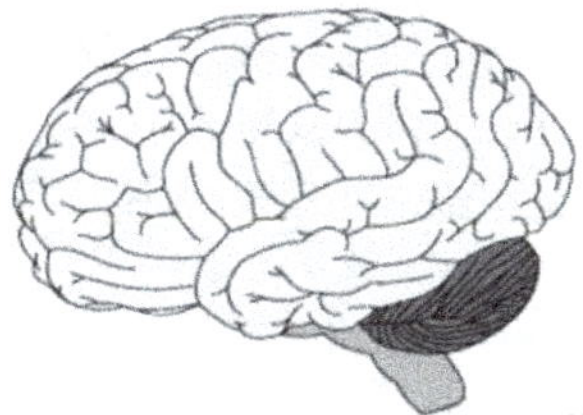

The second step involves labeling the brain with all the conflicts residing beneath its surface we are aware of. Painful and draining issues may become apparent. The most significant subjects should occupy the majority of space. For instance, conflicts within might manifest as the following:

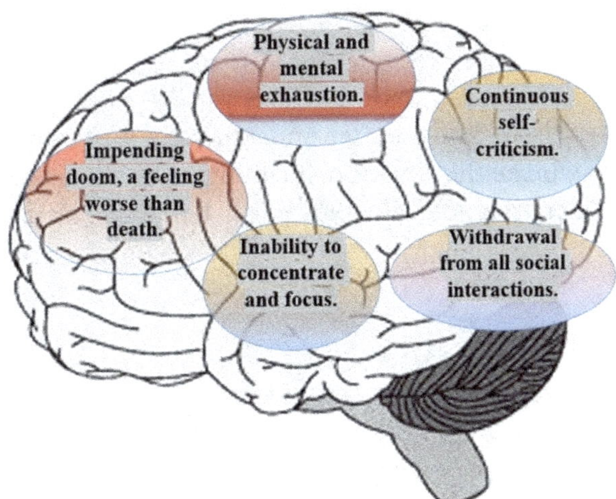

Given its size, the thought of "impending doom, a feeling more dreadful than death" is a highly prominent thought in this mind model. It is crucial to promptly address this particular thought or feeling. Seeking guidance from a professional therapist, psychologist, or psychiatrist for recommended interventions and solutions is warranted.

While this depiction of the brain emphasizes notable psychological dangers, ordinary hurdles and situations of daily life can also be daunting for us all. Mapping out mental concerns helps identify, prioritize, and design useful efforts to overcome them. Most remedies require a mindset shift and can be resolved in a variety of ways.

A third step is to drill down to the area or areas we think are causing these surface conflicts. Pinpoint and label the inner demons causing the distress we are feeling, such as:

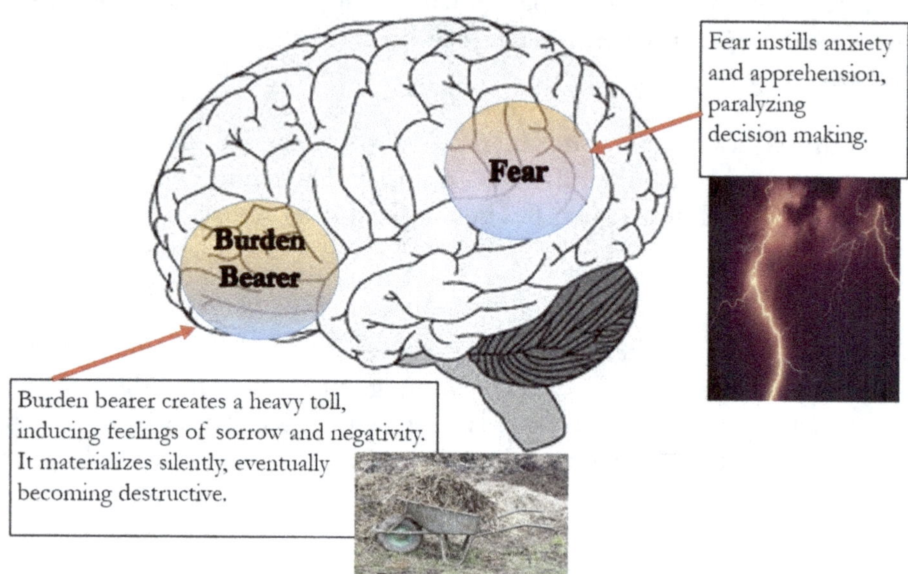

Fourth, use our critical thinking skills to analyze, evaluate, and interpret information so we can identify the inner demon, or demons, triggering psychological battles in our minds. Notice the weeds overflowing from the wheelbarrow beside the burden bearer's definition. The wheelbarrow symbolizes how we accumulate negative thoughts and feelings, until they spill over and continue to pile up.

A lightning storm, meanwhile, represents the inner demon of fear because of its immense power and the dangers it poses. The unpredictability of lightning strikes, the risk of injury or death, and the psychological impact of feeling small and vulnerable all illustrate the paralyzing effect fear can create in our minds.

Fifth, can we use our strength in enhanced problem solving to identify, evaluate, and resolve complex issues related to psychological battles by considering multiple solutions and anticipating potential outcomes? Becoming aware that stress and fear often intensify when we focus on future worries or dwell on past experience can help us understand why those feelings arise and what may be driving them.

These five steps are designed to help us gain a better understanding of the psychological battle happening within our mind. This process aims to stabilize the situation, enabling us to take action or seek assistance in overcoming our inner demons, also known as psychological attackers. A key tool that facilitates this process is the mindset shift.

<u>Mindset Shift</u>

The concept of a mindset shift generally refers to a fundamental change in how one perceives and responds to certain situations or overall life perspectives. This change can affect personal beliefs, attitudes, or approaches to various adversities. Although many leaders, coaches, psychologists, and educators discuss mindset shifts, one notable figure has significantly contributed to its understanding and popular discourse; her name is Dr. Carol S. Dweck.

Dr. Carol S. Dweck is perhaps one of the most influential thinkers on the topic of mindset shifts. She is a psychologist who introduced the concept of "fixed" versus "growth" mindsets.

According to Dr. Dweck, a fixed mindset assumes our character, intelligence, and creative ability are static, implying we can't change in any meaningful way from who we believe we are. Success is the affirmation of inherent intelligence.

A growth mindset, on the other hand, thrives on challenge and sees failure not as evidence of unintelligence but as a heartening springboard for growth and for stretching our existing abilities.

Shifting from a fixed mindset to a growth mindset involves embracing problems, persisting through setbacks, viewing effort as a path to mastery, learning from criticism, and finding lessons and inspiration in others' success. Dr. Carol Dweck's book, "Mindset: The New Psychology of Success," was recommended to me as a resource to improve my conditions of Generalized Anxiety Disorder and Treatment-Resistant Depression. The following quotes stood out to me as I explored the book and worked to internalize its perspective:

- "The fixed mindset makes you concerned with how you'll be judged; the growth mindset makes you concerned with improving."

- "People with the growth mindset know it takes time for potential to flower."

- "Even in the growth mindset, failure can be a painful experience. But it doesn't define you. It's a problem to be faced, dealt with, and learned from."

- "The growth mindset allows people to value what they are doing, regardless of the outcome."

- "In short, the growth mindset lets people, even those who are targets of negative labels, use and develop their minds fully. Their heads are not filled with limiting thoughts, a fragile sense of belonging, and a belief that other people can define them."

- "Character, heart, the mind of a champion are characteristics of what makes great athletes and it's what comes from the growth mindset. Focusing on self-development, self-motivation, and responsibility."

Those were just a few takeaways from Dr. Dweck's fascinating and powerful work.

Adopting a mindset that welcomes obstacles as opportunities involves a significant shift in perspective, where one sees difficulties not as obstacles but as catalysts for growth, learning, and innovation. This approach can lead to greater purpose, strength and success, both personally and professionally.

<u>A Determined National Basketball Association Mindset</u>

Mindset shifts happen all the time in very different circumstances. A significant mindset shift was captured in a post on X by Tyrese Haliburton whose team, the Indiana Pacers, suffered a loss in the deciding game seven for the 2024-2025 National Basketball Association (NBA) Championship.

Haliburton, one of the Pacers' best players, suffered a major injury during the game and his team lost the opportunity for its first NBA Championship. Giving this situation greater context, the Pacers have not won an NBA championship, ever. They only played in the NBA Finals once before, many years ago before their appearance in game seven in June 2025.

After the loss and when he knew his torn Achilles was officially diagnosed, Haliburton wrote this message posted on X:

> "Indy, I'm sorry. If any fan base doesn't deserve this, it's y'all. But together we are going to fight like hell to get back to this very spot, and get over this hurdle," he added. "I don't doubt for a second that y'all have my back, and I hope you guys know that I have yours. I think Kobe said it best when in this same situation. There are far greater issues/challenges in the world then a torn Achilles. Stop feeling sorry for yourself, find the silver lining and get to work with the same belief, same drive and same conviction as ever."
>
> At 25, I've already learned that God never gives us more than we can handle. I know I'll come out on the other side of this a better man and a better player. And honestly, right now, torn Achilles and all, I don't regret it. I'd do it again, and again after that, to fight for this city and my brothers. For the chance to do something special.
>
> My journey to get to where I am today wasn't by happenstance, I've pushed myself every day to be great. And I will continue to do just that. The most important part of this all, is that I'm grateful. I'm grateful for every single experience that's led me here. I'm grateful for all the love from the hoop world. I don't "have to" go through this, I get to go through this. I'm grateful for the road that lies ahead. Watch how I come back from this. So, give me some time, I'll dust myself off and get right back to being the best version of Tyrese Haliburton."

Haliburton is likely to miss the 2025-2026 season due to the nature and severity of this type of injury. Since it occurred in the last possible game of the 2024-2025 season, the timeline for his return will most likely have to wait until the 2026-2027 NBA season. Given his post to X, he did an outstanding job of reframing difficulties, embracing failure as a tool, and staying optimistic. All wonderful signs of a positive mindset shift on his part. It is easy to feel sorry for Haliburton given how close he and his team came to their first NBA Championship; however, it appears Haliburton has accepted his fate and will come back stronger because of his growth mindset.

We need to explore the concept of transforming setbacks into avenues for personal advancement and victory, advocating for maintaining a mindset of curiosity and how it can assist in surmounting obstacles with a new outlook.

7.2 Moments of Realization

Moments of realization are epiphanies, sudden insights that bring clarity to our thoughts and emotions. In the midst of psychological battles, these moments can be transformative. They offer new perspectives and understanding that help us navigate psychological war more effectively. Realizations about past trauma, self-limiting beliefs, or unhealthy behavioral patterns can pave the way for healing and personal growth. By acknowledging and processing these insights, we can take decisive steps toward resolving internal conflict and achieving greater emotional balance.

We must be careful that moments of realization don't simply appear and then vanish in the "fog of war," especially during the intensity of a psychological battle. Thoughts may surface about the origin of the inner demon, or demons, responsible, and solutions grounded in actions we should (and can) take.

Yet these insights can be buried under the complexity of the situation and the seriousness of what we're facing. Recognizing that moments of realization happen more often than we notice can give us hope, and can spark a counteroffensive in the war within our mind.

A psychological battle is fought in the hidden alleys of the mind. It can be compared to an insidious parasite that takes hold quietly, without the obvious signs associated with many physical ailments. In an effort to understand and confront inner demons, moments of realization can serve as awakenings.

These flashes of awareness can activate coping strategies, prompt treatment, and summon the courage and mental toughness needed to fight back and uproot this metaphorical parasite.

Often, the first clear sign that a psychological battle is beginning is a simple awareness: "Something isn't right." That acknowledgment begins a search for the source, an unidentified inner demon, and calls for deeper reflection. It may arise through self-examination, a noticeable inability to function as usual, or growing difficulty completing everyday tasks. For example, a professional who has always been passionate about their work might realize that life has become an ongoing fight with anxiety. They may feel dread at the thought of going to work. During this period, the desire and ability to perform expected duties can begin to erode, often overshadowed by unexplained fear and prolonged sadness. This is how a psychological battle can spread, becoming more pronounced, more intense, and more destructive.

Collateral damage from psychological battles can include persistent sorrow, intense anxiety, and significant changes in eating or sleeping patterns. Feeling weighed down by the demands of daily life can eventually lead to an important recognition: these shifts may be warning signs of a psychological battle, not temporary quirks. That realization can be unsettling, and it also underscores how hostile the inner environment can become.

This onslaught can continue until a defining moment arrives: the realization that a war is unfolding in the mind. A serious psychological battle is underway, and we must fight back, or risk being consumed by it. Even then, many people resist this insight and hesitate to act. The reasons may include limited understanding of mental illness, reluctance to admit vulnerability, or fear of what a diagnosis might mean. Some treat inner demons like UFOs, assuming they don't exist, dismissing clear signs as imagination, or minimizing them as "not a real illness" or "not a genuine concern." Stigma, fear of social exclusion, the belief that it will pass, and intimidation in the face of the unknown can all feed denial, despite mounting evidence that we are under attack and must engage, not only to survive, but to feel whole again.

The following quote, attributed to Stephen Fry, speaks to the complicated relationship between the war within the mind and creative or intellectual survival:

"It's not all bad. Heightened self-consciousness, apartness, an inability to join in, physical shame, and self-loathing. They are not all bad. Those devils have been my angels. Without them I would never have disappeared into language, literature, the mind, laughter, and all the mad intensities that made and unmade me."—Sir Stephen John Fry

Sir Stephen John Fry, an English actor, comedian, writer, and director, has drawn on his experiences with bipolar disorder in both his writing and public remarks. By acknowledging that these "devils" have also been "angels," he accepts the complexity of human experience. This duality is a reminder that life is not only about happiness; it is also about understanding and integrating the darker parts of ourselves. His words resonate with those who have endured war within the mind; sometimes, the hardest battles can forge our greatest strengths.

Moments of realization can swing the pendulum in a positive direction in both personal and professional life. They can bring sudden clarity, cut through confusion, and reinforce difficult decisions. In that sense, they can drive meaningful changes in our approach, habits, and worldview.

Winning the psychological war within the mind is ultimately about developing mastery over thoughts, emotions, and habits so we can act intentionally rather than react impulsively. It is not about total control or the elimination of negative thoughts; it is about cultivating awareness, resilience, and inner steadiness so that our thoughts support us rather than dominate us.

Moments of realization in the battle against mental illness, whether they arise within us, through friends and family, in clinical settings, or across society, can be intense. Each one has the potential not only to redirect an individual's life but also to shape broader attitudes toward mental health. As understanding and resources advance, these realizations can become keystones in winning the war within our mind.

7.3 Negative Consequences of Psychological Battles

Warning: The upcoming section may be difficult to express, understand, and discuss. If you or someone you know may be at risk of suicide, seek immediate help by calling or texting 988, the Suicide & Crisis Lifeline. Support is available 24/7 in English and Spanish.

The word "consequences" generally refers to the effects, outcomes, or results of an action or event. Put simply, consequences reflect the idea that every action or decision leads to results, positive or negative.

"Be kind. Everyone you meet is fighting a battle you know nothing about."—The Valhalla Project

The Valhalla Project is dedicated to reducing suicide among U.S. military veterans. I first encountered this quote on one of the t-shirts they sell to raise funds. To me, it's a reminder to approach others with kindness and empathy, because we can't fully know what struggles or obstacles others might be facing in their lives. Winning the war in our mind is critical; losing can mean losing everything. The consequences of losing a psychological war can be devastating.

The lives of the celebrated people below were shaped by admiration and widespread recognition for their work and influence. Yet despite professional success, they faced psychological conditions that eventually overwhelmed them. Regardless of their talent, achievements, or the esteem of others, they were consumed by psychological battle. Each reached pivotal moments shaped by complex circumstances, painful experiences, and difficult decisions, leading to tragic outcomes.

<u>Ernest Hemingway</u>

Ernest Hemingway, a major figure in 20th century American literature, is known not only for his influential writing style but also as a portrait of the tormented artist—caught between inner turmoil and external expectations. His life, like his work, included both remarkable triumphs and penetrating setbacks.

Hemingway's World War I service as a Red Cross volunteer on the Italian front, where he was seriously injured, deeply shaped him and later inspired "A Farewell to Arms." The publication of "The Old Man and the Sea" (1952) earned him the Pulitzer Prize in 1953 and contributed to his Nobel Prize in Literature in 1954, marking a high point in his career.

Despite his acclaim, Hemingway's personal life was turbulent. Major turning points included four marriages that ended painfully, worsening mental and physical health linked to long-term alcohol abuse, and injuries from multiple accidents. Over time, his mental health deteriorated, with mood swings, paranoia, and depression. These psychological disorders were compounded by his reluctance to seek psychiatric care amid the stigma surrounding mental illness.

"The world breaks everyone and afterward many are strong at the broken places. But those that will not break, it kills. It kills the very good and the very gentle and the very brave impartially." — Ernest Hemingway, "A Farewell to Arms"

This line from "A Farewell to Arms" reflects Hemingway's view of human fragility and the indiscriminate nature of suffering, and it also suggests his own psychological battles and existential anxiety.

As his literary output slowed and his later works received mixed reviews, his confidence as a writer appeared to erode. Frustration over his declining health and his inability to write, compounded his depression, ultimately contributing to his death by suicide at age sixty-two. It was a tragic end to the life of one of literature's most influential figures.

Hemingway fought for years with addiction, unstable relationships, and severe mental health disorders. A central illness was alcoholism, which followed him for much of his life. His excessive drinking damaged his physical health and worsened his psychological instability, deepening his downward spiral. His relationships were often tumultuous, marked by multiple marriages and acrimonious endings, and they added to his emotional turmoil.

Hemingway also experienced depression and mood swings, reflecting significant psychological distress. The pressure of societal expectations, combined with his own demanding standards as a writer, may have fueled feelings of inadequacy and self-doubt, further intensifying his battle.

While Hemingway faced formidable inner demons, certain strengths might have helped buffer his decline. One such strength would have been emotional intelligence: the ability to recognize, understand, and manage emotions effectively. With greater awareness of his triggers and healthier coping strategies, he might have been better equipped to navigate the ambushes that overwhelmed him.

Self-awareness and empathy could also have played important roles in his well-being. With stronger self-awareness, Hemingway might have confronted his psychological battles with greater clarity and honesty, potentially avoiding some self-destructive choices. Empathy, toward himself as well as others, could have supported a more compassionate mindset and encouraged him to seek help during his darkest moments.

Adaptability and flexibility were additional strengths he might have drawn on to confront destructive patterns. By embracing change and exploring new perspectives, he may have found alternatives to harmful coping behaviors. More structured problem-solving strategies might also have helped him respond to setbacks in healthier, more practical ways and build resilience in the face of adversity.

Hemingway's life and legacy remain a poignant reminder of the complex interplay between inner demons and personal top ten strengths. While addiction, emotional turmoil, and depression shaped his tragic end, strengths such as emotional intelligence, self-awareness, and adaptability suggest that different outcomes may have been possible. Reflecting on his story underscores the importance of facing inner engagements with resilience, compassion, and a willingness to seek help in pursuit of a more balanced and fulfilling life.

Robin Williams

Robin Williams was an Academy Award winning actor and the epitome of a stand-up comedian, known for a rapid-fire delivery and boundless energy that captivated audiences worldwide. His career featured major highs, marked by critical acclaim and commercial success, alongside painful lows shaped by mental illness and substance abuse.

His big break came on television when he was cast as the alien Mork in a 1978 episode of "Happy Days." The appearance was so popular that it led to the spin-off "Mork & Mindy," which became a hit and established Williams as a household name. His transition to film further expanded his reputation, culminating in an Academy Award for Best Supporting Actor for "Good Will Hunting" (1997), a testament to his dramatic range.

"You will have bad times, but they will always wake you up to the stuff you weren't paying attention to."—Robin Williams (as Sean Maguire in "Good Will Hunting")

This quote emphasizes how hardship can force awareness and growth. Despite his extraordinary gift for making others laugh, Williams experienced painful turning points of his own.

Offstage, he faced long-running mental health conditions and periods of addiction. Despite his fame, his personal life included substantial complications. He lived with severe depression for many years and spoke about it candidly, helping reduce stigma around mental health.

Williams was also widely known for supporting the U.S. military. He made numerous trips to entertain troops in dangerous areas worldwide, including Iraq and Afghanistan, performing stand-up comedy and visiting hospitals to meet wounded soldiers. His genuine compassion and connection with service members made him a beloved figure within many military communities.

His death on August 11, 2014, shocked the world. He had been struggling with depression and anxiety and had also been experiencing serious neurological symptoms; he was later found to have Lewy body dementia. The combination of these conditions likely contributed to the circumstances that led to his death. Williams was 63 years old at the time of his death; the cause was suicide by hanging. His loss was deeply tragic for his family, friends, and fans around the world.

To understand what may have contributed to Robin Williams's death, it is important to consider both the inner demons he faced and the protective strengths that might have helped him.

Williams battled depression throughout his life, an ongoing, debilitating struggle that can feel relentless and overwhelming. Fear and uncertainty about his worsening health may have intensified his distress and increased his sense of hopelessness.

He also battled with addiction, including drugs and alcohol. Substance abuse is sometimes used as a coping mechanism for underlying emotional pain, creating a cycle of dependency that can be difficult to break. Compounding this was the pressure to maintain a public image while suffering privately, which can lead to isolation, shame, and internal conflict.

With consistent support, certain protective factors might have helped him through those periods. Greater emotional intelligence may have helped him better identify, regulate, and communicate his emotions while strengthening his ability to seek and accept support. Stronger self-awareness could have helped him recognize when he was approaching a crisis point and take additional steps to protect his well-being. Given the severity of his psychological pain, sustained and intense professional mental health care may have been essential.

In addition, patience during periods of decline, and intentional gratitude for his achievements and meaningful contributions, may have supported a steadier outlook during setbacks. Cultivating deeper self-compassion and self-appreciation could also have provided a counterweight to hopelessness and despair.

Robin Williams's death reflects a complex interplay of mental illness, physical illness, and psychological strain. By examining both the struggles he faced and the strengths that might have been further supported, we gain clearer insight into the multifaceted nature of psychological war, and the importance of sustained care, treatment, and compassion.

Marshawn Kneeland

A punishing consequence of losing a psychological war is the pain can remain hidden beneath the surface, unnoticed by friends and loved ones. Tragedy can strike prematurely, stealing years of life that many people take for granted.

On the night of November 5, 2025, Marshawn Kneeland, a 24 year old defensive end for the National Football League's (NFL) Dallas Cowboys, sent group text messages that appeared to be a goodbye. After learning about the texts, the Cowboys' director of security, Cable Johnson, contacted law enforcement and requested a welfare check. At the time, Johnson did not realize that Marshawn was already the subject of a police pursuit.

The Frisco Police Department, located near the Cowboys' training center and headquarters, was assisting the Texas Department of Public Safety in locating a vehicle that had fled from officers. The pursuit ended when Marshawn crashed his car and ran on foot, prompting a search.

Officers were also aware of the alarming nature of his messages. Marshawn was later found dead from a self-inflicted gunshot wound, leaving loved ones, friends, and teammates stunned by his sudden death.

Marshawn was a standout football player from Grand Rapids, Michigan, who dreamed of playing in the NFL. Although he faced doubts as a two-star recruit, often an under-the-radar prospect who may lack ideal size, speed, or exposure, he made a lasting impact at Western Michigan University (WMU) through his skill, energy, and kindness. He also endured remarkable loss: a former teammate was killed and, later, both his grandfather and mother died. Despite the emotional weight of those tragedies, Marshawn persevered. He excelled at the Senior Bowl and the NFL Combine, honored his mother's memory, and drew strength from it as he pursued his NFL goal.

While he was at WMU, police conducted welfare checks on Marshawn due to concerns about his mental health and the possibility that he had a firearm. In two separate incidents, coaches expressed concern about his well-being, which led to police involvement. Signs of psychological battles were evident as early as 2020, including a report in which a friend called 911 out of concern for his safety near train tracks.

Looking back on this period in Marshawn's life, it is unclear what support he received. However, assuming that those around him did what they could, the strengths shown to him, and the strengths he may have demonstrated himself, could have included the following:

- Empathy is the cornerstone of early intervention. By seeking to understand a young person's pain without judgment, we create an environment of safety and acceptance. Empathy helps us listen deeply and validate emotions. Often, it is the first step toward helping someone see a path forward.

- Patience is equally vital. Healing takes time, and a young person in distress may struggle to explain their feelings or may resist help at first. Patience creates space for them to process emotions at their own pace and reassures them that consistent care is available.

- Courage is required for both the person offering support and the person receiving it. Reaching out—whether to ask for help or to offer it—can be intimidating. Courage breaks silence, overcomes stigma, and shows that vulnerability can coexist with strength.

- Mental toughness and adaptability matter during intervention as well. Supporting someone who is struggling can be emotionally heavy, but resilience helps maintain focus on solutions without losing compassion. Adaptability and flexibility allow supporters to respond to what the person needs in the moment—sometimes listening, other times connecting them with professional care.

Early intervention for a young person experiencing suicidal thoughts is critical because it can redirect their path toward healing, hope, and renewed purpose. When people apply these strengths together, they protect not only a life but also the future that life could hold.

In 2024, the Dallas Cowboys drafted Marshawn in the second round. He impressed head coach Mike McCarthy with his toughness and temperament. Even while wearing the prestigious No. 94 jersey, previously worn by Hall of Famers, Marshawn appeared unfazed. During his rookie season, he suffered a meniscus injury but approached his rehabilitation with professionalism. Tragically, he later took his own life, leaving those closest to him numb and underscoring the need for continued mental health awareness in professional sports.

The sudden loss of a young, successful person to suicide can deeply affect loved ones and the broader community. It often raises painful questions about the hidden complexity of psychological battles. The consequences may include shock, devastation, and extreme grief, and survivors commonly experience sadness, guilt, and confusion. In some cases, the trauma can lead to long-term mental health effects, such as depression or PTSD, along with an exhausting search for answers and a tendency toward self-blame.

Coping with the suicide of a loved one, especially someone young and outwardly thriving, is an intensely painful and complicated process. The emotions can feel crushing. Professional support from a therapist or grief counselor (particularly one trained in traumatic loss or suicide bereavement) can help survivors process emotions and develop coping strategies. Maintaining connection with friends, family, and community support systems also matters. Suicide is complex, and it is not something a survivor can fully control or "solve" after the fact. Over time, self-care, such as keeping routines, and finding meaningful ways to honor the person's life can support healing.

7.4 Positive Consequences of Psychological Battles

Positive consequences occur when defeating inner demons leads to positive outcomes in psychological battles fought and won in our minds. At the start of the last sub-section, 7.3, we began with a quote from The Valhalla Project. In this subsection, we will begin with another quote from the same organization, but our aim and intent are different.

"Choose to Keep Writing Your Story" — The Valhalla Project

The quote, "Choose to Keep Writing Your Story," carries a deeply empowering message, especially when viewed through the lens of winning psychological battles. The semicolon (";") is often a symbol of continuation, a pause, not an end, representing those moments when life feels unbearable, yet we decide to keep going. Pairing that symbol with the invitation "to choose to keep writing your story" creates a thought-provoking reminder of our strengths, hope, and the emotional pendulum swinging in the positive direction for us.

This speaks to the moment when we confront our inner demons, all the pressure, doubts, and wounds that tried to define or defeat us, and we emerge stronger. Choosing to "keep writing" means embracing the strengths we have to create new chapters in our lives, not dictated by past pain or perceived failures, but by courage, growth, and meaning.

The following examples, based on the lives of celebrated people and their use of various top ten strengths, reflect how personal and professional psychological battles are not just obstacles, but potential stepping stones to greater achievements and unexpected opportunities. Each of them has managed to redefine success in a myriad of inspiring ways.

<u>Dwayne "The Rock" Johnson</u>

Dwayne "The Rock" Johnson is widely known for his charisma and his roles in blockbuster films. He has also spoke openly about his experiences with depression, including periods of crisis early in his life and career. By sharing his story, he has helped challenge the stigma surrounding mental illness and has encouraged men, in particular, to speak more openly about their mental health.

Few modern celebrities have undergone as dramatic a reinvention as Johnson. Known for his electrifying presence both in the wrestling ring and on the silver screen, his journey from aspiring football player to wrestling icon to one of Hollywood's highest grossing actors reflects determination and resilience.

Johnson was born on May 2, 1972, in Hayward, California. His early life was marked by significant pressure, shaped not only by frequent moves and school changes that disrupted his social stability, but also by periods of financial hardship in his family. These difficulties foreshadowed later bouts with mental health.

His first ambition was to pursue professional football. He earned a full scholarship to the University of Miami, known for its top-tier football program. However, a serious back injury ended his hopes of an NFL career. The injury was more than a setback; it triggered his first major bout with depression. The abrupt shift from potential stardom to uncertainty about the future dealt a heavy blow.

His move into professional wrestling became a turning point after his football dreams collapsed. He rose to superstar status as "The Rock," a charismatic, electrifying figure in the World Wrestling Federation (now WWE). Yet even during this period of success and global fame, he continued to struggle with depression. The physical demands of wrestling, combined with constant travel and pressure to perform, intensified his battle.

Another major turning point came when he transitioned into acting. The move was risky, but it was driven by his desire for new opportunities and a more sustainable career, especially as wrestling's physical toll made long-term stability uncertain. His adaptability and resilience became evident as he refined his acting skills and gradually chose roles that demonstrated range beyond the action genre.

During this time, Johnson also faced personal problems offscreen, managing depression through therapy and wellness routines. His commitment to fitness is widely recognized, but less often discussed is the role exercise has played in supporting his mental health. He has said that training has been essential not only for physical strength, but also as a grounding practice that helps him maintain emotional balance.

In a world where mental health is often stigmatized—especially for men and public figures—Johnson's candid discussions have helped raise awareness. Through interviews and social media, he has emphasized the importance of seeking help, reminding people that mental health struggles can affect anyone (including highly successful people), and highlighting the value of hope and persistence.

"One of the most important things you can accomplish is just being yourself." — Dwayne "The Rock" Johnson

Johnson's life story is one of constant reinvention and mental toughness in the face of adversity. His experiences with depression, alongside his success in sports entertainment and film, show that personal adversities do not determine a person's potential. By speaking openly about his psychological battle, Johnson has shaped his legacy and helped reduce the stigma around mental health. In doing so, he has become a role model not only for aspiring athletes and actors, but for anyone fighting an internal battle. His life reminds us that with determination, support, and openness, it is possible to overcome even the most daunting circumstances.

Johnson has shared feelings about his mental health, particularly depression. His journey highlights the resilience and determination he drew on to confront his condition. The strengths he demonstrated helped him navigate difficult periods and become a source of hope for others facing similar battles. Below are four key strengths, drawn from broader strength areas, that helped him win the war within his mind:

1. Johnson's resilience and mental toughness are evident in both his career transitions and personal difficulties. Despite setbacks such as a career-ending football injury and periods of depression, he persevered, finding success first in wrestling and later in acting. His ability to rebound from adversity while continuing to pursue his goals exemplifies mental toughness.

2. Transitioning from wrestling to acting required significant courage and adaptability. By embracing new prospects and stepping outside his comfort zone, Johnson showed a willingness to evolve and grow professionally. Those risks ultimately paid off: as of recent estimates (around 2024), he has earned more than $800 million, much of it from acting and film production, and he consistently ranks among the world's highest paid actors.

3. Johnson's openness about his mental health reflects strong emotional intelligence and self-awareness. By acknowledging his psychological battles and seeking support, through therapy, fitness routines, and other coping strategies, he showed an ability to recognize and respond to his emotional needs. This self-awareness helped him take proactive steps to manage his mental health.

4. By speaking publicly about mental health, Johnson has demonstrated empathy for others facing similar hurdles. Sharing his experiences and encouraging destigmatization can support people who feel alone in their struggles. His emphasis on gratitude and authenticity also resonates with people working toward self-acceptance and resilience.

By leveraging these strengths, Johnson not only overcame significant inner demons but also encouraged others to seek help and speak openly about mental health. His journey is a reminder that with determination, self-insight, and support, people can endure adversity and emerge stronger. As he said, "One of the most important things you can accomplish is just being yourself." His authenticity has helped create space for meaningful public conversations about mental health and resilience.

<u>Michael Phelps</u>

The most decorated Olympian of all time, Michael Phelps, has openly discussed his struggles with ADHD, depression, and anxiety. After facing personal problems and seeking therapy, he became a strong advocate for mental health, especially among athletes, helping to change the conversation around well-being in sports.

Phelps is an iconic figure in swimming, known not only for his unparalleled achievements in the pool, but also for his willingness to speak candidly about mental health. His story reflects the human capacity to overcome adversity and redefine greatness.

To understand his psychological battles and subsequent metamorphosis, it helps to first recognize the scale of his athletic accomplishments. Born in 1985, he showed exceptional promise from a young age. Under the guidance of coach Bob Bowman, his career flourished, leading to his Olympic debut at the 2000 Sydney Games at just fifteen. Over the next sixteen years, Phelps earned 28 Olympic medals, including a record-breaking 23 gold, an unmatched achievement in Olympic history. His dominance set new standards for excellence and brought him worldwide recognition.

However, behind the public image of invincibility, Phelps faced serious psychological battles. He confronted intense anxiety and depression, disorders that became more visible after his DUI arrests in 2004 and again in 2014. The year after the 2008 Beijing Olympics, where he won eight historic gold medals, was especially difficult. After the ecstasy of Beijing, the following year plunged Phelps into a stark, structureless drift, an all-time low where the roar of expectation drowned out any sense of solid ground.

His experience reflects a common pattern among elite athletes, who wrestle to form an identity beyond their sport. Phelps's sense of self was closely tied to performance, leaving him especially vulnerable during periods away from competition.

A turning point came after his 2014 arrest, which prompted him to seek professional help. After entering a rehabilitation program, Phelps began the difficult process of confronting long-standing emotional pain. That period proved transformative, giving him space to reflect on life beyond swimming.

Therapy—along with support from family and friends—helped him rebuild and develop a healthier perspective on success, fulfillment, and well-being.

With that progress, Phelps returned to competition and capped his career at the 2016 Rio Olympics; yet, his most enduring impact may be outside the pool. In retirement, he has committed himself to mental health advocacy, using his platform to reduce stigma and encourage athletes and others to seek help.

"There will be obstacles. There will be doubters. There will be mistakes. But with hard work, there are no limits." — Michael Phelps

In 2008, Phelps made history by winning eight gold medals in a single Olympic Games. Sustaining that level of achievement required more than physical training; it also demanded inner stability—a battle not measured in medals, but essential to long-term well-being and lasting success.

Phelps's involvement with the Michael Phelps Foundation, which promotes water safety and mental health, underscores his commitment to using his experience for the greater good. His "I'm Fine" campaign encourages open conversations about mental health, with a particular emphasis on seeking help. Through these efforts, Phelps has used his high profile to shine a light on the often overlooked mental illnesses many people face.

Michael Phelps exemplifies mental toughness through his ability to confront and overcome ADHD, depression, and anxiety. His resilience in the face of adversity, along with his determination to seek support and actively work on his well-being, shows what true toughness looks like.

Phelps's journey also reflects strong emotional intelligence as he navigated significant emotional and psychological combat. His decision to seek professional support and commit to therapy demonstrates self-discipline and a willingness to address his psychological battles directly.

He has also shown courage by speaking openly about his mental health and advocating for greater awareness, particularly among athletes. By sharing his story and working to reduce stigma, he demonstrates a commitment to helping others feel less alone.

Phelps's ability to adapt and grow, both personally and professionally, also stands out. From enduring setbacks to making a successful return to competition, he showed flexibility and the capacity to respond constructively to changing circumstances.

Despite his immense success, Phelps has remained grounded and appreciative of the support he received during his darkest periods. His continued emphasis on seeking help and acknowledging his support system highlights how deeply he values the role others played in his recovery.

His journey is also a testament to patience. His perseverance through therapy and self-reflection reflects a commitment to long-term growth, healing, and sustained well-being, rather than quick fixes.

Ultimately, Michael Phelps's story inspires not only athletes but people around the world by reinforcing the importance of seeking help, building resilience, and drawing on inner strength to face confrontations that often remain hidden beneath the surface.

J.K. Rowling

On the brink of despair, before fame and fortune reshaped her life, Joanne Kathleen Rowling struggled through a period of uncertainty while battling depression. After confronting that psychological illness, she emerged as a testament to personal and creative renewal. Rowling's rise from depression to extraordinary success through the creation of the "Harry Potter" series is not simply a story of financial achievement; it is a powerful account of overcoming inner darkness and finding meaning through passion.

J.K. Rowling, the celebrated author of the "Harry Potter" series, has spoken openly about experiencing severe depression, including during the period when she was writing the early novels. Those experiences influenced her work, most notably in the creation of the Dementors, dark creatures that function as a metaphor for depression. Her willingness to discuss her mental health has helped reduce stigma and encouraged others to seek support.

As a single mother living on welfare, Rowling faced depression, poverty, and social stigma. Still, she used her circumstances as a catalyst for creative expression. Her story underscores the importance of perseverance and imagination.

Rowling wrote much of her first book in cafés, often with her infant daughter beside her. She also endured multiple rejections from publishers before finding success. Her books have since grown into a vast universe beloved by millions worldwide, reminding readers that creativity can emerge even amid psychological war.

Rowling's change from someone barely getting by to a source of inspiration illustrates the power of resilience in the face of despair and hardship.

In her early years, Rowling encountered significant adversity. Her mother's long battle with multiple sclerosis and her eventual death deeply affected Rowling's emotional well-being. This period of grief coincided with Rowling's first sustained efforts on major writing projects. She later acknowledged that her emotional state shaped the darker elements of her work, particularly the Dementors, beings that feed on human happiness. As she grappled with clinical depression, she drew on feelings of isolation and despair to portray emotional pain with striking clarity. That difficult chapter ultimately became a turning point, laying the groundwork for a world that would capture the hearts and minds of countless readers.

"Rock bottom became the solid foundation on which I rebuilt my life." — J.K. Rowling

The idea for "Harry Potter" first came to her during a train ride from Manchester to London in 1990, and it developed more fully as she navigated depression in the years that followed. Writing became a therapeutic outlet, not merely a distraction, but a way to process and manage her inner battles. In search of purpose and identity, she immersed herself in the magical world she was creating and refined it in Edinburgh cafés. There, the first book, later published as "Harry Potter and the Sorcerer's Stone," began to take shape. Through both her writing and her lived experience, Rowling confronted her deepest fright.

The immense success of "Harry Potter" transformed Rowling's life. It brought financial stability, enabled her to support her daughter, continue writing, and contribute to charitable causes, and it also represented a personal victory over despair. Rowling has described how this shift helped her move toward greater contentment and hope. It also gave her a platform to speak on behalf of those affected by mental illness, single parenthood, and poverty. Her journey shows that even the most difficult circumstances can spark meaningful personal growth and artistic achievement.

From battling severe depression and financial hardship to achieving remarkable success and personal fulfillment, Rowling's resilience offers insight into the qualities that helped her overcome the psychological war she faced.

J.K. Rowling's mental toughness is evident in her ability to persevere through depression, poverty, and repeated rejection from publishers. Despite numerous setbacks, she continued to pursue her passion for writing, demonstrating determination in the face of adversity.

Drawing on her own experiences of emotional turmoil, she infused her writing with authenticity and emotional depth that resonated with readers.

Her journey from despair to success also demonstrates strong self-confidence. By recognizing her depression and using writing as a therapeutic outlet, Rowling showed an understanding of her emotions and of the role creative expression can play in working through inner turmoil.

As a single mother receiving welfare benefits, Rowling showed courage and adaptability by turning difficult circumstances into an opportunity to write. Her willingness to face uncertainty and fully commit to her fictional world illustrates her capacity to embrace vulnerability and pursue personal growth.

Rowling's quote, "rock bottom became the solid foundation on which I rebuilt my life," reflects her belief in the transformative potential of hardship. By treating challenges as opportunities for growth, she demonstrated a constructive mindset and the problem-solving skills that helped her navigate difficult circumstances with resilience and hope.

The intricate world-building and layered storytelling in the "Harry Potter" series also highlight Rowling's critical thinking and patience as a writer. Even after repeated rejections, she remained committed to refining her work, showing persistence and a clear creative vision.

Overall, J.K. Rowling's journey from darkness to stability illustrates the power of using her strengths in facing her inner demons and building a meaningful life. Through mental toughness, empathy, self-awareness, courage, adaptability, gratitude, and problem solving, Rowling not only overcame her psychological battles but also inspired millions through her perseverance. Her story continues to offer hope, reminding readers that even in the hardest moments, it is possible to rebuild and find purpose.

<u>Lessons Learned</u>

The life paths of Dwayne "The Rock" Johnson, Michael Phelps, and J.K. Rowling vividly show how internal psychological struggles can lead to extraordinary transformation in the face of adversity. Each story reflects a distinct journey shaped by psychological battles and highlights the resilience of the human spirit. Together, these narratives remind us that setbacks, no matter how formidable, do not define our future. Instead, mental toughness, perseverance, and a willingness to grow can open the door to meaningful reinvention.

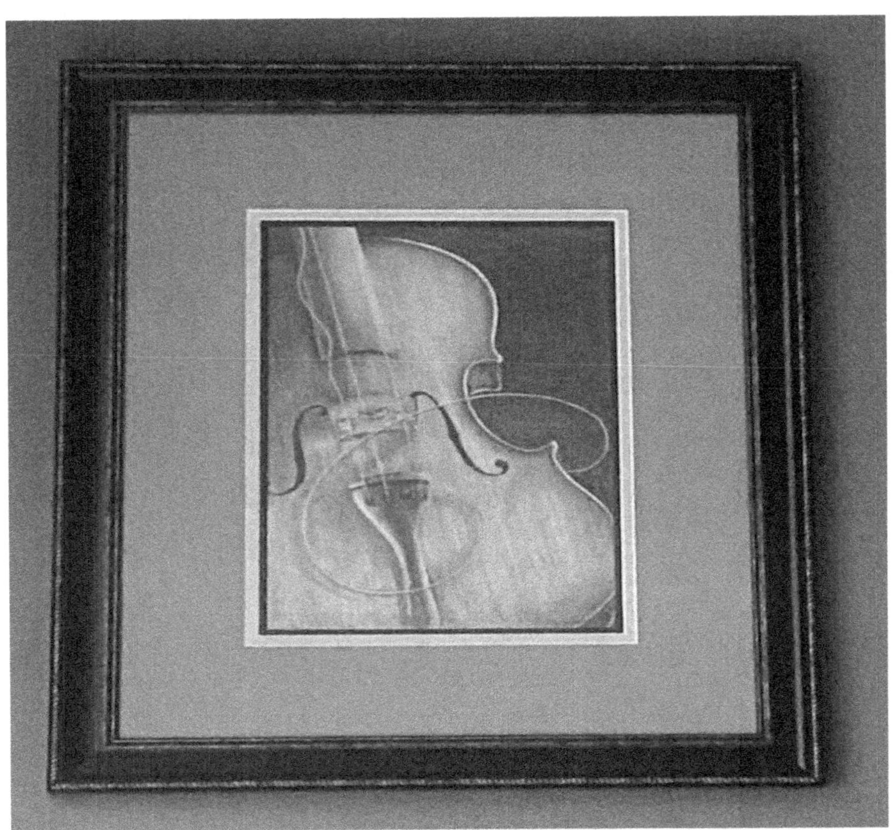

Artist Unknown, Photo by Daniel R. Linden

A violin, when intact, represents harmony, balance, and the capacity to create beautiful music, much like a healthy mind that can think clearly and feel deeply in a balanced way. However, the broken string in this picture signifies disruption, tension, or damage, very similar to how our mind can experience psychological war. Despite the broken string, the violin can be repaired and made to play again, a metaphor for healing, rebuilding, and winning the psychological war within our mind.

Chapter 8: Winning the War Within Our Mind

Winning the war within our mind is a gradual, mostly private process. Conquering our inner demons, by contrast, is often a quiet, personal achievement that may go unnoticed by others.

Even without external recognition, this internal victory can have an intense and lasting impact. The lack of grandeur does not diminish its importance. Though rarely celebrated publicly, it carries deep significance and is often honored privately as a sign of overcoming formidable obstacles and finding inner peace. It can also mark a return to normalcy—the end of a difficult journey out of darkness and into a life shaped by hope, tranquility, and optimism.

Psychological battles can take many forms, including low confidence, anxiety, and feelings of inadequacy. Early efforts to face these conditions are often filled with confusion and fear, and it can feel as though negative emotions are taking over. Overcoming them often begins with a pivotal realization, a moment when we choose to confront the hesitancy in our minds and the thought patterns that keep us stuck. This shift is often fueled by a deep desire to change and grow, along with a longing for inner peace and happiness. Although the journey is challenging, it can also be deeply rewarding, calling for self-reflection, courage, and a willingness to face our deepest insecurities. Strengthening mental toughness involves increasing self-awareness, practicing self-compassion, and seeking support from trusted loved ones or professionals.

As we move through this process, fundamental change can occur, leading to greater self-acceptance, confidence, and inner strength. Embracing that transition means letting go of limiting beliefs, allowing ourselves to be vulnerable, and learning to trust our ability to recover and grow.

The joy that comes from resolving psychological battles is multifaceted, encompassing relief, empowerment, and a deep sense of accomplishment. This joy is not merely temporary; it often endures because it reflects a lasting shift in mindset, one that brings clearer purpose, stronger commitment, and renewed direction.

When doubt and despair loom large, it takes immense courage and resilience to navigate through the storm and emerge on the other side with newfound strength and clarity. One such remarkable individual who exemplifies this triumph over adversity is the legendary Maya Angelou. Through her life's trials and tribulations, Maya Angelou's story serves as a beacon of hope and tenacity, resiliency, and willpower for all those grappling with their psychological battles.

<u>Maya Angelou</u>

A well-known poet, writer, and advocate for civil rights encountered numerous difficulties in her lifetime that tested her determination and strength to the limit. From a troubled upbringing marked by mistreatment, Maya often struggled with uncertainty and hopelessness within herself. The nature of her psychological battles primarily stemmed from traumatic experiences. For instance, after being raped by her mother's boyfriend at just eight years old, Maya experienced an extreme psychological battle with her sense of self-worth and security. Her subsequent muteness was both a shield and a cage, reflecting her loss of trust and the expression of her emotions. The weight of these onslaughts manifested as a substantial psychological war within her mind that posed a lethal threat.

"You may not control all the events that happen to you, but you can decide not to be reduced by them."—
Maya Angelou

The course of her battle was neither straightforward nor swift. Initially, Maya describes how her trauma led to silence; she believed her voice had the power to kill, as the man who molested her was murdered after she named him. Neglecting her voice was a manifestation of her psychological war, a tug-of-war between fear and the yearning to express herself. The resolution of this conflict began to unfold when Maya met Mrs. Bertha Flowers, a cultured and kind woman who introduced her to the world of literature. Mrs. Flowers encouraged Maya not only to read but to speak, emphasizing the power and beauty of words.

Maya's evolution from silence to abundant expression is a vivid depiction of victory over her inner turmoil. Through interactions with literature and supportive figures like Mrs. Flowers, she gradually recognized that her voice was not a weapon of destruction but a tool for empowerment and healing. This metamorphosis allowed Maya to reclaim her identity and her voice, leading her to become a renowned writer, poet, and activist.

Ultimately, Maya's journey illustrates how confronting and overcoming conflicts within can lead to tremendous personal growth and freedom. Her story is a testament to the beauty of human spirit and the power of nurturing environments in resolving inner battles. Maya's life and works continue to inspire countless human beings to face their psychological battles, embracing the painful but rewarding path toward personal harmony and liberation.

"If you don't like something, change it. If you can't change it, change your attitude." — Maya Angelou

Despite the darkness that clouded her path, Maya Angelou embarked on a journey of self-discovery and healing, ultimately leading her to triumph over her inner demons. Through her literary works, most notably her groundbreaking autobiography, "I Know Why the Caged Bird Sings," Maya found solace in the power of words and storytelling. By giving voice to her pain and fight, she not only liberated herself but also inspired countless others to confront their own psychological wars within their mind with courage and grace.

In the annals of history, Maya Angelou's journey stands as a testament to the human capacity for resilience, redemption, and triumph in the face of doubt and despair. By conquering her inner demons with poise and bravery, Maya not only transformed her own life but also touched the lives of countless people who found solace and inspiration in her words. As we navigate our own paths of self-discovery and healing, let us draw strength from Maya Angelou's enduring legacy and remember that the darkest moments often pave the way for the brightest victories.

Photo by Daniel R. Linden

Typically, lambs are viewed as vulnerable creatures due to their youth and small size. They rely on their mother and herd for protection against predators. Despite lacking strong physical defenses, they possess instincts that aid in their safety, such as sticking close to the flock and being vigilant of potential threats. These instincts enable them to survive and thrive. Living a lamb's life has several symbolic meanings for winning. To live a lamb's life could mean winning by rejecting stress, greed, and aggression and by embracing calm, contentment, and harmony.

8.1 Winning

Winning in the context of a psychological war within the mind is intensely personal; those of us who have endured these battles often understand the depth, ferocity, and pain only after emerging victorious. At its core, winning feels like relief: a release from burden and a freedom from what once seemed impossible.

After unlocking the secrets to winning the war within our mind, we often feel a surge of empowerment. Having navigated psychological conflict, we discover a renewed sense of capability and activity. This empowerment is liberating because we are no longer internally divided or paralyzed by unresolved tension. Choices become less burdensome without inner disputes, and our actions become more genuine, aligned with our true desires, values, and vision.

We also gain a richer sense of self-understanding and empathy. Psychological battles can take us into the innermost recesses of the psyche, unearthing insights about our triggers, vulnerabilities, and strengths. This understanding often deepens our sensitivity to the psychological battles others may be experiencing, adding a more human dimension to how we connect, strengthening compassion within the relationships we inhabit.

The complexity of the human mind is revealed when we venture inward to confront inner demons, uncover inherent strengths, and extract life-changing insight. Few writers illustrate this more powerfully than Fyodor Dostoevsky.

<u>Intricacies of the Human Spirit</u>

Fyodor Dostoevsky, a renowned Russian novelist, thinker, and journalist, is celebrated for his deep understanding of human psychology. Born on November 11, 1821, he died on February 9, 1881. Throughout his life, Dostoevsky grappled with personal and financial hardship, experiences that shaped his exploration of ethics, suffering, and salvation. His work goes beyond mere endurance; it probes the intricacies of the human spirit and offers insight into the fragilities and contradictions we must confront to overcome life's greatest obstacles.

Dostoevsky's formative years unfolded in a strict, stifling environment, conditions that later seeped into his literary creations. His emotional and financial burdens intensified in 1849, when he was arrested for his association with the Petrashevsky Circle, a group of intellectuals who read forbidden texts, criticized the ruling system, and imagined a fairer society. After a staged execution, Dostoevsky was exiled to Siberia and sentenced to years of hard labor. This harrowing ordeal left a lasting imprint on his understanding of suffering and human nature.

"To live without hope is to cease to live." — Fyodor Dostoevsky

This quote underscores the central role of hope in human life. When we seek to win the war within our mind, hope is crucial: it sustains motivation, strengthens resolve, and keeps us moving through psychological darkness. Dostoevsky suggests that holding onto hope preserves purpose—an essential force in any inner battle.

Confronted with the harsh realities of prison life, Dostoevsky was compelled to face his innermost thoughts and reassess his philosophical beliefs. That period of forced introspection illuminated the dual nature of humanity—our capacity for both cruelty and virtue. As a result, he developed a sharper understanding of what drives people, a psychological depth that would become a hallmark of his later novels.

Dostoevsky's life and work offer a compelling study of someone who explored the depths of his own mind and emerged with lasting insight into what it means to be human. His characters—often entangled in internal conflict—reflect his relentless pursuit of the mysteries of human nature.

"The greatest happiness is to know the source of unhappiness." — Fyodor Dostoevsky

In the context of winning psychological battles, this quote emphasizes the importance of identifying the root causes of suffering. When we uncover the sources of unhappiness, we can name the "inner demons" at work and recognize the top ten strengths we can use to confront them. Understanding, in this sense, is not passive, it becomes the foundation for growth, emotional well-being, and a more durable inner peace.

"Man is a mystery. It needs to be unraveled, and if you spend your whole life unravelling it, don't say that you've wasted time." — Fyodor Dostoevsky

This speaks directly to the journey for self-understanding that sits at the center of any psychological war. These battles are often clashes between competing parts of the self: rational versus emotional, fear versus courage, doubt versus belief. Recognizing this complexity is essential, we cannot win a battle we refuse to understand. "Unraveling the mystery" means sustained introspection: examining triggers, habits, defenses, and emotional patterns. Dostoevsky also implies that the work may take a lifetime. In that view, winning is not a single, final event, but an ongoing process of learning, failing, and growing. Accepting that this effort is not wasted helps cultivate patience and self-compassion, two of the most effective "weapons" in an inner war.

The Taste of Winning

The taste of winning after psychological battles is sweet, not only because it ends turmoil, but because it initiates a new beginning marked by heightened self-confidence, empowerment, and purpose. This victory is not the end of the journey; it is a meaningful waypoint in a continuing path of growth and understanding. In our individual battles and breakthroughs, we can take solace in the fact that no psychological war must remain at a perpetual impasse, and that the taste of winning, though hard earned, can be deeply transformative.

That taste can be understood in two dimensions. First, there is freedom: liberation from internal demons, not only from the symptoms of conflict but from the constraints those symptoms placed on life's possibilities. Second, there is reinvention. Winning often shifts how we see ourselves, strengthening self-esteem and reshaping identity. Emerging from psychological war can consolidate our top ten strengths and redefine us in more life-affirming terms.

In the theater of personal growth, the hardest battles are often the ones fought in private, far from public scrutiny or social competition. Whether we face fear, self-doubt, addiction, or any other inner adversary, these conflicts are demanding, consequential, and often transcendent. The taste of winning is not merely the absence of battle; it is reformation—a resurgence into greater clarity and power. To truly savor that victory, we must commit to the fight when it comes, stay engaged through setbacks, and remain determined to endure.

8.2 Resolution of Psychological Battles

Psychological battles can be destructive. They can cause severe emotional distress and impair our ability to function in many areas of life. These battles must be resolved so we can regain freedom where discord, discontent, and unease currently reign.

When we confront powerful inner hostilities with the intent to overcome alarming threats, we often encounter suffering. By drawing on our top ten strengths—mental toughness, empathy, emotional intelligence, self-awareness, patience, courage, adaptability, flexibility, critical thinking, problem solving, and gratitude—we give ourselves multiple tools for healing and change. Resolution often unfolds in three stages.

<u>Stage 1: Awareness and Acknowledgment</u>

The first step in resolving psychological battles is recognizing that a battle is taking place. This stage is about admitting there is a problem—that something in our thoughts, emotions, or behavior feels off—and deciding to take action.

For some, this decision takes days, months, years, or even decades. In other cases, hard-to-define factors prevent action altogether; people become overwhelmed, and the outcome can be tragic. Sometimes the inability to keep fighting isn't about capability or willingness, it's simply exhaustion. While that idea may sound harmless, it can become a major stumbling block for those carrying long-term psychological burdens.

Progress in this stage requires deep, sometimes painful introspection. Awareness and acknowledgment are essential starting points; they initiate the hardest battles, often the ones that forge our greatest strengths.

<u>Stage 2: Confrontation and Action</u>

Once awareness is established, the next step is to address the underlying inner demons through confrontation and action. This may include seeing a therapist, joining a support group, using self-help techniques, or making intentional behavioral changes to identify and challenge the "inner demons" at work.

Action can also include cultivating a growth mindset, practicing self-compassion, setting specific and achievable goals, committing to continuous learning, and strengthening self-reflection. The more of our top ten strengths we can draw on, the better our chances of success.

Taking action is the beginning of winning, but early effort is often met with resistance and setbacks. With determination and resilience, we can navigate the complexities of our inner world, unlock more of our potential, and build healthier patterns that positively shape both our lives and those who come after us.

<u>Stage 3: Persistence and Patience</u>

Psychological wars are rarely won quickly. Progress requires willpower, persistence, and patience, especially the willingness to acknowledge setbacks, learn from them, and adjust strategies in the face of obstacles. The mental toughness developed in this phase is crucial; it reflects the human capacity to endure, adapt, and evolve.

At times, the same battle must be fought again and again, creating the feeling that nothing is changing. This is often the point where people are tempted to give in. That is what defeat feels like, and it's what our inner demons "want."

When frustration mounts and hopelessness threatens to overwhelm us, we must continue. With time and consistent effort, victory becomes possible. Even when we can't see it or fully believe it, progress is still within reach. We must keep moving toward resolution to protect our dreams and our well-being. Staying the course is what ultimately leads to winning the war within our mind.

8.3 Celebrating Small Wins

In a relentless psychological war, every small victory brings hope and moves us closer to resolution. Ultimately, these battles aren't won in dramatic leaps, but through the quiet accumulation of small wins.

As in physical war, a brief respite in a psychological war brings relief. The bullets have stopped flying, and for a moment we can lean back and rest. Even if the calm is temporary, we can breathe more easily and steady ourselves. When the weight of the world lifts even slightly and when a small ray of sunshine breaks through the dark clouds of depression that have reduced our visibility to zero, it's time to recognize and celebrate a small win.

Celebrating small wins during psychological battles is a way to fuel motivation and resilience through positive reinforcement. It means acknowledging the progress we've made, no matter how small, and using that momentum to keep moving forward. Just as a runner gains confidence and energy by reaching milestones in a race, recognizing small wins in mental health can strengthen confidence, self-esteem, and determination. It reminds us that we are making progress and that we have the strength and capability to keep pushing through difficult times.

Celebrating small wins can take many forms, depending on what feels meaningful and rewarding. Here are a few ideas:

1. Treat ourselves to something we enjoy, such as a favorite meal, a relaxing bath, or a movie night.

2. Give ourselves a mental high-five—or a literal pat on the back—for our accomplishment.

3. Share our success with a friend or loved one who can encourage us and celebrate with us.

4. Write the achievement down in a journal so we can look back on our progress later.

5. Take a moment to reflect on how far we've come and the effort it took to get here.

6. Reward ourselves with a small gift or purchase we've been wanting.

7. Practice self-care, such as meditation, yoga, or a walk in the park.

8. Set a new goal or challenge to build on our progress.

Celebrating small wins boosts morale and motivation, reinforces positive behaviors, and helps propel us toward larger goals. Recognizing progress, however minor, reminds us that success is a journey, not a destination. This practice can also foster appreciation and gratitude in both personal life and professional environments. Most importantly, celebrating small wins helps us resist the urge to give in or give up.

In psychological battles, recognition from loved ones, encouragement, and the celebration of milestones may seem trivial from the outside, but they matter deeply to those of us learning how to win the war within our mind.

8.4 Learning from Outcomes

During a psychological war made up of multiple battles, it becomes imperative to learn from the outcomes those battles create in order to win the war within our mind, and to sustain success. Some outcomes are painful, while others are transformative. The key to making outcomes meaningful (and benefiting from them) lies in how we process and manage them.

<u>Negative Outcomes from Psychological Battles (and What We Can Learn)</u>

- When battles become consuming, professional support may be needed. If psychological conflict escalates or persists, serious mental health concerns may require help from a therapist or counselor, essential allies when psychological warfare breaks out within the mind.

- Emotional exhaustion; continuous psychological battles can drain emotional energy, leading to fatigue, burnout, or apathy.

- Intensified anxiety and stress; the mind may become overwhelmed, increasing anxiety, dread, restlessness, and difficulty concentrating.

- Identity confusion; intense internal conflict can create uncertainty about values, goals, and direction, raising questions about our true self and genuine aspirations.

- Cognitive dissonance; prolonged consternation can create discomfort from holding contradictory beliefs or thoughts, pushing a person toward resolution, or toward avoidance and isolation.

<u>Positive Outcomes from Psychological Battles (and What We Can Learn)</u>

- Mental toughness; psychological battles can teach perseverance in the face of adversity and reinforce the ability to recover from setbacks.

- Self-awareness; they can deepen understanding of thoughts, emotions, and behaviors, supporting personal growth and development.

- Empathy; difficult experiences can increase compassion for others who are struggling.

- Stronger problem solving; internal battles can sharpen critical and creative thinking, improving the ability to navigate complex battles.

- Vulnerability and support seeking; these can highlight the importance of reaching out, strengthening relationships and connection.

- Gratitude; psychological battles can clarify what matters most to us and cultivate appreciation for what is still good, even during hardship.

- Adaptation; over time, these experiences can foster a stronger sense of self, purpose, and resilience.

Every outcome, negative or positive, contains valuable lessons. Critically analyzing what worked and what didn't helps refine strategies and improve future performance. This growth mindset strengthens adaptability and resilience, which are essential for long-term success. Practicing takes initiative, stamina, courage, and optimism. By reflecting on outcomes and the lessons they provide, we can continue to grow and evolve, unlocking the tools needed to win the war within our mind.

<u>A Tool for Processing Outcomes: The After-Action Review (AAR)</u>

A valuable mechanism for processing and managing outcomes is the After-Action Review (AAR). Originating in the U.S. military and, now, widely used across industries, an AAR is a structured debrief that helps members or teams assess what happened, what went well, what didn't go as planned, and what should change next time.

<u>Key Components of an After-Action Review</u>

1. Set objectives: Clarify the purpose and goals of the review so the discussion stays focused.

2. Conduct the review: Bring together relevant participants to discuss actions, outcomes, and contributing factors.

3. Analyze performance: Examine key events, decisions, and actions to identify strengths and weaknesses.

4. Identify lessons learned: Determine what worked, what didn't, and what could be done differently.

5. Develop action items: Turn insight into specific, actionable next steps.

6. Implement feedback: Apply what was learned to future planning and decision making.

When AARs are used consistently, members and organizations can build a culture of continuous improvement.

<u>Applying an AAR to Psychological Battles</u>

In the context of psychological battles, AAR components can shape both negative and positive outcomes:

1. Setting objectives: Clear, realistic objectives provide direction and purpose; unclear or unrealistic objectives can fuel confusion, low motivation, and wasted effort.

2. Conducting the review: Effective reflection (alone or with trusted support) can increase insight and communication; ineffective review can lead to blame, misunderstanding, or missed learning.

3. Analyzing performance: Honest assessment reveals strengths and gaps; poor assessment risks repeating mistakes or stalling growth.

4. Identifying lessons learned: Clear lessons make our top ten strengths stronger; ignored or vague lessons often lead to repeated failures and lost progress.

5. Developing action items: Specific next steps enable change; vague intentions without follow-through create stagnation.

6. Implementing feedback: Consistent application builds momentum and stability; resistance to change can keep a person stuck in recurring patterns.

Overall, After-Action Reviews can help people (and systems supporting them) learn from experience, adapt, and improve performance over time. By committing to continuous learning, people can better navigate psychological battles and create positive outcomes, even in adversity.

<u>Closing Reflection</u>

In the labyrinthine journey of understanding and combating psychological battles, the metaphor of "war" is used to describe the relentless, often exhausting, conflict experienced by millions. This metaphor can include not only those directly affected, but also caregivers, mental health professionals, and the broader society engaged in the work of support and recovery. The outcomes of these battles, painful and empowering alike, offer insight into the nature of psychological conflict, effective approaches to healing, societal attitudes, and the durability of the human spirit. From these outcomes, lessons emerge and strategies evolve, helping shape the path forward in the ongoing effort to defeat inner demons and win the war within our mind.

Photo by Daniel R. Linden

Flying into the clouds or the fog of psychological war requires mental toughness. Expressing courage and determination in the face of fear reflects the idea of pushing through our fright to achieve our goals or face inner demons, despite being afraid. Triumph over psychological battles is hard fought, and small wins need to be celebrated. Positive outcomes turn psychological battle into inner peace and win the war within our mind.

Part 3: Leading After Psychological Battles and War

Part 3, "Leading After Psychological Battles and War," focuses on what happens after the war within our mind has been faced and won. It explores healing by transforming pain into purpose. Hard-earned wisdom enables us to mentor others and strengthens our ability to thrive in our own lives. This final section of our book emphasizes the growth of our strengths post-psychological conflict. Our mental toughness becomes stronger, and we become better equipped to help others navigate psychological battles of their own.

Part 3 contains the following four chapters: Chapter 9: "Wounds and Scars;" Chapter 10: "Transformation;" Chapter 11: "Imparting Winning the War Within Our Mind;" and Chapter 12: "Thriving After Winning the War Within Our Mind." All of these chapters encourage us to help ourselves, help others combat inner demons, and utilize our top ten strengths to win the war within our mind.

Leading after psychological battles and war is not just about surviving; it's about thriving in the face of past, present, and future adversity, emerging stronger and more resilient. Healing psychological wounds requires deep self-knowledge, which is essential to becoming a better person in every area of life.

The issues of battle wounds and scars are addressed in Part 3. It acknowledges that psychological battles can affect us, even after victory. We explore the impact of these injuries, including emotional fatigue, mistrust, grief, and the lingering effects of stress or trauma. Part 3 also examines the paradox of growth through pain, showing how suffering can deepen character, empathy, and resilience. It emphasizes weathering the storm, enduring an ongoing recovery process rather than expecting immediate relief. Finally, self-reflection guides us to honestly evaluate what we lost, what we learned, and what we must change to prevent a relapse into a war within our mind.

Expanding recovery into transformation describes how people rebuild themselves after psychological battles and war. It explores changes in self-expression, including learning to communicate more honestly, set healthier boundaries, and live authentically. Part 3 also examines how social stigma can be transformed by confronting shame and reshaping how individuals see themselves, and how they believe others see them. This final section reframes setbacks by treating mistakes as information and training rather than a permanent identity. Ultimately, identity is formed in the crucible of life; lasting self-identity is shaped by what a person becomes, not by what tried to break them.

We turn outward in Part 3 by focusing on how to impart what was learned from winning the war within our mind. It explains how to tell our story of psychological victory in a way that is honest, responsible, and useful to others. It provides guidance on offering inspiration without minimizing the struggle, and it outlines a leadership ethos for psychological warriors to build courage, humility, discipline, integrity, and service. This effort closes with mentoring the next generation, emphasizing practical support, example setting, and teaching others the tools to recognize threats, build readiness, and persist through their own psychological battles.

The last chapter defines what it means to thrive after victory, not merely to survive, but to build a stable, meaningful life beyond constant psychological battles. It explores life after victory, including the adjustment to peace, freedom, and new responsibilities. It also examines what it means to live outside the boundaries that once trapped us, stepping beyond old limits, challenging fear-based rules, and shedding identities formed solely through struggle.

We look beyond the battle by encouraging these psychological war veterans to pursue purpose, relationships, and goals that were once blocked by inner warfare. The chapter also emphasizes preparing for future threats to psychological stability by staying aware of triggers and strengthening routines that protect mental health. Finally, it focuses on maintaining hard-won gains and asks the forward-looking question: What comes next? The answer calls us to keep growing, leading, and living a life well lived after the war within our mind ends.

Photo by Daniel R. Linden

Part 3 explores life after winning the psychological war within our mind: healing wounds, turning pain into purpose, and growing stronger. It guides transformation through self-knowledge, resilience, and healthier identity, then shifts outward to responsible storytelling, mentoring, and leadership—helping others fight their own battles and thrive beyond survival.

Chapter 9: Wounds and Scars

Wounds and scars have long served as tangible symbols of triumph over adversity, whether born of physical injury, psychological battle, or emotional turmoil. Those of us that have faced, or are currently facing, psychological battles know how perilous these hostilities can be: isolating, relentless, and mentally exhausting. The decision to hide them often grows out of shame (unnecessary, yet real), social stigma, fear of judgment, or simple fatigue. As a result, we may unintentionally bury what we are going through, relying on defense mechanisms, such as denial or repression to cope. This concealment is complex: it hides the inner war and keeps it unseen and unspoken.

The mind is the battleground where psychological wars unfold, creating hostile terrain marked by discord and contradiction. Navigating these obstacles tests endurance and survival instincts, because each step can feel fraught with danger. The scars such battles leave behind can be lasting reminders, ones that require time, care, and patience to heal.

Emotional scars, though invisible, carry special meaning for those who have confronted their inner demons. They can represent self-discovery and the courage it takes to face psychological battles head on. By acknowledging these wounds, we reclaim our story and draw strength from the journey toward restoration and personal growth. Ultimately, wounds and scars, physical or emotional, stand as symbols of tenacity, resilience, willpower, courage, and the enduring human capacity to win the war within our mind.

An example of overcoming wounds and scars emerged after a shocking event that reverberated across the United States more than sixty years ago. President John F. Kennedy was assassinated on November 22, 1963. The moment shook the nation to its core. The tragedy inflicted deep psychological wounds on Americans. In the aftermath, having lost a popular, young, and ambitious president, the country grappled with grief, shock, and collective trauma. Over time, through resilience, unity, and a shared commitment to honoring Kennedy's legacy, the nation gradually began to heal.

The wounds of President Kennedy's legacy inspired a renewed sense of purpose and resolve. Nowhere was that determination more visible than in America's space program. Two years and five months before his assassination, on May 25, 1961, Kennedy addressed a joint session of Congress and declared his vision of landing a person on the moon before the end of the decade. He famously said, "We choose to go to the moon in this decade, not because it is easy, but because it is hard." The goal would showcase American ingenuity and technological capability while inspiring generations to come. He challenged the nation to reach for the stars.

NASA met President Kennedy's challenge on July 20, 1969, just five months before the decade's end. Apollo 11, commanded by Neil Armstrong, with Lunar Module Pilot Buzz Aldrin, landed the lunar module Eagle on the moon's surface. After descending the ladder and stepping onto the lunar ground, Armstrong declared, "That's one small step for man, one giant leap for mankind." Together, Armstrong and Aldrin explored the surface for a little more than two and a half hours.

The Apollo 11 moon landing was an historic achievement that transcended scientific progress alone. Many factors explain why the fulfillment of Kennedy's goal carried such incredible significance for the United States and the world.

One key reason was the technological capability it demonstrated. The Apollo program pushed the boundaries of what was thought possible in space exploration. Advances in materials, propulsion, and computing drove innovations that later benefited numerous industries. The mission became a catalyst for technological progress, inspiring new generations of scientists and engineers to test the limits of human ingenuity.

The moon landing was also a moment of immense national pride. In the midst of the Cold War, it signaled American technological strength on the world stage. At home, it fostered unity and optimism during a period of social and political upheaval. Images of astronauts walking on the lunar surface resonated across the country, creating a shared sense of achievement.

Beyond national pride, the moon landing symbolized the triumph of human ambition and the spirit of exploration. It showed what determination, collaboration, and innovation can accomplish. The sight of humans on the moon inspired wonder worldwide and affirmed humanity's capacity to overcome obstacles in pursuit of new frontiers, a testament to the enduring drive to discover.

The scientific legacy of the Apollo program continues to reverberate today. Data and samples collected during the missions have deepened our understanding of the moon and the solar system's origins. Technologies developed for Apollo have influenced fields ranging from medicine to communications. In addition, the era's momentum helped lay the groundwork for later cooperative efforts in space exploration, including the International Space Station and future plans for crewed missions to Mars.

President Kennedy's challenge to the space program, his subsequent assassination, and the Apollo program's historic achievement are a reminder of what becomes possible when we overcome past wounds and scars, and work toward motivating goals.

Photo by Daniel R. Linden

The White House's official portrait of John F. Kennedy (JFK), the 35th President of the United States, hangs near the visitor's entrance. The portrait of JFK invites reflection on the somber expression captured in the painting. Before sitting for his official portrait, JFK was assassinated. Jacqueline Kennedy, the president's spouse, enlisted Aaron Shikler to create the artwork during the late 1960s, with its public debut taking place in 1971. In a departure from conventional presidential portraits. Mrs. Kennedy desired a unique representation, a wish realized through Shikler's contemplative portrayal of JFK, featuring a slightly bowed head and crossed arms, not a traditional presidential portrait pose. The portrait's melancholic essence offers a glimpse into the self-reflective mind of JFK, often having been celebrated for his charm and charisma.

9.1 Impact of Injury

Wounds and scars, both visible and invisible, can serve as persistent reminders of injuries we have endured. These remnants, whether physical marks or psychological trauma, often have effects that extend far beyond the initial pain. Physiologically, scars can affect the function and appearance of body tissue; psychologically, trauma can alter behavior, emotional responses, and cognitive functioning. Over time, these lasting effects can shape how we interact with the world, influencing our personal and social lives, and sometimes limiting our ability to perform certain tasks or fully engage in daily activities.

Ongoing psychological battles can also change a person's sense of self and perception of reality. Repeated internal conflict may lead to lowered self-esteem, chronic anxiety, or a lasting shift in outlook, often expressed as pessimism or fatalism. The effects of psychological hardship can also extend into personal relationships: prolonged stress may contribute to isolation and social withdrawal, making it harder to form or maintain connections. Malala Yousafzai, a Pakistani activist for girls' education, who survived a targeted Taliban attack in 2012, exemplifies how such experiences can be transformed into positive change, for herself and for others.

<u>Malala Yousafzai</u>

Malala Yousafzai's experience of being shot in the head by the Taliban at age 15 left deep psychological scars. The trauma led to symptoms commonly associated with post-traumatic stress disorder (PTSD), including flashbacks, nightmares, and anxiety. She underwent extensive therapy to cope with the emotional aftermath. Trauma of this magnitude can have long-lasting effects on mental well-being, shaping a person's ability to trust others, feel safe, and maintain a sense of normalcy.

The attack also had significant social and relational consequences. For safety reasons, Malala and her family relocated to the United Kingdom. This sudden upheaval disrupted her social connections and required her to adjust to a new environment far from her home in Pakistan. The attack also affected her relationships with peers and members of her community, as she became a target for people who opposed her advocacy for girls' education. Despite these pressures and attempts to silence her, she continued to speak out for educational rights.

Malala's activism—and the attempt on her life—also had far-reaching societal repercussions in Pakistan and around the world. The incident drew global attention to girls' education in Pakistan and prompted widespread condemnation of the Taliban's violence and repression. Her resilience inspired millions and helped galvanize international support for education for all children, regardless of gender. At the same time, the attack underscored the risks faced by women and girls in patriarchal societies, where calls for gender equality can be met with intimidation, backlash, and violence.

Malala continues to advance girls' education as executive chair of the Malala Fund and through her production company, which partners with Apple TV+ to create films highlighting women's stories, particularly in Afghanistan. She advocates internationally for educational rights, works to secure funding for girls' education in countries such as Pakistan and Afghanistan, and has returned to her hometown in Pakistan for the first time since the 2012 shooting.

<u>Lady Gaga</u>

Lady Gaga, born Stefani Germanotta, is a global icon known for her musical talent and distinctive style. Like Malala Yousafzai, she also exemplifies many of the top ten strengths we value most: mental toughness, empathy, emotional intelligence, self-awareness, patience, courage, adaptability and flexibility, critical thinking, problem solving, and gratitude.

Behind Lady Gaga's glamorous public image is a story of a number of psychological battles. She has lived with post-traumatic stress disorder (PTSD) following a sexual assault in her late teens, and she has also faced severe depression and anxiety. Despite these inner demons, Gaga has transformed her pain into purpose—building a highly successful career and a meaningful life. Her journey toward healing has made her a symbol of empowerment and inspiration for millions worldwide.

Gaga has spoken openly about her experience of sexual assault and its lasting impact. When she was about 19, she was assaulted by an older music producer. She has described the experience as deeply traumatic and has said she did not fully process what happened at the time. Instead, she tried to suppress the memory and continue pursuing her career.

Years later, after her career was established, the trauma resurfaced. It showed up as intense emotional distress and physical symptoms associated with PTSD. She has described experiencing flashbacks, anxiety, and severe pain. At one point, the trauma felt so overwhelming that it contributed to psychosomatic pain and a period when she felt emotionally unable to function.

Gaga has said that receiving a PTSD diagnosis was a turning point in her healing. She credits therapy, supportive relationships, and creative expression, especially music and performance, with helping her manage the ongoing effects of trauma. She has also emphasized the importance of mental health awareness and trauma-informed care, using her platform to advocate for survivors through efforts such as the Born This Way Foundation.

In addition to PTSD, Gaga has spoken candidly about depression and anxiety. These experiences have become part of her personal narrative and artistic identity, and she has consistently used her visibility to raise awareness about mental health. By sharing her story, she has encouraged others to seek help without fear of judgment. Her advocacy has helped normalize conversations about mental health and has inspired many people to pursue treatment.

Her depression and anxiety have sometimes affected both her personal life and her career. Gaga has described periods of intense sadness, panic attacks, and feeling disconnected from herself and others. She has also discussed the physical pain associated with fibromyalgia, a chronic pain condition she has linked to her trauma history. This connection between physical and emotional suffering underscores how trauma can persist in both mind and body, making recovery an ongoing process.

Through her music, Gaga has pushed boundaries and challenged stereotypes, addressing themes such as self-acceptance, heartbreak, and resilience. By channeling pain into her work, she has shared her vulnerability with the world in a way that feels authentic and relatable to many fans. Her openness has strengthened her artistic impact and has provided catharsis for both herself and listeners.

In her performances and visuals, Gaga often uses avant-garde fashion and dramatic aesthetics to express complex emotions and lived experiences. Her creativity becomes a way to externalize pain and transform it into something meaningful. Through her artistry, she shows that creative expression can be a powerful tool for healing and self-discovery.

Throughout her career, Lady Gaga has received numerous awards, including:

- 11 Grammy Awards

- 1 Academy Award (Best Original Song)

- 1 Golden Globe Award

- 1 MTV Video Music Award for Video of the Year

- 3 Brit Awards

- 13 MTV Europe Music Awards

These are just a selection of the many honors she has earned for her contributions to music and entertainment.

Lady Gaga's journey from trauma to triumph is a powerful reminder of the human capacity to overcome adversity. By confronting her past, seeking support for her mental health, and using her creativity to connect with others, she has achieved both success and healing, and become a source of hope for countless people. Her resilience, authenticity, and commitment to self-expression demonstrate how pain can be transformed into an excellent example of leading after psychological battles and the war.

9.2 The Paradox of Growth Through Pain

The paradox of growth and pain runs deep. Psychological battles can push suffering to unbearable levels while remaining mostly invisible to others; at other times, these issues become highly publicized. Although the latter is rare, we will examine the life of actor Robert Downey, Jr., who serves as a compelling example of growth through pain.

From intense psychological war, meaningful growth is not only possible, it often becomes clearer in hindsight. We learn to navigate the complexities of our inner world, draw strength from hardship, and often emerge as stronger advocates for ourselves and those around us.

The human mind is a complex landscape where inner battles are fought not with physical weapons, but with thoughts, emotions, and perceptions. Pain is often described as a catalyst for change, but an important question remains: How do we endure this paradox while we're still living through it?

Emotional and psychological pain can disrupt our comfort and push us toward change. Adversity forces us to draw on our top ten strengths to confront unease and insecurities, which can build resilience and support personal development. In psychology, discomfort is often seen as potentially transformative, prompting us to reexamine beliefs, habits, and patterns that no longer serve us.

Moving through the tension between pain and growth requires both vulnerability and resilience. Vulnerability helps us acknowledge suffering without judgment, creating space for self-compassion and healing. Resilience, often strengthened through practice and support, helps us recover from setbacks—what once felt destabilizing can become a foundation for greater endurance.

<u>Robert Downey, Jr.'s Pain and Gain</u>

Robert Downey, Jr.'s early life didn't follow a smooth, upward-sloping origin story. Instead, it came in jolts: bright flashes of talent and charisma, interrupted by long, bruising detours. Long before the world knew him as the driving force behind billion-dollar films, he was a kid growing up in a home where art and instability shared the same space, where the atmosphere could feel electric one moment and corrosive the next. That mix gave him gifts—fearlessness, sharp intelligence, and a performer's instinct for timing—but it also left him with issues that weren't cinematic at all: the slow, grinding kind, fought in private, when we're trying to outrun ourselves.

In entertainment and showmanship, he broke through early because he was unmistakable. On screen, he didn't just play a character; he seemed to bring one to life—fast talking, watchful, and funny in a way that hinted at both charm and damage. Hollywood noticed. Critics noticed.

Early momentum can be dangerous when it takes hold in a life without much stability beneath it. His career began to compete with his personal inner demons and, eventually, those battles eclipsed his work. Substance abuse issues, arrests, legal problems, and missed opportunities followed—the kind of headlines that can turn an actor into a cautionary tale. Yet his story is also one of great success.

Downey's return to sustained Hollywood success is closely tied to overcoming a long, very public period of the pain and agony of substance addiction and legal trouble in the late 1990s and early 2000s.

Below are specific, widely reported incidents that defined that era.

- Long-term addiction began in his youth. Downey has said he began using drugs at a very young age and struggled for years with addiction, including cocaine, heroin, and alcohol.

- Repeated attempts at rehabilitation and relapses occurred throughout the 1990s. Despite professional success, he cycled through arrests, treatment programs, and relapse.

- In June 1996, in the Malibu / Los Angeles area, Downey was arrested after police found him in possession of heroin, cocaine, and a firearm. This arrest is often cited as the beginning of his most visible legal spiral.

- Later in 1996, he was arrested again after an incident in which he entered a neighbor's home and fell asleep. Reports said he was intoxicated or under the influence of substances that rendered him unconscious.

- Probation violations in 1997 led to escalated penalties. A judge ordered him to undergo drug treatment and placed him on probation. Contemporary reports indicate that he repeatedly violated probation by failing drug tests and/or failing to comply with court-ordered conditions.

- Between 1999 and 2000, after repeated probation violations, Downey was sentenced to a California state prison term. He served roughly one year before being released.

- After his release from prison in 2000, he was arrested in a widely reported incident for cocaine possession.

- In 2001, Downey was arrested again in Culver City, California, for being under the influence in an incident described as suspected drug use.

These episodes led to significant professional fallout, including the loss of a high-profile television role and difficulty securing insurance for film work. The hard truth about that period is that talent didn't save him. Fame didn't soften the blow. If anything, the spotlight made every stumble more visible.

The setbacks weren't only professional, they were existential: trust eroded, options narrowed, and Downey was trapped in a loop where consequences arrived faster than hope. From the inside, psychological battles often look like this: we wake up promising ourselves that today will be different, and by night we're staring at familiar wreckage, exhausted by our own patterns. It isn't a single dramatic showdown; it's attrition.

Then, slowly, the industry began to notice a different pattern, one that had nothing to do with scandal and everything to do with reliability. Downey showed up. He delivered. He came prepared. He became someone people could bet on again, not because the past had vanished, but because it no longer controlled him. When he returned to major roles, he did so with a sharper edge to his craft, as if the hard years had sanded away anything superficial and left something more concentrated: lived-in humor, controlled intensity, and real stakes, even when the lines were playful.

His growth was shaped by a mix of court-mandated treatment, personal commitment and, over time, a more stable, sustained recovery. His career rebounded as he became insurable and consistently employable again, with mid-2000s comeback roles culminating in a blockbuster era. Downey's success is "magnificent" not only because he became a star again, but because of the scale and rarity of what he achieved.

- He became the cornerstone of one of the most successful franchise eras in modern film. As Tony Stark / Iron Man, he wasn't just in a hit series, he helped define the shared universe blockbuster model that studios spent the next decade trying to replicate.

- Downey was now able to balance prestige with blockbuster stardom. Many actors become either awards season favorites or blockbuster leads; Downey sustained both, earning Oscar nominations for "Chaplin" and "Tropic Thunder," while also anchoring global tentpoles like the Marvel Cinematic Universe (MCU) and "Sherlock Holmes."

- "Iron Man" (2008) effectively launched the MCU as a full-scale franchise, and the character's portrayal became one of modern blockbuster filmmaking's defining performances. The character appeared throughout the MCU in "Iron Man" (2008), "Iron Man 2" (2010), "The Avengers" (2012), "Iron Man 3" (2013), "Avengers: Age of Ultron" (2015), "Captain America: Civil War" (2016), "Avengers: Infinity War" (2018), and "Avengers: Endgame" (2019).

- At the height of the MCU, he was widely reported to be one of Hollywood's highest-paid actors, with compensation tied to box-office performance, an indicator of rare leverage and bankability.

Public estimates vary and are highly unreliable, but Downey's net worth is most often placed in the $250 million to $350 million range (as of the mid-2020s). What changed wasn't a single lucky break, but a sustained decision to rebuild. Recovery, when it's real, can be unglamorous: routines, accountability, humility, and the long work of repairing relationships and earning back credibility. It means learning to sit with discomfort instead of fleeing into old escapes. It also means confronting the parts of our mind that whisper fatalism— "This is who we are; this is all we'll ever be"—and responding with action instead of argument. Over time, that kind of fight becomes a different kind of performance: not for applause, but for survival.

That's part of why his later dominance in Hollywood didn't feel like a fluke. When he stepped into the roles that defined an era, most famously as the face of a massive franchise, he brought more than quips and charisma. He carried the weight of someone who knows what it is to fall and still get back up.

We can feel it in the rhythm of his performances: the way confidence and vulnerability braid together, and how bravado sometimes functions as armor. He didn't just portray characters who were brilliant and broken; he made that combination believable, almost familiar.

Based on Robert Downey, Jr.'s public story and achievements, some of his most notable life accomplishments include:

- Sustained recovery and rebuilt stability: After years of addiction and legal trouble, achieving long-term sobriety, consistent work habits, and a stable life was the foundational accomplishment that made everything that followed possible.

- One of Hollywood's most significant career comebacks, returning not just to work but to the top tier of the industry by becoming an A-list lead again after being considered uninsurable, is rare.

- Creating an iconic, era-defining character, his portrayal of Tony Stark / Iron Man became one of the most influential pop culture performances of the 21st century and helped set the tone for an entire cinematic era.

- Elite artistic recognition across decades: Being Oscar nominated (and broadly awards respected) while also carrying global blockbusters is an unusual dual achievement.

- Downey built a durable life and family. He often credits his marriage to Susan Downey and family life as central to his recovery and success, something many would rank above career milestones.

- Becoming a business/creative partner beyond acting: Expanding into producing (Team Downey) is a long-term accomplishment that adds influence and sustainability beyond on-camera roles.

To "rise above psychological wars" isn't to erase them, and it isn't to win once and declare victory forever. It's to learn our triggers, build a life that doesn't rely on denial, and keep choosing the habits that support clarity, especially on days when clarity feels costly. It's replacing chaos with structure and impulse with intention. Robert Downey, Jr.'s story, in that sense, reads less like a miracle and more like something rarer: a sustained, earned comeback.

Today, his prominence isn't only about box office numbers or iconic scenes. It's also about the emotional resonance of watching someone reclaim authorship of his own life. The setbacks didn't disappear from the record; they became part of the texture. And when we see him command the screen now, it lands with extra weight—the sense that behind the performance is a person who has walked through psychological fire, learned how to live with his mind instead of against it, and kept going until "surviving" turned into "building."

Robert Downey, Jr. exemplifies the paradox of growth through pain. He achieved one of Hollywood's most prominent career revivals. More than the money or awards, his restored reliability and return to A-list status—after years of legal troubles and substance abuse—have become a benchmark for a "true comeback."

9.3 Weathering the Storm

Haruki Murakami, a contemporary Japanese writer renowned for his surreal, thematic novellas, offers a layered exploration of the trials and tribulations his characters endure. One of his notable quotes encapsulates the idea of personal metamorphosis—of weathering psychological storms and the inner war that follows:

"Once the storm is over, you won't remember how you made it through or how you managed to survive. You may not even be sure whether it's truly over. But one thing is certain: when you come out of the storm, you won't be the same person who walked in. That's what the storm is all about." — Haruki Murakami, Japanese Writer

Murakami's metaphorical "storm" relates not only to tangible hurdles but also to the tumultuous confrontations within our mind—psychological battles often unseen yet deeply impactful. It explores the reassurance embedded within Murakami's words that suggests these internal conflicts, while often painful, are conduits for meaningful personal growth and positive identity reformulation.

Murakami's depiction of the storm serves as a versatile metaphor not restricted to physical or external threats but expansively encompassing the psychological war that besieges human consciousness. In psychological terms, these storms can be identified as periods of intense emotional turmoil, cognitive dissonance, depression, anxiety, or any psychological battle that disrupts mental homeostasis. Such storms are daunting; they are the embodiments of our deepest pressures, unresolved conflicts, and the darkest sides of our psyche.

Murakami astutely observes that post-storm, there remains a lingering doubt about whether the turmoil has truly ceased. This mirrors the recovery or reconciliation phase from psychological war, where doubt and uncertainty prevail. Recovery is rarely absolute or devoid of relapses.

The questioning of whether the storm is truly over reflects a realistic portrayal of human psychological recovery processes, where healed wounds can occasionally reopen or leave lasting scars. It underscores a critical phase where we grapple with the fear of reverting to the prior state or facing new storms.

The crux of Murakami's observation lies in the innovative experience by those of us who endure these storms. "You won't be the same person who walked in" speaks to a fundamental change in identity, perception, or understanding that arises from enduring and overcoming psychological battles. Psychological theories like post-traumatic growth support this notion, suggesting that we can emerge from periods of suffering with increased resilience, a deeper sense of meaning in life, and a restructured set of personal beliefs. The storm's ability to fundamentally alter and reregulate us is both a testament to the human capacity for growth and a solace, indicating that the endured pain was not in vain. It serves as a pathway to a new, perhaps more enlightened, healed self.

The acknowledgment of inevitable change provides a form of reassurance. It offers a perspective that the tumult and torment experienced during psychological battles have a purpose. This can be crucial for those in the throes of such turmoil, providing us with a lens to view our suffering as an evolutionary journey rather than a perpetual state of despair. The metaphor of the storm offers solace by reframing the narrative from victimhood to one of survival and eventual victory over our inner demons, unlocking the secrets of winning the war within our mind.

The psychological battles we fight are deeply personal and inherently invisible. They range from conflicts of morality, identity crises, and existential queries, to the struggle against mental health disorders. The path through these storms is often nonlinear and obscured, characterized by bouts of confusion, distress, and solitude. Like navigating a real storm, there are periods of calm interspersed with moments of overwhelming chaos. Murakami's suggestion that "you won't remember how you made it through, how you managed to survive" points toward the disorienting nature of these battles, where survival often necessitates a moment-by-moment coping mechanism, sometimes leaving little room for a cohesive memory of the journey.

Murakami's metaphor of the storm eloquently encapsulates the essence of psychological war and the psychological evolution triggered by such experiences. By interpreting these conflicts as storms, we see them not only as burdens but also as opportunities for significant personal growth and self-discovery. The reassurance embedded within Murakami's words lies in the acknowledgment that these painful experiences are revolutionary, reshaping us into human beings forged with greater strength, insight, and compassion. Thus, as we navigate the storms within, we are concurrently constructing our refined selves, equipped to face the world with renewed vigor and understanding. In tunnelling through these psychological battles with an awareness of their groundbreaking potential, we can find the courage to endure and the hope to evolve.

9.4 Self-Reflection

Self-reflection may seem laid back on the surface, an easy going and innate process. It doesn't imply an exceptionally proactive powerful experience requiring significant mental or physical strength. It would appear to be a natural, relaxed, and passive process. However, self-reflection, after experiencing psychological battles and a psychological war, demands extensive mental stamina and dedication, consuming a tremendous amount of physical and emotional energy.

Self-reflection's importance in fighting and winning psychological battles in our minds has been emphasized many times before in our examination. Practicing effective self-reflection is a valuable skill. Here are five steps to help us engage in meaningful self-reflection:

1. Find a quiet and comfortable space where to reflect without distractions. Set aside regular time for self-reflection, whether it's daily, weekly, or monthly.

2. To prompt deeper reflection, we need to ask ourselves open-ended questions such as "what are my values and beliefs?" or "what are my strengths and areas for growth?" Reflect on the thoughts, emotions, and experiences that surface.

3. Writing down our reflections can help us track our progress and gain insights over time. Consider keeping a journal to record thoughts, feelings, and revelations during the reflection.

4. Mindfulness techniques, such as deep breathing or meditation, can help us stay present and focused during self-reflection.

5. Reflecting with the perspective of others can provide valuable insights and new perspectives. Consider seeking feedback from trusted friends, family members, or mentors to gain greater insight for self-reflection.

The importance of self-reflection in shaping our greatest strengths to fight psychological battles cannot be overstated. Despite its myriad of benefits, self-reflection is not without limitations. Time constraints, societal pressures for quick results, inexperience, and unawareness can impede this process. Self-reflective practice requires patience, motivation, commitment, and the development of a self-structured approach to process our experiences effectively.

Effective self-reflection is not an intuitive process for everyone. It requires structured thinking and specific methodologies that need to be learned and practiced. Unfortunately, explicit training in reflective practices is not universally integrated into our upbringing. Without guidance on how to engage in productive self-reflection, we may find ourselves unsure of what questions to ask ourselves, what aspects of our experiences to focus on, or how to use our reflections to improve our performance.

Time management is essential for deep, thoughtful self-reflection to learn from involvements and efforts regarding psychological distortions negatively impacting our mindscape. Some of us may feel that every minute spent in self-reflection is one less minute available for completing tangible tasks that contribute directly to success. This misconception hurts our opportunities to fully embrace our experiences from psychological battles that help our self-confidence and strengthen a sustained and successful victory of the war within our mind.

Engaging in self-reflection often involves recognizing our failures and shortcomings, which can be uncomfortable or even painful. Many of us avoid deep self-reflection because it forces us to confront aspects of our personality or work habits that we may not be proud of. This emotional discomfort can be particularly acute in the competitive environments we find ourselves in, where there is high pressure to succeed. As difficult as self-reflection might become under these circumstances, the reward is uncovering and eradicating inner demons initiating psychological battles within our thoughts and feelings.

In today's digital age, constant notifications and the allure of instant information can be significant distractions hindering deep, meaningful self-reflection. Social media, emails, and other digital tools can pull us away from reflective practices, making sustained attention and introspection increasingly challenging. Disconnecting and carving out time for solitude may be one of the most important skills we can develop to support our mental health and self-understanding.

Self-reflection has the propensity to propel self-compassion and self-acceptance. Additionally, effective self-reflection improves emotional intelligence, professional expertise, ethical decision making, and self-confidence. It stands as a cornerstone of lifelong learning and continuous improvement, essential for us aiming to realize our best selves.

Self-reflection also deepens the capacity for empathy and understanding toward others. By exploring our own vulnerabilities, insecurities, and difficulties, we develop a more compassionate outlook, fostering meaningful connections and relationships based on mutual respect and support.

Design and Artist Unknown

The quote, "The ocean does not apologize for its depth and the mountains do not apologize for the space they take, and so, neither shall I," is attributed to Becca Lee, a writer and poet known for her empowering and introspective quotes. When reflecting on past psychological battles, embracing our true selves without apology is the first step toward inner peace and self-empowerment. Just as nature stands unapologetically in its magnificence, so too can we stand tall in our journey toward self-discovery and winning the war within our mind.

Chapter 10: Transformation

This chapter explores the transformation of our lives as we become veteran warriors of psychological wars. Some psychological battles may persist for years or even decades. Coming from a world where self-doubt and the fog of psychological warfare clouded our decision making, we found courage to embrace our true selves. Having survived life-altering experiences, our rewards include enhanced perceptibility, improved instincts to navigate threats, and enhanced self-confidence resulting from winning the war within our mind.

The grueling journey of overcoming the war within our mind meant each step we took along the way represented progress, albeit often indistinguishable inching along the path. Sometimes we had to fight the same battle over and over again. Some psychological battles have the potential to fester indefinitely, requiring a continuing series of adjustments. Transformation indicates we learned to navigate the dangers inherent in psychological battles. Grasping realities made us healthier in mind and body.

The transformation was marked by progress, using as many of our top ten strengths as possible to overcome inner demons' intent on waging war against us. Each step we took represented a victory and should not be minimized or underestimated because of the courage it took to fight back against a wicked invisible opponent threatening everything that matters to us. This journey is not linear; it is a process of growth and self-discovery that requires mental toughness, empathy, emotional intelligence, self-awareness, patience, courage, adaptability and flexibility, critical thinking, enhanced problem solving, and gratitude. It takes everything we have to fight for our lives.

Transformation involves acknowledging a plethora of inner demons that we may be facing. These demons may include fear, addiction, anger, a poisonous tempter demon, envy, passionate emotion impulsive reactions, sadness, confusion, burden-bearing, deceiving, and trickery. We have identified and analyzed these inner demons. Understanding and recognizing the unique peculiarity that each of these enemies brings to the psychological battle, and knowing what it takes to overcome each, is the result of maturity gained from our transformation into veterans of psychological war.

A result of our transformation is having the maturity to fully embrace the journey. Overcoming the war within our mind is usually not a quick fix; it may become a lengthy excursion requiring significant time and extensive effort. Our maturity means we become able to accept and tolerate ups and downs, wins and setbacks, with an open heart and a willingness to grow. Each battle won, no matter how small, equips us to face future obstacles with greater valor and increased determination.

After our psychological battle transformation, we realize it is essential to remember that we do not have to fight our psychological battles alone. Seeking support from friends, family, therapists, or support groups provides invaluable guidance, encouragement, and unique perspectives to assist us. In combination with building an outside team to help us in psychological battles, another powerful tool in overcoming the war within our mind is self-compassion. While at first, it may sound trivial, being committed to treating ourselves with kindness, understanding, and forgiveness allows us to heal from past wounds and move forward with a sense of peace, acceptance, and purpose. While we have been taught to show others respect and treat people with courtesy, we do not always extend the same favor to ourselves, and it is important that we do so to win the war within our mind.

The journey of overcoming the war within our mind is a fundamental and transformative experience that has the potential to positively impact every aspect of our lives. We learn to navigate the complexities of our inner worlds with cleverness and poise.

Our transformative stage is about re-integration into areas of life that may have been neglected or impaired by our condition. This could involve re-establishing social connections, returning to work or school, and engaging in hobbies and interests previously abandoned or newly discovered.

Emergence from psychological war is seldom marked by a definitive endpoint; rather, it is a continual process of managing health and brain space. This recovery process incorporates learning to dismantle old, harmful structures and replace them with healthier, sustainable ones. Emotional intelligence fortifies our ability to face future stressors and triggers without a debilitating reprise of psychological war.

Our fight leads to a new purpose or direction, such as advocacy for mental health, a deepened understanding of personal mental health needs, and a refined sense of empathy toward others. Transformation is not a sign of an end but a new beginning. A testament to the human spirit's capacity to transcend its fiercest battles and evolve knowing that our toughest battles forge our greatest strengths.

Photo by Daniel R. Linden

Picture a mountain paradise undergoing a remarkable change. Picture yourself at the summit of a snow-covered peak, feeling the brisk air on your face while looking down the sparkling slopes, imagining the exhilarating journey that lies ahead. Now, fast forward a couple of months, and that once snowy mountain has transformed into a verdant haven, embellished with majestic pine trees sharing mysteries of concealed trails down the slopes. This metamorphosis serves as a tribute to the perpetual allure of nature and the transformative capability of the human mind to win the war within our mind.

10.1 Transformation of Self-Expression

Self-expression plays a deeply transformative role in healing from trauma and reclaiming personal independence. Trauma often fragments a person's sense of self and narrative; it can silence us, distort memories, and erode trust in our own voice. Through self-expression, whether through writing, art, music, movement, or dialogue, we begin to piece together our experiences in ways that restore coherence, meaning, and ownership of our story.

One of the core functions of self-expression in trauma recovery is externalization. Translating painful internal experiences into external forms like journaling, painting, or storytelling, creates psychological distance from the trauma.

This shift helps transform overwhelming sensations and emotions into something observable and, therefore, more manageable. Expression becomes both a release of pent-up emotion and a means of re-establishing control over what once felt uncontrollable.

Additionally, self-expression fosters integration, which is essential for post-traumatic growth. Trauma can split off aspects of memory and identity, but creative or reflective expression allows for the weaving together of past, present, and future selves. By articulating our experiences, we link emotion and cognition, facilitating understanding and, ultimately, transforming a narrative of victimization into one of survival and resilience.

Self-expression also provides a platform for connection and validation. Sharing our story, whether privately in a journal or publicly in a safe community, can counteract the isolation that trauma often creates. Being witnessed in our truth helps restore trust in others and reinforces the belief that our experiences and emotions are legitimate and meaningful.

Reclaiming our narrative through self-expression is an act of empowerment. It asserts that it is us, not the trauma, defining our identity through positive transformation. Choosing how we frame and share our story helps us see ourselves through the lens of survival, reshaping our understanding of the past and revealing strength, creativity, and purpose pain once hid.

In essence, self-expression is not only a therapeutic tool but also a declaration of self-determination. It transforms suffering into a story, silence into a voice, and disempowerment into authorship, allowing us to reclaim our narratives and, ultimately, our sense of wholeness.

Tyler, The Creator – An Openly Evolving Person

Tyler, The Creator, exemplifies the power of self-expression in fostering personal growth and positive change, both artistically and individually. Born Tyler Okonma, he adopted the moniker "Tyler, the Creator," to symbolize his role as a music and media innovator. Renowned for his pioneering work in hip-hop, Tyler transitioned from provocative shock rap to a more refined, alternative sound, gaining acclaim for his involvement in the Odd Future collective, unique fashion sense, and contributions as a producer, director, and songwriter. His impact is evident in critically acclaimed albums like "Flower Boy" and "IGOR."

Tyler is recognized for his dynamic musical evolution, spanning from experimental hip-hop to soul-infused melodies. Co-founding the influential Odd Future collective, he has garnered multiple Grammy Awards for his solo ventures and earned accolades for his fashion endeavors. Despite initial controversies surrounding his early lyrics, Tyler's artistry evolved into a personal exploration of themes like loneliness and identity, reshaping his own narrative and the landscape of hip-hop culture.

In the realm of hip-hop during the early 2000s, Tyler, then known as Tyler Okonma, faced backlash for his explicit storytelling, which set him apart from mainstream rap artists. Through his work with Odd Future, Tyler initially provoked mixed reactions. However, as time progressed, his music and creative ventures increasingly reflected a genuine and introspective approach, evident in albums like "Wolf" and "Cherry Bomb," signaling a shift toward using self-expression as a means of self-discovery.

From 2013 to 2021, Tyler underwent a significant transformation in his music and public persona. Albums like "Flower Boy" and "IGOR" marked pivotal moments where he delved into themes of self-acceptance and vulnerability, garnering widespread acclaim for his emotional depth. Subsequent releases, such as "Call Me If You Get Lost," showcased further personal growth, emphasizing complex emotions and artistic sophistication, steering away from earlier anger-driven expressions toward confidence and maturity.

Tyler's journey serves as a testament to the transformative power of authentic self-expression, illustrating how embracing our true self and evolving publicly can lead to personal and professional advancement.

His narrative from a controversial figure to a multifaceted artist underscores the importance of challenging norms and celebrating individuality as a catalyst for positive change and artistic innovation.

10.2 Transforming Social Stigma

Going into the shadows due to psychological battles is an extremely challenging journey, but returning to a sense of normalcy within our society may become even more demanding. Facing psychological battles, navigating dangerous circumstances, and overcoming social stigma are all essential skills for those of us who have won the war within our mind, creating a new positive direction for our lives. Social stigma associated with mental health maladies is like any form of discrimination. There is a tendency for many people to place all of us who wrestle with inner demons into the same category. This is the easiest, safest, and most natural thing to do for those who have never fought psychological battles or, worse, those who believe psychological battles result from weakness instead of an illness. Unfortunately, these obstacles are way too common. To preserve our victory over the war within our mind, we have to stand ready for whatever threatening, biased, and prejudicial external forces come at us or we stumble into.

Surviving psychological war in our mind is a journey that requires immense strength; however, the journey doesn't end there. For many of us who have overcome psychological battles, other dangerous difficulties of societal misconceptions and judgments surrounding mental health disorders create barriers for those who have bravely faced and overcome their inner demons. Some of the best ways to cope with and overcome these unwelcome and unwarranted stigmas persisting in our society include the following:

1. One of the most effective ways to combat social stigma is through education and awareness. Individuals who have overcome psychological battles can take the initiative to educate their friends, family, and community about mental health. By sharing their stories and experiences, they can help break down stereotypes and misconceptions surrounding mental illness.

2. It is essential for those of us who have dealt with psychological battles to surround ourselves with a supportive network of friends, family, or support groups. Having a strong support system can provide a safe space to discuss feelings, seek guidance, and receive encouragement during unexpected, unwelcome, uneducated, and unfair critique of mental health issues we have faced or are facing. Connecting with others who have battled similar experiences in psychological war can also help reduce our vulnerability toward unjust bias regarding mental illness.

3. Self-compassion is crucial for those of us who have overcome psychological battles to combat social stigma. It's essential to treat ourselves with kindness, understanding, and acceptance. Engaging in self-care activities, practicing contemplation, and acknowledging our progress and achievements are all ways to cultivate self-compassion and boost self-esteem.

4. In dealing with social stigma, it is important for us to set boundaries with others. This may involve limiting interactions with people who perpetuate stigma or negativity surrounding mental health. Setting boundaries also means prioritizing our well-being and mental health above societal expectations, social platforms or judgments.

5. Those of us who have triumphed over psychological battles can become advocates for mental health awareness and destigmatization. By sharing our stories publicly, participating in mental health advocacy campaigns, or supporting organizations that promote mental health education, we can contribute to creating a more understanding and accepting society.

Overcoming social stigma after dealing with psychological battles is a gradual process. It's essential to remember that our mental health journey is valid, and seeking help or support is a sign of strength, not weakness. Together, we can work toward a society that embraces mental health with compassion and understanding.

<u>Muhammad Ali – "The Greatest of All-Time"</u>

A world class example of personal growth and development is an iconic figure, a person who was once the most recognized and well-known individual on the planet, and this was long before the advent of social media platforms. He shaped and waged his own psychological battles on the world's stage, on his own terms and conditions. He was able to reach such great heights due to his imagination, creativity, determination, physical prowess, mental acuity, intuitiveness, showmanship, personal conviction, and sheer will.

Muhammad Ali, born as Cassius Clay on January 17, 1942, in Louisville, Kentucky, is widely recognized as one of the greatest athletes of all time and a cultural icon. Throughout his life, Ali achieved countless triumphs inside and outside of the boxing ring, leaving an enduring legacy. From his boxing career to his outspoken advocacy for civil rights and his contributions to humanitarian causes, Muhammad Ali's life is filled with notable highlights, inspiring and resonating with people from all walks of life.

Boxing became the focal point of his life, as Ali gained fame in the 1960s for his exceptional abilities, graceful movement, and fast reactions. His path to becoming the greatest heavyweight boxer of all time started with a notable triumph at the 1960 Summer Olympics in Rome, where he won the gold medal in the light-heavyweight division at just 18 years old. Following his Olympic success, Ali faced racial prejudice upon returning to Louisville, enduring the humiliation of being denied service at a nearby restaurant solely due to his African American heritage.

Ali encountered a stark illustration of racial bias, which was widespread during that era. Even with his great accomplishment in the Olympics and his role in enhancing America's athletic reputation, he still had to deal with the unfair segregation of the time. This event highlighted the contradiction of proudly representing his nation internationally while simultaneously grappling with racial inequities domestically. Ali may have faced inner turmoil triggered by racial discrimination, leading to feelings of self-doubt, anger, and resentment. These emotions could have impeded his drive and aspirations. Nevertheless, rather than being consumed by these psychological battles, Ali directed his focus toward realizing his dream of becoming the World Heavyweight Boxing Champion and so much more.

One of the defining moments in Ali's boxing career was his legendary "Fight of the Century" against Joe Frazier in 1971. This bout was highly anticipated, as it pitted two undefeated heavyweight champions against each other. The fight went the full fifteen rounds and was a brutal battle between two extraordinary fighters. Although Ali lost by a unanimous decision, the fight showcased his tenacity, resiliency, and unwavering determination to win.

"Only a man who knows what it is like to be defeated can reach down to the bottom of his soul and come up with the extra ounce of power it takes to win when the match is even." — Muhammad Ali

Ali won the heavyweight boxing title three times in his career. He first won it in 1964 by defeating Sonny Liston. He regained the title in 1974 by defeating George Foreman in the famous "Rumble in the Jungle" fight. Ali utilized his "rope-a-dope" technique, absorbing Foreman's powerful punches by leaning against the ropes, and then launching his own counterattacks when his opponent tired. This victory showcased Ali's ability to consistently adapt and outthink his opponents. Ali won the title for a third time in 1978, when he defeated Leon Spinks in their rematch.

"I am the greatest. I said that before I knew I was." — Muhammad Ali

Muhammad Ali's impact extended far beyond his boxing achievements. He was not only an athlete but also a powerful advocate for civil rights and social justice. During the civil rights movement, Ali became increasingly vocal about his convictions, denouncing racial segregation and discrimination. In 1964, he controversially converted to the Nation of Islam and changed his name from Cassius Clay to Muhammad Ali, which reflected his religious beliefs.

Ali refused to be drafted into the U.S. Army during the Vietnam War. In 1967, he became a conscientious objector to the war. He cited his religious convictions that found the war to be immoral and unjust. Consequently, he was systematically denied a boxing license in every state and stripped of his passport.

As a result, he did not fight in the ring from March 1967 to October 1970—between the ages of 25 and almost 29—as his case worked its way through the appeal process. In 1971, the United States Supreme Court overturned his conviction in a unanimous 8-0 ruling (Justice Thurgood Marshall abstained from the case). This decision subjected him to public scorn and led to a three-year hiatus during the prime of his career.

Throughout his life, Ali raised awareness and funds for numerous charitable initiatives, including the Muhammad Ali Center, which promotes education, social justice, and cultural understanding. His commitment to philanthropy extended to humanitarian efforts worldwide, particularly in developing countries. In 1990, he visited Iraq during the Gulf War to negotiate the release of American hostages, showcasing his dedication to peace and diplomacy.

His dedication to humanitarian causes remains a testament to his character and compassion. He demonstrated his empathy and compassion toward the most vulnerable populations around the world. At the 1996 Summer Olympics in Atlanta, Georgia, he lit the opening torch. The appearance came 12 years after Ali was diagnosed with Parkinson's disease, which slowed his movement and quieted his voice but couldn't overpower his epic stature. Muhammad Ali died at age seventy-four on June 4, 2016. His legacy continues to resonate, inspiring us to strive for greatness, stand up for justice, and leave a lasting impact on the world.

10.3 Transforming Failure

Understand that setbacks are natural components of any endeavor in the learning and growth process. The ability to handle failure positively involves adopting a growth mindset, where failures are seen as opportunities for learning and development. This perspective encourages mental toughness, urging us to persist, despite losses.

Analyzing failures critically but constructively can pinpoint areas for improvement, reducing the likelihood of recurring mistakes. This approach involves stepping back, assessing what did not work, and strategizing on better approaches for future endeavors; hence, turning painful moments into proactive steps toward success. While failure can be disheartening and challenging, it also presents an opportunity for learning and improvement. Here are three essential steps to overcome failure.

1. The first step in handling failure effectively is to accept it. Denying or avoiding failure can lead to frustration and limit personal growth. In contrast, seeing failure as a natural part of learning shifts our focus from the setback to the lessons it can provide. Reflection is essential at this stage to consider why the failure happened, what went wrong, and what factors contributed. This kind of self-acceptance can offer valuable insight for future attempts, support personal development, and reduce the likelihood of repeating the same mistakes.

2. The second key step in dealing with failure is to cultivate mental toughness and perseverance. Mental toughness is the ability to recover from setbacks, while perseverance is the commitment to keep moving forward despite obstacles. We can strengthen mental toughness by developing a positive mindset, practicing self-care, and seeking support from others. It's also important to remember that failure does not define our worth or abilities; it is a temporary setback on the path to success. By staying resilient and continuing to persevere, people build strength, character, and confidence in their ability to overcome future difficulties.

3. The third step in effectively dealing with failure is to focus on adaptation and growth. Failure can be an opportunity to improve, prompting people to reassess their goals, strategies, and approaches. Instead of seeing failure as the end of the road, view it as a catalyst for change and innovation. Adapting after failure involves shifting our mindset, setting new goals, and applying strategies informed by lessons learned from past setbacks. Embracing a growth mindset, one that treats problems as opportunities for development, can help people turn failure into success and reach their full potential.

Failure is not the end, but a stepping stone on the journey to success.

<u>Michael Jordan's Return to the Chicago Bulls and Meeting Failure</u>

In the annals of sports history, few stories captivate the imagination quite like Michael Jordan's departure from basketball to play minor league baseball, followed by his triumphant return to the National Basketball Association (NBA) and the Chicago Bulls. Michael's exit from basketball in 1993 was a shock to the sports world; his return in 1995 and the subsequent rebuild of the Chicago Bulls is a profound narrative of mental toughness, leadership, and strategic transformation.

In October 1993, Michael Jordan, at the height of his basketball prowess, stunned the world by announcing his retirement from the NBA. Michael's decision was not just a personal challenge but also a substantial blow to the Chicago Bulls, who under his leadership had secured three consecutive NBA Championships from 1991 to 1993.

Michael's stint in baseball lasted until March 1995, when he decided to return to the NBA. Announcing his comeback with an iconic press release stating simply, "I'm back," Michael rejoined a Bulls team that was struggling to find its former glory.

Michael's return was not without its obstacles. His basketball skills had rusted during his time away, evident in his first few games back. However, the playoffs were approaching, and there was little time for a gradual adjustment. The 1995 playoffs presented a harsh welcome back, as the Bulls were eliminated in the second round by the Orlando Magic. This failure was pivotal, as it highlighted the areas needing improvement and set the stage for one of the most impressive comebacks in sports history.

The defeat by the Orlando Magic served as a pivotal learning moment for Michael and the Bulls organization. Following the loss, Michael resolved to make immediate preparations for the upcoming season and inspired his teammates to do the same, foregoing any off-season break. Motivated by their shared ambition to reclaim their NBA Championship status, the Bulls players commenced their collective training without delay. Their united commitment highlighted the importance of physical conditioning, team cohesion, and strategic improvements. They undertook the subsequent steps, showcasing exemplary efforts in constructing a championship-caliber team.

Michael regained his physical form and worked tirelessly on his basketball skills, reminding the world of his work ethic and determination. Michael set an excellent example for his teammates to follow. The Bulls finished the new 1995-1996 NBA season with a record-breaking 72 wins and just 10 losses, the best regular-season performance in NBA history at that time. The playoffs saw the Bulls decisively vanquishing all competitors, culminating in a championship victory against the Seattle SuperSonics.

Michael Jordan's return to basketball and the subsequent transformation of the Chicago Bulls symbolize a compelling saga of confrontation with failure and the pursuit of greatness. Through meticulous planning, unwavering dedication, and strategic foresight, Michael and the Bulls not only reclaimed their position at the pinnacle of the NBA but also engraved their saga as one of the most inspiring in the annals of sports. The Bulls went on to win three more consecutive NBA Championships.

Michael Jordan's story reflects losing psychological battles along the journey to winning the psychological war within our mind.

The story of Michael's retirement, his stint in minor league baseball, and return to basketball, leading the Chicago Bulls to multiple championships, serves as a poignant narrative of losing psychological battles but ultimately winning the psychological war within our mind. Michael's experiences mirror the process of encountering setbacks, overcoming challenges, and emerging victorious in the realm of the psychological war within the mind.

Michael's retirement in 1993 marked a significant setback for the Chicago Bulls. The loss of a legendary teammate with the magnitude of skill, leadership, and dedication of Michael posed a psychological challenge for the team, forcing them to adapt to a new reality. Michael's initial uncharacteristic difficulties upon his return to basketball highlighted the psychological toll of being away from the game and facing a competitive disadvantage after developing his body and mind for baseball, where the physical and mental capabilities are completely different from basketball.

Even though Michael is one of the greatest basketball players of all time, he has learned from setbacks and embraced change on the road to becoming one of the best to ever play the game. After abandoning his baseball quest and rejoining the Bulls, the defeat by the Orlando Magic in the 1995 playoffs served as a critical turning point for Michael and the Bulls. Michael's response to the loss exemplified a growth mindset as he immediately focused on improvement and inspired his teammates to do the same. The willingness to learn from failures and adapt to new circumstances reflects a crucial aspect of winning the psychological war within our mind.

Michael's relentless work ethic and commitment to excellence shone through in his rigorous training regimen post-playoff exit after he returned to the NBA. By setting an example through his dedication and work ethic, Michael motivated his teammates to elevate their performance and strive for greatness. The transformational journey of the Bulls was fueled by the collective dedication of team members toward a shared goal, showcasing the power of unity and perseverance.

Through resilience, learning from failures, unwavering dedication, and strategic foresight, Michael and the Bulls exemplified the transformative power of perseverance and mental toughness. Their story serves as an enduring reminder of how confronting setbacks, embracing change, and staying committed to excellence can lead to triumph in the face of adversity. Michael's legacy extends beyond the basketball court, inspiring us to overcome our own psychological battles and emerge victorious in the pursuit of greatness.

10.4 Self-Identity Formed in the Crucible of Life

The alchemy of intense heat and pressure is a remarkable phenomenon that showcases the transformative power of nature. One of the most iconic examples of intense heat and pressure transforming raw substances into something valuable is the formation of diamonds. Diamonds, known for their brilliance, clarity, and rarity, are created deep within the Earth's mantle. Carbon atoms are subjected to extreme heat and pressure, reaching temperatures of over 2,200 degrees Fahrenheit and pressures of around 725,000 pounds per square inch. Over millions of years, these conditions cause the carbon atoms to crystallize and form the precious gemstone. The evolution of self-identity through psychological battle is similar to the refinement of human character in a crucible. The intense heat and pressure of psychological war within the crucible of life shapes our character. This alteration redefines personal narratives, often aligning our identity much closer to our core values and beliefs, ultimately leading to a congruent self-concept.

The issue of self-identity and its formation through the psychological battles we encounter present a complex debate. This debate especially focuses on how our internal conflicts shape us. As we relate our inner demons to the evolution of self-identity, it's crucial to consider the intricate interplay between our experiences, societal influences, and biological factors. A psychological war is more than merely striving for mental balance; it represents a journey that significantly molds our self-perception and identity. To fully understand the scope of this adaptation, we must intensely analyze the nature of the psychological battles we have fought. By employing psychological theories, personal stories, and social contexts, we aim to unravel how these intense experiences influence and reshape our self-identity.

Self-identity is fundamentally our understanding of who we are – a blend of self-perception, physical, emotional, and social attributes forming an internalized narrative.

Identity development is a cornerstone of adolescent and adult psychological development, deeply influencing how we interact with our social world and making a plethora of important choices to determine our path in life.

People may struggle with feelings of aimlessness and confusion, grappling with the challenge of finding meaning and purpose in their lives. Finding activities that interest us, even if we are uncertain about them, is crucial. Setting small and achievable goals gives us a sense of accomplishment and direction. It is important to accept that not everything is meant to be understood; it is okay to not have everything figured out, and that life's journey is ongoing.

A psychological battle emerges when we face challenges that question the authenticity of our self-identity. The clash between imposed commitments and our evolving self can guide us on our quest for self-discovery. It is beneficial to map out different paths to consider, along with the positives and negatives associated with each. Embracing new ideas without resistance aids in exploring fresh options and opportunities, fostering new areas for personal growth and additional methods for well-being. New adventures bring about new opportunities.

Accept that life is a test when we are attempting to get ahead or when we may be falling behind. We need to do our best to fall forward, meaning being deterred in one dimension of life can lead to greater accomplishments we never imagined possible.

Continuing to choose paths that reflect our true values leads to personal growth. Remaining calm is also crucial for maintaining the psychological progress we've made. Establish healthy boundaries to create space for authentic connections. Leveraging strengths to build on our achievements helps prevent complacency and manage potential issues before they undermine our progress.

Embracing the challenges and victories inherent in the process of identity formation can lead to a deeper understanding of ourselves and a more authentic way of engaging with the world around us, assisting us to win the war within our mind.

Photo by Daniel R. Linden

This is a photo of a very small Norfolk Terrier with a huge sense of self-identity and inspiring character. His transformation from a puppy over the years transcended from being inquisitive about many different things to embodying self-confidence. His tendency was never to back up or back down, even when much larger dogs or strangers approached. When he encountered situations filled with new circumstances that he was unfamiliar with, he was undeterred. If we look closely at the expression on his face and the way his body is positioned in this picture, his poise and pride as a Norfolk Terrier are obvious. This was his manner, the way he chose to live his life.

Chapter 11: Imparting Winning the War Within Our Mind

Making our stories known has always been at the heart of human communication, providing a way for us to connect, empathize, and influence each other. Storytelling can shape identities and rewrite the internal dialogues that might otherwise be dominated by disorder and despair.

When we share how we have navigated the treacherous landscapes of psychological warfare within our mind, we can throw a lifeline to those drowning in similar experiences. This connection is vital, not only for support but sometimes for survival. By presenting psychological battles through the lens of a personal journey, the storyteller humanizes the condition, educating the listeners that psychological distress is not a sign of weakness but a complex interplay of biological, psychological, and social factors. Acknowledging this and seeking assistance are definite signs of strength. The battlegrounds of psychological warfare are as diverse as those of us who fight them; each has a unique story that holds potential lessons and inspiration for others.

It's important to acknowledge that psychological battles are a natural part of the human experience. The mind is a complex landscape where conflicting ideas, desires, and beliefs often collide. While the battles within us may never fully end, seeking understanding and resolution can bring moments of peace and renewal. Learning from those who have overcome psychological wars is invaluable; their experiences offer insight, guidance, and inspiration as we navigate our own psychological battles. Overcoming psychological warfare is a significant personal achievement, perhaps one of life's greatest victories, and it often requires drawing on our key top ten strengths we discussed.

Learning from the triumphs of others can ignite hope and purpose within us, propelling us forward on our path to healing, growth, and success. By reflecting on the experiences of those who have prevailed, we gain valuable insight into psychological battles and the inner demons that intensify them. We may never reach a state of permanent resolution, but we can strive for moments of peace amid the turmoil created by the war within our mind. Stories of determination, vulnerability, and self-discovery also teach practical lessons about coping skills, self-care, and emotional regulation.

Experiences from those who have dealt with psychological battles offer a wealth of knowledge, inspiration, and guidance that can empower us to confront our own inner demons with courage and conviction. By incorporating these lessons into our own lives, we can develop the strength and emotional awareness needed to navigate the complexities of our minds with grace and spirit.

Sharing our innermost setbacks and breakthroughs with trusted people can deepen relationships and strengthen bonds of hope and understanding. It encourages open and honest communication and fosters empathy and compassion among friends and family. When we share our vulnerabilities and victories, we invite others to do the same, creating space for authentic, meaningful connection grounded in mutual respect and support. Putting our psychological battles into words can also bring clarity and insight into our values, principles, and aspirations, paving the way for continued personal growth, self-improvement, and ultimately winning the inner psychological war.

Surviving serious psychological battles instigated by inner demons is an immense achievement and deserves to be recognized and celebrated. The journey of overcoming such intense conflict is a testament to the power of the human spirit. In light of this, sharing our victory story becomes not only a personal catharsis but also a source of inspiration and hope for others who may be fighting related battles. It is important to remember that if we have survived or experienced one psychological battle, we understand just one psychological battle. All battles are unique.

Sharing our victory in a psychological war involves acknowledging substantial adversities that have been confronted and the maximum efforts that have been expended in overcoming them. Humbly sharing the details of our dangerous expedition with others validates our experiences and emotions, which helps reinforce our self-confidence based on the challenging situations we have survived.

This allows for inner celebration, emotional maturation, and character development, making all of our top ten strengths stronger. Our progress demonstrates that it is possible to overcome inner demons and emerge stronger on the other side. Keep in mind the following words of Albert Camus:

"Nobody realizes that some people expend tremendous energy just to appear normal." — Albert Camus, French Philosopher

Few statements in the realm of human psychology capture the essence of the psychological battle as accurately as this insightful observation made by Albert Camus. This quote from the French philosopher and writer encapsulates a deep truth about the psychological war we face that is mostly hidden from the outside world. The simplicity of seeming "normal" masks the intricate and draining efforts many undergo. Camus, who won the Nobel Prize in Literature in 1957 at the young age of forty-four, invites us to reflect on the unseen conflicts within people's minds. Sharing our narratives of internal turmoil reassures others that they are not alone in their journey, and through patience and self-awareness, moments of tranquility can be discovered amid the chaos.

Sharing our journey of overcoming psychological war serves not only as a cathartic experience for the storyteller, but also as an inspiration for others. It imbues hope and encourages others facing similar battles, providing tangible proof that obstacles can be overcome and that suffering can be transcended to win the psychological war within our mind.

Photo by Daniel R. Linden

Purposefully advancing through our own adversities inspires others as long as we stay humble, positive, and realize that everyone's experiences are unique.

11.1 Telling a Story of Winning the War Within Our Mind

Winning the war within our mind springs from an inspirational story of overcoming the inner demons we have identified. Each is not purely evil but a distorted reflection of something human, a test rather than a curse. The victory comes by utilizing our top ten strengths. Passing each test is not to be underestimated, it is heroic.

The following story conveys a deep and introspective emotional journey for the protagonist, Erin, as she confronts and navigates through various emotional ambushes represented by demons in their realm. The story emphasizes the importance of facing fears with courage, understanding anger, empathizing with sadness, practicing gratitude, maintaining clarity of thought, and embracing adaptability and self-awareness.

"Embracing the Demons Within: Erin's Quest for Inner Peace"

There was once a traveler named Erin, who lived in a realm where the heart shaped the world. Every thought left a print on the land, every emotion a ripple through the sky. Those who lost balance summoned shadows—demons born not from evil, but from the neglect of their own truth.

Erin's realm had grown dark. Fear whispered from the trees, addiction sang from a silver pool, anger seethed beneath cracked earth. Envy stirred storms, sadness soaked the valleys, and tricksters spun illusions of comfort and pride. Erin had run from them all once, but running only thickened the shadows. One quiet morning, a voice deep within spoke: "You cannot escape what lives in you. You can only walk through it." So, Erin set forth.

The first demon awaited among whispering branches—fear, tall and cloaked in smoke. "Walk back," it hissed. "Here lies only failure." Erin's legs trembled, but a spark inside replied, "I walk anyway." Step by step, the whispers softened. Each heartbeat was a declaration of courage, each breath a reminder of strength. When Erin reached the forest's edge, the smoke dissolved. Where fear had stood now rested a clear path forward—a reminder that courage is not the absence of fear, but movement through it.

Soon came the Pool of Temptation, its waters sweet, shimmering with promises of ease. Addiction's voice purred, "drink, and you'll forget every ache." Erin knelt, the reflection rippling with every pulse of longing. Yet instead of reaching, Erin breathed. The craving passed like a wave. In that moment of patience, Erin realized that every craving is just a wish for peace. Turning from the pool, Erin set out to create peace from within, not borrow it from illusions.

Beyond the pool rose mountains of fire and, within them, roared anger, a molten giant. "The world wronged you!" it thundered. Erin clenched her fists but then looked closer. Beneath the giant's flames flickered pain and sorrow. "You only wanted to be heard," Erin whispered. Reaching out with empathy, the traveler offered understanding instead of battle. The giant's blaze cooled, transforming into a soft glow of purpose. Anger became passion, purified and steady.

Next stood a great mirror where envy lived, showing visions of others soaring, smiling, succeeding. Each vision whispered what Erin lacked. For a while, the traveler felt small… until noticing something: the mirror only reflected light. Erin knelt, touching the ground. "I have my own light," she said. "Different, but real." With gratitude, Erin thanked the mirror for showing what to cherish, not what to covet. The glass cracked, and from it poured golden light.

Rain fell endlessly. Sadness waited there, not monstrous, but weary. She looked up at Erin and said, "will you sit with me?" For the first time, Erin did not run from sorrow. Together they sat in silence until the rain softened. Sadness smiled faintly and whispered, "Thank you for listening." She dissolved into mist, leaving the ground lush and green.

Mist led to a labyrinth with shifting walls. The trickster and deceiver lurked here, painting paths of false hope and false fear. Erin paused to analyze, using critical thinking. Every time the maze changed, Erin adapted, questioning illusions instead of reacting. Over time, the maze's power weakened, unable to mislead a mind anchored in truth. At the center stood a single door marked simply: "Know Yourself."

Beyond the door knelt a giant carrying stones carved with names—regret, responsibility, and expectation. The Burden Bearer groaned, "Take them, so others may rest." Erin placed a hand on the stones, feeling their weight. "I will share the load, but not all of it is mine." Carefully setting down what belonged to others, Erin felt strength return. Gratitude welled up, not for ease, but for discernment, the wisdom to know what to carry and what to release.

At last, Erin reached the mountain's summit where all the demons gathered, not as enemies, but as parts of the whole. Fear guarded vigilance. Anger breathed passion. Sadness gifted empathy. Envy became humility. Even the trickster bowed, now a teacher of discernment. Erin finally understood:

"I am not broken. I am becoming." With self-awareness, mental toughness, and gratitude, Erin opened her heart. Light and shadow joined, balancing into wholeness. The realm brightened, not perfect, but beautifully alive.

The moral of this story is that our demons are not there to destroy us. They reveal where our greatest strengths can grow. Gratitude turns pain into wisdom, and self-insight transforms struggle into peace. When Erin descended from the mountain, the realm responded. Forests bloomed where fear once grew. Rivers shimmered clear again, no longer poisoned by anger or envy. The people, seeing this change, asked how the land had healed.

Erin smiled. "It was never the world that was broken, it was the mirror inside me. When I mended that, the reflection changed too." And so, Erin became known not as a warrior or conqueror of demons, but as the keeper of shadows—one who learned that light thrives because of the dark, not in spite of it.

Erin taught others the path:

- To face fear with courage, not avoidance.

- To meet anger with understanding, not resistance.

- To soothe sadness with empathy, not denial.

- To balance hope with patience, not haste.

- To practice gratitude, not comparison.

- To think with clarity, not impulse.

- To meet every trial with adaptability and self-awareness.

The story of Erin invites us to see that inner mastery is not about banishing our flaws, but transforming them. Each shadow—fear, anger, envy, sadness—carries the seed of its opposite virtue.

- Where fear dwells, courage waits.

- Where anger burns, passion longs to serve.

- Where envy whispers, gratitude speaks truth.

- Where sadness weeps, compassion grows.

And when all are integrated, we walk, not without darkness, but with light that knows its depth.

11.2 Inspiration to Win Psychological Battles

There are many inspirational leaders throughout history who converted their personal difficulties into bold leadership strategies. One of those leaders is known best for fighting the Civil War and less so for the psychological war he fought in his mind.

<u>President Abraham Lincoln</u>

Abraham Lincoln was born on February 12, 1809, in a one-room log cabin in Hodgenville, Kentucky. His family endured economic difficulties, living in a frontier area with scarce resources and limited comforts. These humble beginnings marked the early life from which he would rise to become the sixteenth President of the United States. His formative years in Kentucky exposed him to the difficult life on the frontier, which helped forge his strong character.

Leading during one of the most tumultuous times in American history, President Abraham Lincoln faced immense personal and national dread during the Civil War. His fear of the destruction of the Union and the continued practice of slavery led him to adopt decisive measures, including the Emancipation Proclamation. Lincoln's leadership was marked by significant moral and strategic decisions that proved essential in maintaining the Union and freeing millions of slaves.

President Lincoln struggled privately with the intense psychological battle of depression. His ability to overcome personal adversity and lead the nation through its most perilous period is as instructive as it is inspiring. His depression is well documented, with numerous anecdotes and personal correspondence indicating periods of sadness and despair. Biographers such as Joshua Shenk, in his detailed analysis "Lincoln's Melancholy," suggest that Lincoln's depression was both clinical and severe, noting it could be classified today as major depressive disorder.

President Lincoln exhibited an admirable sense of purpose that seemed inextricably linked to his depressive realism. His commitment to the Union and to the principles of liberty and equality helped him to focus on his goals, despite personal despair. President Lincoln also leaned heavily on a network of close confidants like his wife, Mary Todd, and his friend and law partner, William Herndon, who provided emotional support and political advice. This small tight knit support team was crucial in helping him through his darkest times.

President Lincoln's management of his depression had direct implications for his leadership. His empathy, derived from personal suffering, equipped him with the ability to relate to the pain and suffering of others, whether they were war-torn soldiers or enslaved human beings. This empathy shone through in his leadership style, characterized by compassion, patience, and moderation.

"In the end, it's not the years in your life that count; it's the life in your years." — Abraham Lincoln, 16th President of the United States of America

The assassination of President Abraham Lincoln, an event that sent shockwaves through a nation already torn by four years of civil war, stands as a pivotal moment in American history. It occurred on the night of April 14, 1865, just days after the Confederate surrender at Appomattox Court House, which effectively ended the Civil War. He was fifty-six years-old at the time of his death.

Gaining inspiration from individuals like President Lincoln who have successfully conquered mental fights can offer valuable insights and motivation. Overcoming personal psychological battles leads to a deep comprehension of the complexities and complications involved in these conflicts. Drawing lessons from the triumphs of others in psychological warfare serves as a strong affirmation that prevailing over significant mental hurdles is possible, even when faced with overwhelming obstacles.

11.3 Leadership Ethos of Psychological Warriors

It takes strong leaders to impart winning the war of the mind onto others. Ethos is the characteristic spirit of a culture manifested in its beliefs and aspirations. Psychological warriors are made, not born. Their leadership stems from overcoming inner demons whose desire is to break the warrior down and keep them inoperative until they surrender their freedom, dreams, and love of life.

At times, psychological warriors make difficult leadership decisions under extreme pressure. Each move made may have significant costs and substantial positive or negative ramifications associated with it. Most decisions in life are made without complete information beforehand. Navigating between following our gut instincts and relying on analytical programmed algorithms can create psychological battles in our lives. The circumstances surrounding situations involve a delicate balance between risk taking and caution. To alleviate tension, confusion, and uncertainty, psychological warriors follow proven leadership principles.

Psychological warriors overcome obstacles as opportunities for growth. By facing their worst terror, warriors gain the courage to take decisive actions and remain resolute in their beliefs. The warrior's mindset creates a heightened sense of self-assurance perceived as legitimacy and authenticity by others. A warrior's aspiration for a better existence empowers them to craft a captivating vision for their future, occasionally motivating others to reach remarkable results.

The leadership spirit of a psychological warrior is not about wielding power but about empowering ourselves and others. Their warrior ethos comes alive by overcoming invisible inner demons enacting daunting difficulties upon them. Most people will never notice the dangerous difficulties they faced, until the proud warrior extends a helping hand or the warrior's confidence compels others to keep their own hopes and dreams alive.

Psychological warrior's leadership is perfected in a war of the mind involving battles against doubts, alarm, and insecurities. For unbeatable warriors, winning does not mean just victory but an insightful realization of inner strengths. Triumph for the warrior means finding inner peace amid chaos. Winning does not come with a forever guarantee, nor a pardon that excuses warriors from future battles or psychological wars. Winning the war in our mind means remission that requires toughness to maintain and subsequently succeed and thrive.

Winning a psychological war in our mind means conquering inner demons that seek to incapacitate and destroy us. This process hardens leadership skills. Warriors become wise enough to realize that uprisings can begin again at any time and humble enough to never forget what it took to prevail through the toughest battles that forged our greatest strengths. These are two constructs of the psychological warrior ethos.

Post-triumph, psychological warriors may find themselves in positions of leadership, drawn from the wisdom and strength they have gained. This leadership is characterized by authenticity, empathy, and a deep understanding of human frailty. Such leaders are seen as relatable and inspirational, having turned previous troubles into testimony.

The ethos of psychological warriors includes the following leadership qualities necessary to impart the story of winning the war within the mind onto others:

- Acceptance and complete ownership of their decisions.

- Demonstration of humility, acknowledgment of our own fallibility, and the realization that nobody is perfect or correct 100% of the time.

- Maintain openness to diverse perspectives, experiences, and suggestions all encourage others to listen to their stories.

- Fosters a positive environment to lead others to sustainable success.

- Stays informed and committed to continuous learning that inspires others.

- Recognized as open to change and innovation.

- Upholds the highest ethical standards and demonstrates integrity in decision making.

- Capable to build trust and credibility.

- Open to accepting unfiltered feedback and takes action to improve effective dynamics involved in psychological battles.

- Adaptable to achieve the best possible outcomes despite overwhelming circumstances.

The ethos of successful leadership by a psychological warrior hinge on possessing advanced emotional intelligence and acute self-awareness. Warriors need to manage their own emotions while comprehending the sensitivities of others. This involves an ongoing process of introspection. It is their credibility and integrity that win the war within our mind.

11.4 Mentoring the Next Generation

Mentoring becomes a natural leadership progression and phenomenon for many of us who have overcome psychological battles fought in our minds. We have learned valuable life lessons, strategies, and gained wisdom through experiences in cruel and challenging circumstances. By mentoring the next generation and passing on sincere reasons for developing a sense of purpose and instilling hope for a fulfilling future, we serve everyone's best interests by fortifying future leaders.

Before stepping into the role of a mentor, it is crucial to grasp the contemporary mental health landscape facing our young population. The escalation in rates of depression, anxiety, self-harm, and other mental health disorders among teens and young adults is alarming. Factors contributing to this rise include cyberbullying, post-pandemic lifestyles, academic pressures, social isolation, and an overall more competitive world. The 21st century technological engulfment adds layers of complexity with constant connectivity, leaving little room for personal reflection and development.

Mentors play an essential role in the lives of young people. They provide more than guidance, they offer validation, listening ears, and paths to understanding ourselves in deeper ways. To be effective in mentoring someone, one must adopt three intricate key roles:

- An effective mentor listens without judgment, acknowledging the mentee's feelings and experiences as valid and significant.

- While it's vital to listen and validate, providing informed advice on dealing with emotional and psychological strains is equally crucial.

- Sometimes, mentoring means advocating for finding professional help, educating others about mental health resources, or supporting them in familial and academic situations.

A supportive environment is key to helping young minds thrive in the face of societal pressures. By fostering open communication, providing mentorship, and creating a safe space for expression, we can empower young people to seek help when needed and build resilience against external stressors. We can help empower the next generation to thrive in an ever-changing world and build a brighter future for themselves and those around them. Most importantly, we can make the concept of asking for help a sign of strength rather than one of intimidation and weakness.

We can not only hope but must actively work to support new generations in recognizing and triumphing over psychological battles—one resilient individual at a time—to win the psychological war within our mind.

Photo Collection of Daniel R. Linden

Each of us faces our own psychological battles, insecurities, and uncertainties that threaten to hold us back. For those of us who are veterans of these conflicts, it is our responsibility to help others navigate the complex landscape of winning the war within our mind. Sharing what we have learned helps to tell a story that inspires others. Our stories prove it is possible to conquer inner demons and emerge stronger on the other side. By sharing our journeys, we offer a roadmap for others to follow, giving them the courage and motivation to utilize their own specific strengths to confront inner battles. This initiates a ripple effect that transcends time, influencing generations to come, and fosters a culture of empathy, support, and growth.

Chapter 12: Thriving After Winning the War Within Our Mind

After confronting one of life's toughest tests, the war within our mind, we have achieved a sense of contentment. Our worst imaginable nightmare is now in remission. What comes next?

Finding meaning and purpose amid psychological battle requires a combination of self-reflection, acceptance, support, mental toughness, tenacity, resilience, willpower, and growth. By engaging in this process with openness and courage, we transcend the limitations of daily living and personal boundaries, ultimately leading to a more authentic, fulfilling, and purpose-driven life. Embracing the battle we fought, we have won; it now acts as a catalyst, paving the way for a deeper understanding of ourselves and the world, fostering a sense of connection, resolve, and meaning that supersedes individual psychological battles and limitations.

The previous eleven chapters invited us to enter into the world of psychological warfare not on a distant battlefield but within the recesses of our own mind. Life is an adventurous path filled with hurdles and trials that put our endurance and fortitude to the test. At some point, we encounter the most daunting battle of our lives, grappling with seemingly insurmountable circumstances. Winning this war means we are able to move onward, having healed with scars worn as badges of honor. We evolved as caring people, transformed by newly found moments of joy after fearing for our lives, livelihood, family, and friends.

Upon emerging victorious from the demanding war within our mind, it is crucial to allocate time for contemplation and rejuvenation. Reflecting on the ordeal enables introspection and comprehension of the lessons learned during the strife. It serves as a period to acknowledge the emotions that surfaced during the battle and cement our journey of healing. Recovery encompasses rest, self-nurturing, and self-compassion.

Having moved past all psychological battles necessitates tapping into our resilience and tenacity. The war unveiled inner reservoirs of bravery and resolve that might have otherwise remained undiscovered. Harnessing our tenacity is pivotal in propelling us forward, fully energized for reconstructing our life post-battle. Our successful stand turns into a testament to our human spirit, God's grace, and the ability to persevere and triumph over adversity.

The aftermath of a strenuous battle presents an opportunity for reconstruction and innovation. This phase involves delineating fresh objectives, redefining priorities, and envisioning a future beyond the end of the war. It might entail instigating changes in various facets of life, such as relationships, career, or personal development. Reconstruction is a gradual process that demands patience, persistence, and a readiness to embrace revolution.

Venturing beyond the battle entails uncovering significance and direction in the experience. It revolves around transmuting pain and suffering into wisdom and growth. This phase may encompass seeking meaning from psychological battles, identifying silver linings, and utilizing our experience to aid others grappling with psychological distress. Discovering significance and direction can furnish a sense of closure and empowerment as one progresses in life.

By transcending the battle, we unearth the depths of our inner integrity and the top ten strengths to confront whatever psychological battles that may cross our path in the future.

Photo by Daniel R. Linden

To determine whether this is a picture of a sunset or a sunrise, we need to know our direction of travel. We could be embarking on the day heading east into the sunrise or journeying west later in the day, driving into the sunset. Astronomically, these principles are certain. After winning the war in our mind, the direction of our travel becomes inconsequential. What holds the most significance is our survival. We are presented with a wonderful opportunity to continue scripting the narrative of our lives. Grateful that the battles are behind us and peace reigns while danger has subsided. Once more, we can guide ourselves and others toward a life not consumed by internal war but one focused on passion and purpose.

12.1 Life After Victory

Thriving after winning the war within our mind begins symbolically by standing victorious on the battlefield of life, with fragments of defeated inner demons having been exploded and scattered around us. We begin to understand the fundamental impact these battles had on our lives. Having traversed difficult and dangerous terrain, we gained insight into the root causes of the psychological battles we fought and the reasons why we won our psychological war. We have learned to take nothing for granted and realize that the fighting may not end and our winning will not end either.

This book has led us through the intricacies of psychological battles and has helped to identify our limitations; more importantly, we have become aware of how to best utilize our top ten strengths to win the psychological war within our mind. Emerging victorious over life's adversities means identifying inner demons attempting to limit us, but more importantly the significance of making our strengths stronger. An ultimate reward for those of us who have previously fought and won the psychological war in our mind is to utilize our top ten strengths and inspire others to tackle their own inner demons, mentoring them to achieve victories in their psychological battles.

What begins with unraveling the origins of inner demons and continues with examining our thoughts, instincts, and feelings, we gain an understanding of the impact of a psychological battle on our life. It ends with overcoming fear and transforming adversity into opportunities for enhancing personal growth. By thriving after winning the war in our mind, we learn to stay motivated under pressure, harness essential strengths, and adapt to obstacles with grace by shedding layers of illusion and limitation. This process reveals the radiant essence within, characterized by confidence, clarity, and security, enabling us to positively influence and support others, experiencing inner peace.

Life after victory signifies the ongoing journey of self-discovery and growth even after overcoming the psychological battles within our mind. It involves fully understanding and acknowledging the combat we faced and the impact it had on us. It means gaining insight into the underlying causes of our psychological trauma and recognizing the reasons behind our triumph.

Additionally, life after victory highlights the importance of continuous vigilance and utilization of our strengths: mental toughness, empathy, emotional intelligence, self-awareness, patience, courage, adaptability and flexibility, critical thinking, enhanced problem solving, and gratitude. It requires a willingness to confront future battles with the same courage and determination that led to our past successes. It is about realizing that the path to personal growth and well-being is a never-ending process of learning, adjusting, and evolving.

12.2 Living Outside of the Boundaries

What does it mean to live outside the boundaries of what is considered reasonable, given the war within our mind? Having survived, the war reveals new dimensions of life that bring peace and tranquility to those whose minds had once become battlefields. Imagine a life where we break free from societal norms and expectations, applying a new scope of calm and serenity. This concept holds significant potential to deliver unparalleled liberation and happiness to us and all of those we deeply care about.

Living beyond the confines of reasonability does not imply recklessness or chaos; rather, it signifies a departure from limitations we impose on ourselves and society dumps on us. It involves daring greatly and dreaming bigger. Pursuing passions seeming far-fetched, listening to the whispers of our hearts that guide us toward our true calling. This shift in perspective opens doors to opportunities previously unseen, leading to a life rich in fascinating experiences and personal growth.

Allow harmony and composure to become our companions. Embrace authenticity, follow our inner compass to align with our true self and find peace within. The noise of unwanted internal disturbances and external expectations fade away, allowing us to focus on what truly matters. Inner peace radiates outward, creating a ripple effect that touches not only our lives but those around us.

Thriving after winning the war within our mind requires courage and willingness to challenge the status quo. It beckons us to question norms confining us, traveling on our chosen path based on our values and aspirations. While the journey may be daunting at times, the rewards of living authentically and in alignment with our true self are immeasurable.

Contemplate what it would feel like to venture into a dimension of life, recharging dreams previously considered improbable. Necessary changes include embracing uncertainty, enhancing trust in our inner wisdom, and daring to live life rising above perceived boundaries of reasonability. Traveling beyond the battle in our minds to discover new paths toward personal growth and understanding.

After overcoming psychological battles, it behooves us to set ambitious yet achievable goals. These goals act as beacons, guiding us toward new horizons and pushing us to surpass our limitations. By establishing clear objectives, we create a roadmap for success and channel our inner strength toward tangible outcomes.

Here's a list of ten quick Specific, Measurable, Action-Oriented, Realistic, and Timed (SMART) goals to stimulate our thoughts regarding going outside boundaries on a path to personal growth and prosperity:

1. Develop a daily mindfulness practice: Meditate for 10 minutes every morning for the next 30 days to maintain mental clarity and emotional resilience.

2. Rebuild physical stamina: Complete three 30-minute workouts each week for the next two months to increase energy and strength.

3. Pursue continuous learning: Read one self-improvement or personal development book per month for the next six months.

4. Strengthen social connections: Schedule one meaningful conversation or meet up with a friend or mentor each week for the next eight weeks.

5. Enhance emotional awareness: Journal for 15 minutes at the end of each day for the next 60 days to reflect on progress and feelings.

6. Advance career growth: Enroll in one professional development course and complete it within the next three months.

7. Build financial stability: Save $200 per month for the next six months toward an emergency fund or personal project.

8. Improve sleep quality: Establish a bedtime routine and aim for 7 to 8 hours of sleep nightly for 30 consecutive days.

9. Nurture a new creative skill: Dedicate one hour each week for the next two months to learning a new artistic or creative skill (e.g., painting, guitar, writing).

10. Give back to others: Volunteer for one local or online cause at least twice per month for the next three months to foster purpose and connection.

Stepping outside our comfort zones is where true growth occurs. Embracing change and problems allows us to expand our horizons, acquire new skills, and cultivate resilience. By confronting unfamiliar situations with courage and adaptability, we open doors to opportunities that lead to personal and professional development.

Going outside established and maintained healthy boundaries doesn't mean breaking them recklessly. It means knowing when to stretch beyond our comfort zone to grow.

- Expansion of boundaries is healthy only when it is anchored in self-confidence; otherwise, it becomes self-sabotage.

- Take calculated risks. Try something just beyond our current ability (a difficult project, difficult conversation, or confronting a fear).

- Extending new positive boundaries can be exhausting. Allow ourselves sufficient periods of rest and recovery after extensive periods of intense activity.

Pushing past boundaries in a controlled way helps us expand our resilience and adaptability.

12.3 Beyond the Battle

Beyond the battle emerges in the context of successfully enduring years of a psychological war within our mind and emerging as a better person than before the fight began. In the journey of life, we often find ourselves entangled in persistent psychological battles. These battles may not be visible to the outside world, but they shape our thoughts, actions, and overall well-being. Beyond the battle signifies getting past the inner demons that attempted to destroy us.

Living beyond the battle provides excellent prospects for growth and healing. Engaging in self-reflection, therapy, contemplation practices, and creating outlets for diminishing frustration enables a healthy inner transformation. All of this facilitates reinvigoration, making for a more fulfilling life.

Amid psychological battles, discovering meaning and purpose provides a sense of direction and contentment. Contemplating on our values, passions, and aspirations help us align our actions with our innermost desires. Finding meaning in the midst of hardship fuels human motivation and inspires a strong self-purpose.

In the intricate tapestry of life, navigating the torments of psychological battles requires courage, mental toughness, and self-discovery. Life's journey is seldom a linear path; it is more often a complex traversal across emotional landscapes and mental barriers. Psychological war casts a long shadow that can touch even the brightest days, but transformative victory illuminates and exposes weaknesses of fear and doubt to set us free to go beyond the battle.

Psychological warfare is exhausting. Sometimes, the same battle needs to be fought over and over again. The energy spent on psychological conflicts may leave us drained, isolated, and, at times, despondent. Going beyond the battle brings us to a significant personal understanding and spirituality. Facing our deepest horror requires extreme courage that acts as a catalyst, fueling our passion in at least five distinct ways.

1. We learn about our personal triggers, boundaries, and coping mechanisms. This newly formed self-knowledge facilitates a more authentic life where personal choices are aligned synergistically with our true self, leading to increased enthusiasm and optimism.

2. Becoming able to articulate our needs and boundaries clearly, we improve our connections with others. Clear communication and enhanced empathy strengthen existing relationships and help establish new allies with a stronger foundation to grow in the future to support everyone's efforts, all of which bolster our attitude, boldness, and assurance.

3. Winning the war within our mind ignites the desire and ability to contribute meaningfully to others. We find renewed purpose using our hard-earned experience to understand and support others who generously supported us through the toughest of times and those who made need our help.

4. Having navigated the tumultuous terrain of psychological battles, we develop enhanced mental toughness. This mental toughness increases our resiliency and improves our capability to handle future stressors more effectively. We approach life's tests with a steadier hand, a more balanced perspective, becoming even more grateful for opportunities we can spot, create, and build on.

5. It's not uncommon for those of us who have experienced significant psychological battles to channel our past experiences into passionate creative expression. Whether through art, writing, music, or additional forms of representation, these creative outlets not only serve as therapeutic modalities but also, going beyond the battle, make a contribution to the cultural fabric of society lending themselves to inspiration for others.

Life beyond the battle is not an ultimate destination but an ongoing positive process that puts our psychological battlefield involvement to use. We understand a war waged in our mind involves embracing a narrative of mental toughness and personal transformation to overcome future threats.

12.4 Preparing for Future Challenges to Psychological Stability

Gaining experience in fighting past psychological wars within our mind prepares us well for future challenges from inner demons. This preparation involves acknowledging the top ten strengths involved in our fight and making those strengths stronger.

Here is a reminder of the strengths we have used as our foundation to win the war within our mind.

	Strength	Summary Statement
1.	Mental Toughness	Mental toughness gives us the ability to withstand the intense pressure, chaos, and trauma that characterize psychological combat situations.
2.	Empathy	Empathy's superpower lies in its ability to offer and receive psychological support, making it vital to grasp our psychological needs and those of others.
3.	Emotional Intelligence (EI)	The ability to maintain our composure and make sound judgments amidst the chaos during intense psychological battles is a gift given by possessing effective EI.
4.	Self-Awareness	Self-awareness serves two important functions: one is to recognize, and the other is the capability to analyze and understand our own emotions.
5.	Patience	Patience is not just about waiting; it's about how we behave while we're waiting. Not everything is within our control and important endeavors take time to progress.
6.	Courage	When dealing with inner conflict, having courage to face one's inner demons and insecurities is crucial for personal growth and overcoming threats and challenges.
7.	Adaptability and Flexibility	Adaptability involves the capacity to adjust to new conditions. Flexibility refers to the ability to bend or adjust easily to changing circumstances.
8.	Critical Thinking	Critical thinking enables us to analyze, evaluate, and interpret information effectively. It becomes essential when inner demons start psychological battles.
9.	Enhanced Problem Solving	Identifying, analyzing, and resolving complex problems involve approaching psychological battles by considering multiple solutions and anticipating potential outcomes.
10.	Gratitude	Having the courage to face one's inner demons is crucial for personal growth and overcoming psychological battles and winning the war within our mind.

Focusing on identifying our unique strengths and leveraging them for personal and professional growth is the best way to get strong and stay that way. Maximizing strengths leads to enhanced performance, engagement, and overall well-being.

The principle of making strengths stronger emphasizes that we should invest our time and energy in areas where we naturally excel. By capitalizing on innate talents and abilities, we can significantly enhance our performance levels, experiencing higher levels of productivity, efficiency, and effectiveness in preparing for future challenges that may affect our psychological stability. Examples of this phenomenon include:

- When we align with our strengths, we are more likely to experience a sense of fulfillment and engagement in our tasks. Strengths-based development encourages us to pursue activities that energize and inspire, leading to a deeper sense of passion and commitment.

- Making strengths stronger plays a crucial role in personal growth and well-being. By focusing on what we do best, we can build confidence, resilience, and self-consciousness.

- Embracing our strengths allows us to cultivate a positive self-image and leverage our unique qualities to navigate challenges and achieve our goals. This holistic approach to development promotes a sense of fulfillment and satisfaction, leading to overall well-being and life satisfaction.

- In addition to individual benefits, the concept of making strengths stronger also underscores the importance of leveraging collective strengths. By recognizing and appreciating diverse strengths, we foster a culture of collaboration that sustains psychological stability.

The importance of making strengths stronger cannot be overstated. Ultimately, leveraging strengths leads to a more engaged, productive, and harmonious environment, sustaining our psychological stability.

12.5 Maintaining Hard Fought Gains

Maintaining gains after winning the war within our mind refers to the process of sustaining the positive mental and emotional progress we have made after overcoming psychological battles. This internal conflict often involves psychological battles with fear, self-doubt, negative thinking, anxiety, depression, or other threats to our well-being. We do not want to relinquish any ground we have gained because we aim to avoid fighting the same battle again if possible.

Winning the war within our mind is not about receiving a championship victory parade at the end of the season because we were the best team in the league. There isn't a specified season or number of games or psychological battles scheduled. There are no opening days where each team starts out with zero wins and zero losses, and all teams are tied for first place when a new season begins. We have to be ready whenever a psychological battle starts and have the endurance to fight as long as necessary with the ultimate goal of achieving remission and peace of mind.

Sustaining this state of remission demands ongoing dedication, self-reflection, and revisiting successful strategies. The aim is to transform these achievements into enduring habits. Past experience guides future choices to make better decisions. Lasting remission requires continuous effort and a healthy, highly functioning sense of purpose.

Motivation plays a crucial role in sustaining efforts to maintain remission from psychological warfare. Staying proactive is incredibly important because one of the pitfalls of psychological warfare is the loss of motivation. Different people may be driven by various types of motivation, such as intrinsic (personal fulfillment, growth), extrinsic (external rewards, recognition), or both. Understanding our motivational drivers can help us remain committed to our journey toward inner peace and remission, even in the face of future setbacks and challenges.

The dynamics involved in achieving a state of remission in psychological warfare are multifaceted and complex, sometimes mirroring strategies employed in military operations. Just as soldiers undergo rigorous training to deter war, when in remission from psychological warfare we must equip ourselves with the necessary skills and coping mechanisms to prevent the recurrence or appearance of newly activated inner demons. This training may involve therapy, self-reflection, focused practices, or cognitive behavioral techniques. By honing these skills, we can better navigate future inner turmoil and develop mental toughness in the face of confrontation.

12.6 Life After Victory – What Comes Next?

From the depths of pain arising from our toughest psychological battles to the heights of triumph, the scars of yesterday forge our greatest strengths for today. In the future, there will be new goals, innovative pursuits, and peaceful acceptance of our journey. Slated ahead, life sequences will include gratitude and harmony. Beyond the narrative arc, from enduring wounds and hurt to transformative victory is a journey of personal growth. We move beyond the war within our minds to reshape our lives, radiating the enduring power of the human spirit.

The war held in the battleground of our mind is an intensely personal struggle. The victory of remission marks a fundamental shift in our path. After confronting multifaceted dimensions filled with complex circumstances restraining us, overcoming significant doubts and hesitancy results in the wonderful feeling of freedom. When the chains constraining us are broken, new optimism is born. This defining moment fuels the desire to propel us to draft new trajectories in our life. Newly discovered paths lead us to design bold new missions, prepare accordingly, and execute successfully. Once stuck in the morass of agony, new missions forge greater strengths of enhanced problem-solving skills, courage, critical thinking, and patience.

The major transition from a state of consternation to one of discovery is a delicate phase where we re-learn, re-adapt, and redefine our own existence in relation to ourselves and the world around us. In accordance with Darwin's theory of survival of the fittest, prosper or perish, our toughest battles have been fought, forging our greatest strengths of self-awareness, mental toughness, flexibility, and adaptability.

Long-term recovery is seldom an isolated journey. Family, friends, mental health professionals, and community support systems play integral roles in sustaining health and well-being in order to win the war within our mind.

Photo by Donna R. Linden

Exploring life after winning the psychological war within our mind offers not just hope, but also illuminates the richness of human spirit and the sincere potential for personal transformation and growth. When we walk into the future proud and confident, future generations will follow. Winning the war within our mind helps ensure their success.

Epilogue

My goal when writing this book was to construct a detailed model that mirrored a real battlefield in the mind. The imagery I sought to evoke in the reader's mind was meant to resemble the harsh realities of war. My motivation originated from the psychological war that was waged and raged in my mind from 2010 until 2024.

To sincerely and accurately reflect the battlefield, it was necessary to incorporate a range of psychological elements, including emotions, uncertainties, aspirations, and danger. Scenes of psychological conflict required representation through a theater of operations where blood is shed, wounds are grave, and fighting for survival is a stark reality. The stakes are high, and morbidity and mortality are real. A psychological war deserves reverence because many warriors make a supreme sacrifice and pay the ultimate price. The serious nature of these consequences motivated me to assist others in taking positive action, seeking options, and persevering until winning is the only choice and victory becomes the norm.

This book dared to look into the crossfire of conflicts within our mind, battles fought in our brains. The mind serving as host for both conscious and subconscious clashes we grapple with. No two battles are identical, just as no two minds are alike. Each struggle is unique.

Reflecting on the moral of this story, it is about winning a fight often unseen and difficult to understand. Psychological battles leading to the war within our mind stem from the inner workings of the brain influenced by both internal and external factors. We identified twelve inner demons that act as perpetrators of the pain, distress, and misery psychological battles inflict on people. Given the broad spectrum and vast universe of inner demons, these twelve inner demons most likely represent a small sample size of the myriad of agitators that exist. To counter these enemies causing negative thought processes and patterns, we identified ten top strengths. Making these strengths stronger is the basic premise and foundation on which Winning the War Within Our Mind is built.

My next book will convey a sense of reassurance and optimism, providing a message of hope, resilience, and faith in the face of suffering. It will explore themes of overcoming setbacks, finding inner strength, and believing in a brighter future, despite present uncertainties or setbacks. The process of unlocking the secrets within our mind will be the catalyst for this transformation, leading to a meaningful shift in perspective and a renewed sense of urgency to gain a deeper understanding of inner peace and well-being in our life. Until then, win the war within your mind.

www.ingramcontent.com/pod-product-compliance
Lightning Source LLC
Chambersburg PA
CBHW081144130726
47996CB00009B/2983